CIVIL PROCEDURE
2015
Third Cumulative Supplement
to the
2015 Edition

Up–to–date generally to June 18, 2015

TO ACCESS THE WHITE BOOK UPDATING SERVICE VIA
HTTP://WWW.SWEETANDMAXWELL.CO.UK/WHITEBOOK
YOU NEED TO ENTER THE FOLLOWING PASSWORD:
WB2015

SWEET & MAXWELL  THOMSON REUTERS

Published in 2015 by Thomson Reuters (Professional) UK Limited
(Registered in England & Wales, Company No. 1679046.
Registered Office and address for service:
2nd Floor, 1 Mark Square, Leonard Street, London EC2A 4EG)
All typesetting by Hobbs the Printers Ltd., Totton, Hampshire.
Printed and bound in the UK by CPI Group (UK) Ltd, Croydon, CR0 4YY.
For further information on our products and services, visit
http://www.sweetandmaxwell.co.uk.

*No natural forests were destroyed to make this product; only farmed timber was used
and replanted.*

British Library Cataloguing in Publication Data
A catalogue record for this book is available from the British Library

ISBN–978–0–41403–930–8
Crown Copyright material is reproduced with permission of the Controller of HMSO
and the Queen's Printer for Scotland. Thomson Reuters and the Thomson Reuters
Logo are trademarks of Thomson Reuters.

Thomson Reuters and the Thomson Reuters logo are trademarks of Thomson Reuters. Sweet & Maxwell® is a registered trademark of Thomson Reuters (Professional)
UK Limited.

PUBLISHER'S NOTE

Civil Procedure 2015 published on March 30, 2015. The Third Cumulative Supplement contains updating material for both Volumes of *Civil Procedure 2015* and brings the work up–to–date to June 18, 2015. It is a cumulative Supplement so it includes the text of the previous two Supplements.

This Supplement updates *Civil Procedure 2015* in the following respects.

1. Updates to case law in commentary including *Singh v Thoree, Yeo v Times Newspapers Ltd*, *CIP Properties (AIPT) Ltd v Galliford Try Infrastructure Ltd* and *Purser v Hibbs* (Part 3 – The Court's Case and Costs Management Powers); *Ashley v Tesco Stores* and *Dunbar Assets Plc v BCP Premier Ltd* (Part 6 – Service of Documents); *Tchenguiz v Grant Thornton UK LLP* (Part 16 – Statements of Case); *American Leisure Group Ltd v Olswang LLP* (Part 19 – Parties & Group Litigation); *JX MX v Dartford and Gravesham NHS Trust* (Part 21 – Children & Protected Parties); *JSC Mezhdunarodniy Promyshlenniy Bank v Pugachev* (Part 25 – Interim Remedies and Security for Costs); *Big Bus Company Ltd v Ticketogo Ltd* (Part 31 – Disclosure and Inspection of Documents); *Novoship (UK) Ltd v Mikhaylyuk* (Part 40 – Judgments, Orders & Sale of Land); *Excalibur Ventures LLC v Texas Keystone Inc* (Part 44 – General Rules About Costs); *Spliethoff's Bevrachtingskantoor BV v Bank of China* and *Christofi v National Bank of Greece (Cyprus) Ltd* (Part 74 – Enforcement in Different Jurisdictions); *Brown v Haringey LBC* (Part 81 – Contempt of Court).

2. New and revised commentary has been produced for:
– Part 19 under Death of a party (r.19.8(1));
– Part 29 (The Multi–track) under Rule 29.2 (Case management) on Fixing the Trial Date and Directions for a Speedy Trial;
– Part 30 (Transfer) on the *Chancery Masters' Guidelines for the Transfer of Claims*; Part 39 (Miscellaneous Provisions Relating to Hearings) on the *Practice Direction (Audio Recordings of Proceedings: Access)* and the *Practice Direction (Committal for Contempt: Open Court)*;
– Part 52 (Appeals) under Rule 52.3 on Permission on when and where should the application for permission be made and how the appeal court deals with such applications;
– To Practice Direction 53 on Defamation Claims;
– On Money Claims under Part 70 on General Rules about Enforcement of Judgments and Orders.

3. The publication of various pieces of Chancery Division guidance in Section B of Volume 1 (Miscellaneous Practice Directions and Practice Statements), such as:
– A Practice Note on Fixed–End Trials;
– Chancery Masters' Guidelines for the Transfer of Claims;
– Guidance for Masters concerning the Grant of Injunctions and other Interim Relief;
– Guidance concerning the Type of Claim which are suitable for Trial by a Master.

4. Footnoted amendments to the Admiralty & Commercial Courts Guide under 'Ordinary Applications' and 'Heavy Applications'.

5. Commentary in Companies Act Proceedings includes a Note on listing and criteria for the transfer of work from the registrars to The County Court sitting in Central London and a note on Unfair Prejudice Applications, along with a new form, following consultation by the Chancery Modernisation Review Implementation Committee.

The Fourth Supplement to *Civil Procedure 2015* will publish in the Autumn. *Civil Procedure News* will continue to keep you abreast of developments for the remainder of the subscription year.

For Rule updates, please see the White Book Updating Service accessed via **http://www.sweetandmaxwell.co.uk/whitebook**: click on 'Log in to the White Book Updating Service' and enter your subscriber password 'WB2015'. This site contains the latest Civil Procedure Rules and Practice Directions. Changes that have been introduced since the *White Book* published are highlighted in red. Court forms and *Civil Procedure News* are also published here.

We welcome feedback from subscribers – please email *whitebook@sweetandmaxwell.co.uk* with any comments or suggestions.

The White Book Team
June 2015

LIST OF EDITORS

EDITOR–IN–CHIEF

THE RIGHT HONOURABLE LORD JUSTICE JACKSON
Lord Justice of Appeal; Honorary Fellow of Jesus College, Cambridge

GENERAL EDITORS

SENIOR MASTER B. FONTAINE
Senior Master of the Senior Courts in the Queen's Bench Division and Queen's Remembrancer; Central Authority for the Hague Conventions on Service and Taking of Evidence; Central Body under the EC Service and Evidence Regulations; Former Member of the Civil Procedure Rule Committee

PROFESSOR I. R. SCOTT
Emeritus Professor, University of Birmingham; Honorary Bencher of Gray's Inn

EDITOR OF CIVIL PROCEDURE NEWS

PROFESSOR I. R. SCOTT
Emeritus Professor, University of Birmingham; Honorary Bencher of Gray's Inn

SENIOR EDITORIAL BOARD

SENIOR COSTS JUDGE A. GORDON–SAKER
Senior Courts Costs Office

THE HONOURABLE MR JUSTICE HAMBLEN
Judge of the Queen's Bench Division of the High Court

ROBERT N. HILL
Recorder, Deputy District Judge and Regional Costs Judge, North Eastern Circuit; Former District Judge and Former Member of the Civil Procedure Rule Committee

HIS HONOUR JUDGE NIC MADGE
Inner London Crown Court and Central London Civil Justice Centre

EDITORS

JONATHAN AUBURN
Barrister, Thirty Nine Essex Street

MR REGISTRAR BAISTER
Chief Bankruptcy Registrar of the High Court

DR STUART BARAN
Barrister, Three New Square

V. C. BELL
Barrister, High Court Chancery Chambers

HIS HONOUR JUDGE NIGEL BIRD
Manchester Civil Justice Centre

DISTRICT JUDGE SUZANNE BURN
A District Judge on the South Eastern Circuit; Former Member of the Civil Procedure Rule Committee

MARTIN CHAMBERLAIN Q.C.
One of Her Majesty's Counsel

SARA COCKERILL Q.C.
One of Her Majesty's Counsel

MASTER DAVID COOK
A Master of the Senior Courts, Queen's Bench Division

THE HONOURABLE MR JUSTICE COULSON
Judge of the Queen's Bench Division of the High Court; Presiding Judge of the North Eastern Circuit; Member of the Civil Procedure Rule Committee

REGISTRAR DERRETT
A Bankruptcy Registrar of the High Court

PAUL DOBSON
Barrister

MASTER R. EASTMAN
A Master of the Senior Courts, Queen's Bench Division

M. GIBBON Q.C.
One of Her Majesty's Counsel, Maitland Chambers

JOAN GOULBOURN
Of the Public Guardianship Office

DISTRICT JUDGE MICHAEL HOVINGTON
Manchester County Court; Member of the Civil Procedure Rule Committee

R. JAY
Solicitor

E. JEARY
Of the Court Funds Office

MASTER JERVIS KAY Q.C.
Admiralty Registrar and a Master of the Senior Courts, Queen's Bench Division; One of Her Majesty's Counsel

CHRISTOPHER KNIGHT
Barrister, 11 King's Bench Walk

DISTRICT JUDGE M. LANGLEY
A District Judge of the Central London County Court; Chair of the London Association of District Judges

THE HONOURABLE MR JUSTICE LEWIS
Judge of the Queen's Bench Division of the High Court

CHIEF MASTER M. MARSH
Chief Master of the Senior Courts, Chancery Division

SARA MASTERS Q.C.
One of Her Majesty's Counsel

MASTER VICTORIA MCCLOUD
A Master of the Senior Courts, Queen's Bench Division

DISTRICT JUDGE SIMON MIDDLETON
Truro Courts of Justice and Bodmin County Court

KARON MONAGHAN Q.C.
One of Her Majesty's Counsel

HELEN MOUNTFIELD Q.C.
One of Her Majesty's Counsel

MASTER J. O'HARE
A Master of the Senior Courts Costs Office

HIS HONOUR JUDGE RICHARD PARKES Q.C.
A Circuit Judge on the South Eastern Circuit

HER HONOUR JUDGE PATRICIA PEARL
A Circuit Judge on the South Eastern Circuit

ED PEPPERALL Q.C.
One of Her Majesty's Counsel

MASTER N. PRICE
A Master of the Senior Courts, Chancery Division

MASTER ROBERTS
A Master of the Senior Courts, Queen's Bench Division; Member of the Civil Procedure Rule Committee

DISTRICT JUDGE RICHARD ROBINSON
Principal Registry of the Family Division

C. SANDERS
Solicitor

CONTENTS

TABLE OF CASES

TABLE OF STATUTES

TABLE OF INTERNATIONAL AND EUROPEAN LEGISLATION, TREATIES AND CONVENTIONS

*References in **bold type** are to the paragraph at which that article is set out in full.*

VOLUME 1

CIVIL PROCEDURE RULES

SECTION A

CIVIL PROCEDURE RULES 1998

PART 1

OVERRIDING OBJECTIVE

Application by the court of the overriding objective

In rule 1.2 for "and 82.2" substitute:

, **82.2 and 88.2**   1.2

PART 2

APPLICATION AND INTERPRETATION OF THE RULES

Editorial introduction

Delete the second paragraph and substitute:

Part 2 is also supplemented by Practice Direction 2B—Allocation of Cases to Levels **2.0.1**
of Judiciary (see para.2BPD.1 below); for explanation, see notes following r.2.4 below.
This Practice Direction has been amended on a number of occasions since it was first
published in March 2000. A number of specific amendments consequent to the coming
into force of provisions in the Crime and Courts Act 2013 s.17 and Sch.9 creating the
single County Court, from the commencement date for those provisions. By CPR
Update 79 (April 2015), an updated, revised, version came into force on April 6, 2015.

Delete Practice Direction 2B and substitute:

PRACTICE DIRECTION 2B—ALLOCATION OF CASES TO LEVELS OF JUDICIARY

Section I—Scope and Interpretation

1.1 Rule 2.4 provides that Judges, Masters and District Judges may **2BPD.1**
exercise any function of the court except where an enactment, rule
or practice direction provides otherwise. In respect of proceedings in
the High Court, Section II of this Practice Direction sets out the matters over which Masters or District Judges do not have jurisdiction or
which they may deal with only on certain conditions. References to
Circuit Judges include Recorders and references to Masters and
District Judges include Deputies.

1.1A Circuit Judges and District Judges may exercise any jurisdiction conferred on the County Court or on a judge of the County

Court. Section III of this Practice Direction sets out the matters that will be allocated to a Circuit Judge as well as those that may, or will normally, be allocated to a District Judge.

1.1B This Practice Direction does not affect jurisdiction conferred by other enactments. Reference should also be made to other relevant Practice Directions (e.g. Part 24, paragraph 3 and Part 26, paragraphs 12.1–10). The jurisdiction conferred on Masters and District Judges by this Practice Direction shall be exercised in accordance with directions from time to time provided by the President of the Queen's Bench Division, the Chancellor of the High Court, the Presiding Judges, or the Chancery Supervising Judges.

1.1C This Practice Direction is not concerned with family proceedings. It is also not concerned with proceedings in the Family Division except to the extent that such proceedings can be dealt with in the Chancery Division or the Family Division, e.g. proceedings under the Inheritance (Provision for Family and Dependants) Act 1975 or under section 14 of the Trusts of Land and Appointment of Trustees Act 1996. District Judges (including District Judges of the Principal Registry of the Family Division) have jurisdiction to hear such proceedings, subject to any Direction given by the President of the Family Division.

1.2 Masters or District Judges who have jurisdiction to hear a matter or to whom a matter has been allocated, may refer that matter to a Judge instead of dealing with it themselves.

1.3 For the purpose of this Practice Direction, in the County Court—

    (a) "Circuit Judge" means, in addition to a Circuit Judge, all judges of the Senior Courts, including retired and deputy judges of those courts, Recorders and Upper Tribunal judges (including the Senior President of Tribunals, Chamber Presidents, deputy Presidents of the Upper Tribunal and deputy judges of the Upper Tribunal, but excluding District Judges and District Judges (Magistrates' Courts)) and the Judge Advocate General; and

    (b) "District Judge" means all other Courts and tribunal judges, and High Court Officers (for example, Masters and Registrars), including deputy or temporary High Court Officers, who are judges of the County Court under section 5 of the County Courts Act 1984.

Section II—The High Court

Injunctions, Pre–trial Orders and Interim Remedies

2BPD.2   **2.** Search orders (rule 25.1(1)(h)), freezing orders (rule 25.1(1)(f)) and an ancillary order under rule 25.1(1)(g) may only be made by a Judge.

3.1 A Master or District Judge may not make orders or grant interim remedies—

    (a) relating to the liberty of the subject;

    (b) relating to criminal proceedings or matters except procedural applications in appeals to the High Court (including appeals by case stated) under any enactment;

(c) relating to a claim for judicial review, except that interim applications in claims for judicial review may be made to Masters of the Queen's Bench Division;

(d) relating to appeals from Masters or District Judges;

(e) in appeals against costs assessment under Parts 44 to 47, except on an appeal under rule 47.21 against the decision of an authorised court officer;

(f) in applications under section 42 of the Senior Courts Act 1981 by a person subject to a Civil or a Criminal or an All Proceedings Order (vexatious litigant) for permission to start or continue proceedings; or

(g) in applications under section 139 of the Mental Health Act 1983 for permission to bring proceedings against a person.

3.1A Notwithstanding the provisions of paragraph 3.1 a Master of the Crown Office or a Master of the Administrative Court may–

(a) make orders and grant interim remedies relating to claims for judicial review (including claims for judicial review relating to criminal causes, appeals under the Extradition Act 2003 and applications to vary bail conditions, provided the prosecutor does not oppose the variation);

(b) determine liability for costs and make summary assessments of costs in relation to claims for judicial review; and

(c) make orders and grant interim remedies relating to applications under section 42 of the Senior Courts Act 1981 for permission to start or continue claims for judicial review.

Early Trials

4.1 A Master or District Judge may only give directions for early trial after consulting the Head of the relevant Division or a Judge nominated by the Head of Division.

2BPD.3

Assignment of Claims to Masters and Transfer between Masters

6.1 The Senior Master and the Chief Master will make arrangements for proceedings to be assigned to individual Masters. They may vary such arrangements generally or in particular cases, for example, by transferring a case from a Master to whom it had been assigned to another Master.

2BPD.4

6.2 The fact that a case has been assigned to a particular Master does not prevent another Master from dealing with that case if circumstances require, whether at the request of the assigned Master or otherwise.

Freezing Orders: Cross Examination of Deponents about Assets

7 Where the court has made a freezing order under rule 25.1(f) and has ordered a person to make a witness statement or affidavit about his assets and to be cross–examined on its contents, unless the Judge directs otherwise, the cross–examination will take place before a Master or a District Judge, or if the Master or District Judge directs, before an examiner of the Court.

2BPD.5

Human Rights

7A A deputy High Court Judge, a Master or District Judge may not try—

2BPD.6

(1) a case in a claim made in respect of a judicial act under the Human Rights Act 1998, or

(2) a claim for a declaration of incompatibility in accordance with section 4 of the Human Rights Act 1998.

Chancery Proceedings

2BPD.7 **7B.1** In proceedings in the Chancery Division, a Master may not deal with the following without the consent of the Chancellor of the High Court—

(a) granting an indemnity for costs out of the assets of a company on the application of minority shareholders bringing a derivative action; or

(b) making orders in proceedings in the Patents Court except—

(i) orders by way of settlement, except settlement of procedural disputes;

(ii) applications for extension of time;

(iii) applications for permission to serve out of the jurisdiction;

(iv) applications for security for costs;

(v) other matters as directed by a judge of the court; and

(vi) enforcement of money judgments.

7B.2 In proceedings in the Chancery Division, a District Judge may not deal with the following without the consent of the Supervising Judge for the region in which the District Judge is sitting, or without the consent of their nominee—

(a) approving compromises (other than applications under the Inheritance (Provision for Family and Dependants) Act 1975) (i) on behalf of a person under disability where that person's interest in a fund, or if there is no fund, the maximum amount of the claim, exceeds £100,000 or any larger sum specified by the Chancellor of the High Court and (ii) on behalf of absent, unborn and unascertained persons;

(b) making final orders under section 1(1) of the Variation of Trusts Act 1958, except for the removal of protective trusts where the interest of the principal beneficiary has not failed or determined;

(c) giving permission to executors, administrators and trustees to bring or defend proceedings or to continue the prosecution or defence of proceedings, and granting an indemnity for costs out of the trust estate;

(d) granting an indemnity for costs out of the assets of a company on the application of minority shareholders bringing a derivative action;

(e) making an order for rectification, except for—

(i) rectification of the register under the Land Registration Act 1925; or

(ii) alteration or rectification of the register under the Land Registration Act 2002.

7B.3 The consent of the Supervising Judge for a District Judge to deal with proceedings specified in paragraph 7B.2 may be given either in respect of an individual case, or in respect of the categories of cases listed at 7B.2(a) to (e). The consent of the Supervising Judge's nominee may only be given in respect of an individual case.

7B.4 Where a winding–up order has been made against a company, any proceedings against the company by or on behalf of debenture holders may be dealt with, at the Royal Courts of Justice, by a Registrar and, in a District Registry with insolvency jurisdiction, by a District Judge.

Section III—The County Court

Injunctions, Anti–social Behaviour Orders, Committal and Freezing Orders

8.1 Applications for orders and interim applications which may not **2BPD.8** be made or granted by a District Judge in the High Court may not be allocated to a District Judge in the County Court. In the first instance, the following applications for orders and interim remedies will be allocated to a District Judge—

- (a) proceedings which have been allocated to a District Judge pursuant to paragraph 11.1 below;
- (b) injunctions sought in money claims which have not yet been allocated to a track and the amount claimed does not exceed the fast track financial limit;
- (c) injunctions that are to be made under any of the following provisions—
  - (i) section 153A, 153B or 153D of the Housing Act 1996;
  - (ii) section 3 of the Protection from Harassment Act 1997;
  - (iii) sections 34, 40 or 41 of the Policing and Crime Act 2009; or
  - (iv) Part 1 of the Anti–Social Behaviour, Crime and Policing Act 2014.

8.1A An application for an order under—

- (1) section 1B or 1D of the Crime and Disorder Act 1998 (anti–social behaviour);
- (2) section 26A, 26B or 26C of the Anti–social Behaviour Act 2003 (parenting orders); and
- (3) section 4 or 9 of the Violent Crime Reduction Act 2006 (drinking banning orders), may be allocated to a District Judge.

8.2 An application for an order varying or discharging an injunction or an undertaking given to the court may be allocated to a District Judge.

8.3 Any proceedings in which the Court may make an order committing a person to prison or attach a power of arrest to an injunction or remand a person will be allocated to a Circuit Judge, unless the order, power of arrest or remand is made pursuant to section 23 of the Attachment of Earnings Act 1971, section 14 and section 118 (but only in relation to proceedings before a District Judge) of the County Courts Act 1984, sections 153C,153D and 154–158 of and Schedule 15 to the Housing Act 1996; sections 36, 40–45 and 48 of, and Schedule 5 to, the Policing and Crime Act 2009, or Part 1 of the Anti–social Behaviour, Crime and Policing Act 2014, and the relevant rules.

8.4(1) An application for a freezing order will be allocated to a Circuit Judge authorised for the purpose by the Master of the Rolls or the Deputy Head of Civil Justice.

(2) If a Circuit Judge makes a freezing order, paragraph 7 applies as appropriate.

Homelessness Appeals

2BPD.9 **9** Appeals under section 204 or section 204A of the Housing Act 1996 will be allocated to a Circuit Judge.

Other pre–trial Orders and Interim Remedies

2BPD.10 **10** The proceedings specified paragraph 3.1(d) and (e) above will be allocated to a Circuit Judge.

Trials and Assessments of Damages

2BPD.11 **11.1** The following proceedings referred to in paragraph 8.1(a) will normally be allocated to a District Judge—

(a) any claim which has been allocated to the small claims track or fast track or which is treated as being allocated to the multi–track under rule 8.9(c), or any claim referred to in the table at Section B of Practice Direction 8A, except claims:

  (i) under Part I of the Landlord and Tenant Act 1927;

  (ii) for a new tenancy under section 24 or for the termination of a tenancy under section 29(2) of the Landlord and Tenant Act 1954;

  (iii) for an order under section 38 or 40 of the Landlord and Tenant Act 1987;

  (iv) under paragraph 26 or 27 of Schedule 11 to or section 27 of the Agricultural Holdings Act 1986;

  (v) under section 45(2) of the Matrimonial Causes Act 1973 for a declaration of legitimation by virtue of the Legitimacy Act 1976;

  (vi) under section 35, 38 or 40 of the Fair Trading Act 1973; or

  (vii) under Part II of the Mental Health Act 1983.

(b) proceedings for the recovery of land, proceedings under section 82A(2) of the Housing Act 1985 or section 6A(2) of the Housing Act 1988 (demotion claims) or proceedings in the County Court under Chapter 1A of the Housing Act 1996 (demoted tenancies);

(c) the assessment of damages or other sum due to a party under a judgment without any financial limit; and

(d) any other proceedings with the direction or permission of the Designated Civil Judge or Supervising Judge or Supervising Judge's nominee.

11.2(1) A case allocated to the small claims track may only be assigned to a Circuit Judge to hear with their consent.

(2) A case may only be referred to a Circuit Judge under section 65 of the County Courts Act 1984 with their consent.

Other proceedings

2BPD.12 **12**(1) Proceedings under the following enactments will be allocated to a Circuit Judge—

(a) sections 29 and 30 of the Literary and Scientific Institutions Act 1854;

    (b) the Bankers Books Evidence Act 1879;

    (c) section 1 of the Law of Distress Amendment Act 1895;

    (d) the Stannaries Court (Abolition) Act 1896;

    (e) section 6 of the Allotments Act 1922;

    (f) the Chancel Repairs Act 1932;

    (g) paragraph 7(b) of Schedule 8 to the Opencast Coal Act 1958;

    (h) sections 57, 66, 101(3) and 121 of the County Courts Act 1984; and

    (i) paragraph 6 of Schedule 18 to the Housing Act 1985.

(2) A request for the appointment of a court officer to take affidavits under section 56(1)(c) of the County Courts Act 1984, will be made to a Circuit Judge.

(3) Proceedings referred to in the following enactments will be allocated to a District Judge—

    (a) sections 85, 101(1), 104 and Part VI of, and Schedule 1 to, the County Court's Act 1984;

    (b) section 49 of the Vehicle Excise and Registration Act 1994;

    (c) paragraphs 9 and 10 of Schedule 1 to the London Local Authorities Act 1996;

    (d) paragraphs 6 and 7 of the Local Authorities and Transport for London Act 2003; and

    (e) section 64 of the Tribunals Courts and Enforcement Act 2007.

(4) In respect of any proceedings not referred to in this Section, if an enactment which specified the level of judge having jurisdiction to deal with those proceedings was amended by Schedule 9 to the Crime and Courts Act 2013 to confer jurisdiction on the County Court or a judge of the County Court, the proceedings will be allocated to a Circuit Judge or District Judge as if the enactment had not been so amended, unless any other enactment, rule or practice direction provides for the allocation of those proceedings.

Distribution of Business between Circuit Judge and District Judge

13 In any case where proceedings may be allocated to either a **2BPD.13** Circuit Judge or a District Judge, allocation is subject to any arrangements made by the Designated Civil Judge for the proper distribution of business between Circuit Judges and District Judges.

14.1 In district registries of the High Court and in the County Court, the Designated Civil Judge may make arrangements for proceedings to be assigned to individual District Judges and may vary such arrangements generally or in particular cases, save that in cases proceeding in the Chancery Division or the County Court Chancery Business List those arrangements shall be made by the Supervising Judge or their nominee.

14.2 The fact that a case has been assigned to a particular District Judge does not prevent another District Judge from dealing with the case if the circumstances require.

Human Rights

15 A case in which an allegation of indirect discrimination is made **2BPD.14**

against a public authority that would, if the court finds that it occurred, be unlawful under section 19B of the Race Relations Act 1976 will be allocated to a Circuit Judge.

Appeals

2BPD.15 **16** The appeal of any decision by a District Judge in proceedings which, under this Section, should have been allocated to a Circuit Judge, will be determined as if that decision had been made by a Circuit Judge.

PART 3

THE COURT'S CASE AND COSTS MANAGEMENT POWERS

Extending or shortening time limits

In the fourth paragraph, for "(R. (on the application of Hysaj) v Secretary of State for the Home Department [2014] EWCA Civ 1633)" substitute:

3.1.2 (R. (Hysaj) v Secretary of State for the Home Department [2014] EWCA Civ 1633; [2015] 2 Costs L.R. 191)

Interim orders

Add new paragraph at end:

3.1.9.1 In *Islamic Investment Company of the Gulf (Bahamas) Ltd v Symphony Gems NV and Others* [2014] EWHC 3777 (Comm), Hamblen J., *Tibbles* was applied and r.3.1(7) invoked to set aside the activation of a suspended committal order where the solicitor acting for the contemnor was clearly shown to have been engaged in a course of fraudulent conduct including misconduct in the preparation and presentation of the committal hearing.

Effect of rule

In the eighth paragraph, for "Walsham Chalet Park Ltd v Tallington Lakes Ltd [2014] EWCA Civ 1607" substitute:

3.4.1 Walsham Chalet Park Ltd v Tallington Lakes Ltd [2014] EWCA Civ 1607; [2015] C.P. Rep 15

Collateral attacks upon earlier decisions

In the final paragraph, for "Secretary of State for Business, Innovation & Skills v Weston [2014] EWHC 2933 (Ch)" substitute:

3.4.3.3 Secretary of State for Business Innovation and Skills v Weston [2014] EWHC 2933 (Ch); [2014] B.C.C. 581

Pointless and wasteful litigation

In the seventh paragraph, for "Ansari v Knowles [2013] EWCA Civ 1448" substitute:

3.4.3.4 Ansari v Knowles [2013] EWCA Civ 1448; [2014] C.P. Rep. 9

After the ninth paragraph ending "an abuse of process" add as new paragraphs:

In *James v Spamhaus Project Ltd* [2015] EWHC 127(QB); [2015] E.M.L.R. 13, Warby J. refused to strike out a libel claim brought by a US resident on *Jameel* principles given that he had a real prospect of demonstrating that the publication within England and Wales might be read by people whose opinion was of serious consequence to him and his business prospects and that it had therefore caused serious harm to his reputation. The judge made the point that the assessment of whether a real and substantial tort had been committed was not a 'numbers game'; even a publication to a single individual could be highly damaging and make a substantial and costly libel action proportionate. Where a libel claimant had a real prospect of establishing a tort which was real and substantial, the court should be slow to find that it could not devise a proportionate means of trying the claim, and that the only way of dealing with it justly was to dismiss it. That was particularly so after the implementation of costs budgeting procedures to help the court perform the duty of dealing with cases justly and at proportionate cost.

The judge stated that Section 1 of the Defamation Act 2013 did not abolish the foregoing principles. It introduced a new requirement whereby there was no tort unless and until serious harm to the claimant's reputation had either been caused or was likely to be caused by the publication. Accordingly, an assessment of whether a defamation claim in respect of a publication on or after January 1, 2014 should be dismissed on the ground that the actual or likely harm to reputation was too slight to justify the claim ought normally to start with consideration of the serious harm requirements in s.1 of the 2013 Act. The question was whether one of those requirements was satisfied or had a real prospect of being, satisfied. If the answer was no, then there was no tort and the claim would be dismissed. If the answer was yes, then it might be hard for a defendant to establish that the alleged tort failed the "real and substantial tort" test. The factors relevant to the question of whether serious harm had been caused or was likely were the same as those which came into play in assessing whether a tort was real and substantial for *Jameel* purposes.

In *James* Warby J. provided guidance as to the appropriate procedure to adopt: issues as to (i) serious harm and (ii) *Jameel* abuse were best resolved as preliminary issues together with (iii) any disputes as to meaning. This guidance was subsequently followed in *Lachaux v Independent Print Ltd* [2015] EWHC 915 (QB) (Nicola Davies J.).

Other forms of abuse

After the sixth paragraph (ending "action to the claimant"), add as a new paragraph:

In *Munday v Hilburn* [2014] EWHC 4496 (Ch), Nugee J., *Pathania* was followed. An **3.4.3.6** order striking out a claim for abuse of process on the basis that it was not vested in the claimant, who was an undischarged bankrupt when proceedings were issued, was set aside given that it was not shown by the defendants that the claimant had actual knowledge of his lack of entitlement to sue.

After the seventh paragraph (ending "Towler v Wills [2010] EWHC 1209 (Comm)"), add as a new paragraph:

In *Tchenguiz v Grant Thornton UK LLP* [2015] EWHC 405 (Comm), Leggatt J., the claimants served particulars of claim which were 94 pages long and thereby flagrantly failed to comply with the principles set out in the Commercial Court Guide (which states that statements of case must be no longer than 25 pages unless the court has given permission for a longer document, see Vol. 2 para.2A–161). On an application for retrospective permission to serve particulars of claim exceeding 25 pages the learned judge struck out the particulars of claim, disallowed the costs of drafting them and ordered fresh compliant particulars of claim to be served.

Claim "totally without merit"

In the third paragraph, for "R (Grace) v Secretary of State for the Home Department [2014] EWCA Civ 1091" substitute:

R. (Grace) v Secretary of State for the Home Department [2014] EWCA Civ 1091; [2014] **3.4.10** 1 W.L.R. 342

Formulation of rule since April 2013

In the last paragraph, for "Denton v TH White Ltd [2014] 4 Costs L.R. 752" substitute:

Denton v TH White Ltd [2014] EWCA Civ 906; [2014] 1 W.L.R 3296 **3.9.3**

Effect of Mitchell/Denton principles on applications to set aside default judgments

In the second paragraph, for "Samara v MBI & Partners UK Ltd [2014] EWHC 563 (QB)" substitute:

Samara v MBI & Partners UK Ltd [2014] EWHC 563 (QB); [2014] 3 Costs L.R 457 **3.9.5**

After the final paragraph, add as new paragraphs:

In *Avanesov v TOO Shymkentpivo* [2015] EWHC 394 (Comm), Popplewell J., despite a defendant having established a realistic defence, the court refused to set aside judgments totalling about $11 million after concluding that the delay in making the set aside application was the result of a conscious decision to ignore the proceedings and judgments until faced with the risk of enforcement. The court applied the *Mitchell/Denton* principles on the question whether the application to set aside had been made promptly and, taking into account the reason why the defendant had not applied earlier, held that the application had not been made promptly. The judge observed that the need for the efficient conduct of litigation, and the need to ensure compliance with court orders and the rules, was not served by indulging the defendant which deliberately ignored a timetable set out in his order and which failed to engage in the proceedings until it perceives a risk of enforcement.

In *Singh v Thoree* [2015] EWHC 1305 (QB) William Davis J. ruled that the *Mitchell/Denton* principles apply as much to r.13.3 as to any other part of the CPR. In doing so he cited paragraph 34 in the judgment of Christopher Clarke L.J. in *Regione Piemonte* (above). In *Singh* the time for filing the defence had expired on January 28, 2014 but, on that day, the defendant had received amended particulars of claim. The defendant (Mr Singh) did not serve a defence until February 14, 2014 and did not file a defence until February 27, 2014 at the earliest. Judgment in default was entered on February 24, 2014. Allowing the defendant's appeal from a deputy master's refusal to set aside that default judgment, the learned judge held that the defendant had established a realistic defence and had applied promptly to set aside the default judgment (i.e., within one day of first becoming aware of it). Although the default of defence in this case had endured for several weeks it was nevertheless right to grant relief; that delay had occurred because the defendant had assumed, wrongly, that the service of amended particulars of claim had recommenced the time limit for his defence.

Relief from sanctions cases decided after Mitchell

For "Denton v TH White Ltd [2014] EWCA Civ 906; [2014] 4 Costs L.R. 752" substitute:

3.9.6   Denton v TH White Ltd [2014] EWCA Civ 906; [2014] 1 W.L.R 3296; [2014] 4 Costs L.R. 752

Matters of form, not substance

In the first paragraph, for "Denton v White Ltd [2014] EWCA Civ 906; [2014] 4 Costs L.R. 752" substitute:

3.9.6.3   Denton v TH White Ltd [2014] EWCA Civ 906; [2014] 1 W.L.R 3296; [2014] 4 Costs L.R. 752

In the first paragraph, for "Yeo v Times Newspapers Ltd [2014] EWHC 2853 (QB)" substitute:
Yeo v Times Newspapers Ltd [2014] EWHC 2853 (QB); [2015] 1 W.L.R. 971

Breach which does not imperil future hearing dates or otherwise disrupt the conduct of litigation

In the first paragraph, for "Decadent Vapours Ltd v Bevan [2014] EWCA 906" substitute:

3.9.6.4   Decadent Vapours Ltd v Bevan [2014] EWCA 906; [2014] 1 W.L.R 3296

In the second paragraph, for "Utilise TDS Ltd v Davies [2014] EWCA Civ 906" substitute:
Utilise TDS Limited v Davies [2014] EWCA Civ 906; [2014] 1 W.L.R 3296

Breach where a deadline was only narrowly missed

For "Utilise TDS Ltd v Davies [2014] EWCA Civ 906" substitute:

3.9.6.5   Utilise TDS Limited v Davies [2014] EWCA Civ 906; [2014] 1 W.L.R 3296

Substantial breach of a deadline

In the third paragraph, for "Denton v TH White Ltd [2014] EWCA Civ 906; [2014] 4 Costs L.R. 752" substitute:

3.9.6.6   Denton v TH White Ltd [2014] EWCA Civ 906; [2014] 1 W.L.R 3296; [2014] 4 Costs L.R. 752

Extension of time: out–of–time application

In the third paragraph, for "R. (on the application of Hysaj) v Secretary of State for the Home Department [2014] EWCA Civ 1633" substitute:

3.9.6.7   R. (Hysaj) v Secretary of State for the Home Department [2014] EWCA Civ 1633; [2015] 2 Costs L.R. 191

After the last paragraph, add as a new paragraph:
Altomart and Hysaj were followed in *Elliott v Stobart Group Ltd* [2015] EWCA Civ 449 (and see further, para.3.9.6.9, below).

No good reason for breach

After the first paragraph, add as a new paragraph:

Inability to pay for legal representation cannot be regarded as a good reason for **3.9.6.9** delay (*R. (Hysaj) v Secretary of State for the Home Department* [2014] EWCA Civ 1633; [2015] 2 Costs L.R. 191). Being a litigant in person with no previous experience of legal proceedings is not a good reason for failing to comply with the CPR (*R. (Hysaj)*, above) or court orders, (*Elliott v Stobart Group Ltd* [2015] EWCA Civ 449).

Delay in applying for relief

In the second paragraph, for "Denton v TH White Ltd [2014] EWCA Civ 906; [2014] 4 Costs L.R. 752" substitute:

Denton v TH White Ltd [2014] EWCA Civ 906; [2014] 1 W.L.R 3296; [2014] 4 Costs **3.9.6.10** L.R. 752

In the third paragraph, for "Durrant v Chief Constable of Avon & Somerset [2013] EWCA Civ 1624; [2014] 2 All E.R. 757" substitute:

Durrant v Chief Constable of Avon & Somerset [2013] EWCA Civ 1624; [2014] 1 W.L.R. 4313; [2014] 2 All E.R. 757

Relevance of "all the circumstances"

In the first paragraph, for "Denton v TH White Ltd [2014] EWCA Civ 906" substitute:

Denton v TH White Ltd [2014] EWCA Civ 906; [2014] 1 W.L.R 3296   **3.9.6.11**

In the fourth paragraph, for "British Gas Trading Ltd v Oak Cash & Carry [2014] EWHC 4058 (QB)" substitute:

British Gas Trading Ltd v Oak Cash & Carry Ltd [2014] EWHC 4058 (QB); [2014] 6 Costs L.R. 1122

In the fifth paragraph, for "R. (on the application of Hysaj) v Secretary of State for the Home Department [2014] EWCA Civ 1633" substitute:

R. (Hysaj) v Secretary of State for the Home Department [2014] EWCA Civ 1633; [2015] 2 Costs L.R. 191

Orders granting partial relief from sanctions

In the last paragraph, for "Motor Vessel Coal Hunter v Motor Vessel Yusho Regulus 20 November [2014]" substitute:

Motor Vessel Coal Hunter v Motor Vessel Yusho Regulus [2014] EWHC 4406   **3.9.6.12**

Non–compliance cases not governed by Mitchell/Denton principles

In the second paragraph, for "Stoute v LTA Operations Ltd [2014] EWCA Civ 657" substitute:

Stoute v LTA Operations Ltd [2014] EWCA Civ 657; [2015] 1 W.L.R.79   **3.9.6.14**

Failure to comply which is intentional

Add at end:

See also *Avanesov v Shymkentpivo* [2015] EWHC 394 (Comm), Popplewell J.; under **3.9.8** 3.9.5 above.

Whether the defaulting party's claim or defence has merit

In the second paragraph, for "R. (on the application of Hysaj) v Secretary of State for the Home Department [2014] EWCA Civ 1633" substitute:

R. (Hysaj) v Secretary of State for the Home Department [2014] EWCA Civ 1633; [2015] **3.9.11** 2 Costs L.R. 191

Consequence if relief from sanctions is refused

In the second paragraph, for "Associated Electrical Industries Ltd v. Alstom UK [2014] EWHC 430 (Comm)" substitute:

Associated Electrical Industries Ltd v Alstom UK [2014] EWHC 430 (Comm); [2014] 3 **3.9.13** Costs L.R. 415

Meaning of "procedural error"

In the fourth paragraph, for "Stoute v LTA Operations Ltd [2014] EWCA Civ 657" substitute:

Stoute v LTA Operations Ltd [2014] EWCA Civ 657; [2015] 1 W.L.R. 79   **3.10.3**

Civil restraint orders

Add new paragraphs at end:

3.11.1   The Court of Appeal in *Connah v Plymouth Hospitals NHS Trust* [2006] EWCA Civ 1616, stated that the threshold for an extended civil restraint order, which required persistent totally without merit applications or claims, was higher than that for the grant of a limited civil restraint order, which required the making of two or more such applications. That was because the effect of an extended civil restraint order is more draconian. It was further stated that a civil restraint order should usually be made on notice to the person affected being given sufficient time to prepare his defence. A court can make an interim order on its own initiative without hearing the parties or giving them an opportunity to make representations (see CPR r.3.3(4)), but only in an exceptional case where the situation really warrants it.

In *Society of Lloyd's v Noel* [2015] EWHC 734 (QB), Lewis J., it was held that when a court was considering whether it had the power to grant an extended civil restraint order, and in particular whether a party had persistently issued claims or made applications which were totally without merit, it was entitled to have regard to all such claims and applications, including those which had been made prior to the making of an earlier extended civil restraint order.

Costs management to be prospective not retrospective

3.12.2   *In the first paragraph, delete the sentence beginning "Where the court concludes".*

Add new paragraphs at end:

In *Yeo v Times Newspapers Ltd* [2015] EWHC 209 (QB) Warby J. provided guidance on costs budgeting including the following: (i) The court's approval would relate only to the total figures for each phase of the proceedings. The process was intended to be swift, economical and somewhat impressionistic. (ii) The court may reduce a budget for reasons which apply equally to incurred costs. In such cases, it is likely to help the parties reach agreement without detailed assessment later on if these reasons are briefly recorded at the time the budget is approved. (iii) Where costs ran to six or seven figures, it may be appropriate to have regard not only to the factors listed in CPR r.44.3(5) but also to the number of hours claimed and the hourly rates claimed (paras 62–67). In this case the learned judge considered some of the solicitors' hourly rates to be too high by 20–25%, and that, in some instances, excessive partner time had been provided for (para.72). (iv) In some libel, privacy and some harassment cases, the costs may become disproportionate before the time for costs budgeting. While early intervention was not to be regarded as routine, the court might appropriately exercise its powers to give directions for the filing and exchange of budgets at an early stage (paras 75–77). If a budget is required at an early stage it need not be for the entire litigation: in substantial cases, it may be limited initially to part only of the proceedings (see 3EPD.6).

In two other cases guidance has been given where the court considers that the amount claimed as incurred costs is excessively high. In *Redfern v Corby Borough Council* [2014] EWHC 4526, HH Judge Seymour QC held that if the court concludes that the costs already incurred appear to be excessive, it may approve all subsequent costs at lower levels than would otherwise have been approved.

In *CIP Properties (AIPT) Ltd v Galliford Try Infrastructure Ltd* [2015] EWHC 481 (TCC) Coulson J. had, at an earlier hearing, exercised the court's discretion to make a costs management order even though the claim value exceeded £10 million. Subsequently the claimant filed a budget totalling almost £9.5 million of which about £4.3 million had already been incurred. Coulson J. declared this costs budget to be a wholly unreliable document and that its figures for costs already incurred and future estimated costs were disproportionate and unreasonable. In his judgment there were four available options for the court to consider: to order the claimant to prepare a new budget; to decline to approve the claimant's costs budget; to endeavour to set costs budget figures on a phase by phase basis, looking primarily at estimated rather than actual costs; or to simply refuse to allow anything more in the costs budget beyond that which had already been spent. He decided that only the option of endeavouring to set costs budget figures on a phase by phase basis was workable, but, in the unusual circumstances of the case, that option needed modification to arrive at a better approximation to justice. He reduced the total budget from £9.5 million to about £4.3 million, roughly the amount said to have been already incurred. Whilst setting totals for each phase of the budget the learned judge recorded the amounts which he considered it had been reasonable for the claimant to have already incurred. If, on a subsequent detailed assessment, larger sums were allowed for any of these items, corresponding reductions would have to be made to the sums approved as reasonable for the claimant to incur in the future.

"file and exchange budgets"

In the third paragraph, for the sentence beginning "The Ministry of Justice" to the end of the paragraph substitute:

The Ministry of Justice has published a leaflet entitled "Precedent H Guidance **3.13.1** Notes" which gives guidance as to the completion of Precedent H (*http:// www.justice.gov.uk/forms* [Accessed May 24, 2015]).

Delete paragraph 3.13.2 and substitute:

Statement of truth for use in Precedent H

Practice Direction 3E, para.6 states that a budget in the form of precedent H must **3.13.2** be dated and verified by a statement of truth signed by a senior legal representative of the party on whose behalf it is submitted (see PD3E.2, below). Practice Direction 22, para.2.2A sets out the form of words to be used (see para.PD22.2, below). Reliance upon a budget which is unsigned may well lead to the imposition of some sanction unless the statement is signed at, if not before, the case management conference by someone who has authority to sign it (see above, r.3.4(2)(c) and the commentary thereto).

In *Americhem Europe Ltd v Rakem Ltd* [2014] EWHC 1881 (TCC); [2014] 4 Costs L.R. 682 (TCC), Stuart–Smith J., a solicitor had served and filed a costs budget in the form of Precedent H in time, but it was signed by a costs draftsman and not by a senior legal representative within the meaning of PD3E. It was held that the error did not render the budget a nullity. The document suffered only from an irregularity and CPR r.3.14 was not applicable. The learned judge stated that while CPR r.3.14 provides a sanction in the event that a party "fails to provide a budget", it does not include the additional words "complying in all respects with the formal requirements laid down by PD3E".

Effect of rule

For "Mitchell v News Group Newspapers Ltd [2013] EWCA Civ 1537; [2013] 6 Costs L.R. 1008" substitute:

Mitchell v News Group Newspapers Ltd [2013] EWCA Civ 1537; [2014] 1 W.L.R. 795; **3.14.1** [2013] 6 Costs L.R. 1008

"Unless the court otherwise orders"

For "Mitchell v News Group Newspapers Ltd [2013] EWCA Civ 1537" substitute:

Mitchell v News Group Newspapers Ltd [2013] EWCA Civ 1537; [2014] 1 W.L.R.795 **3.14.2**

Revising costs budgets

In the third paragraph, for the sentence that begins "The court may take the view" substitute:

The court may take the view that the failure to declare this expenditure earlier **3.15.3** improperly invalidated the statement of truth which was or should have been given earlier that "This budget is a fair and accurate statement of incurred and estimated costs..." (as to this statement, see para.3.13.2, above). However, in *Purser v Hibbs* (QBD, May 19, 2015, unrep.) HH Judge Moloney (ruling on costs following the acceptance of a Pt. 36 offer after a disclosure of some surveillance evidence) remarked that the costs budgeting rules made no express provision for what should be done with regard to the costs of surveillance evidence; that, whereas most litigation was conducted on a cards–on–the–table basis, some degree of cunning was required in the administration of surveillance evidence; and that the court would not wish to do anything to discourage the judicious use of surveillance evidence, or to alert fraudsters to the use of surveillance. Therefore, the learned judge suggested that no allowance for surveillance need be made in a defendant's costs budget.

Effect of rule

In the first paragraph, for "Henry v Newsgroup Newspapers Ltd [2013] EWCA Civ 19, January 28, 2013, CA, unrep." substitute:

Henry v News Group Newspapers Ltd [2013] EWCA Civ 19; [2013] 2 Costs L.R. 334 **3.18.1**

PRACTICE DIRECTION 3D—MESOTHELIOMA CLAIMS

"Mesothelioma"

In the fourth paragraph, for "Master Eastman and Master McCloud, two" substitute:

3DPD.1.1   Master Eastman, Master Fontaine and Master Gidden,

Delete paragraph 3DPD.1.4 and substitute:

Pre–Action disclosure of HMRC work records of deceased parties

3DPD.1.4   With the passing of section 85 of the Deregulation Act 2015, the need for the *Yates v Commissioners for Her Majesty's Revenue & Customs* [2014] EWHC 2311 QB unrep. applications has passed and such records should be provided by HMRC upon proper request.

"standard interim payment"

3DPD.2.2   *Delete the last sentence beginning "In future".*

PART 5

COURT DOCUMENTS

Add new paragraph 5.0.2.1:

Electronic working—Technology and Construction Court

5.0.2.1   Practice Direction 51J (Electronic Working Pilot Scheme), see para.51JPD.1 and following below, was made under CPR rr.5.5, 7.12 & 51.2. It provides for a pilot scheme ("Electronic Working") to operate in the Technology and Construction Court in the High Court at the Royal Courts of Justice, Rolls Building, London, from April 27, 2015, and to apply to existing claims and claims started on or after that date. See further para.51.2.12 below.

Limits to application of r.5.4B and r.5.4C

At the end of the seventh paragraph, before the full stop, add:

5.4C.9   ; Part 88 (Proceedings Under the Counter–Terrorism and Security Act 2015) (r.88.33)

Filing by electronic means

Add at end:

5.5.1   Practice Direction 51J (Electronic Working Pilot Scheme), see para.51JPD.1 and following below, was made under this rule; see further para.5.0.2.1 above and para.51.2.12 below.

PART 6

SERVICE OF DOCUMENTS

Methods of service on company permitted by Companies Acts

Add new paragraph at end:

6.3.8   Where, for the purpose of serving a claim form on a defendant company registered in Scotland or Northern Ireland, a claimant adopts a method of service permitted by s.1139(1) of the 2006 Act, that is a method of service "permitted by Section II" of Part 6 within the meaning of r.6.40(2), and is valid service out of the jurisdiction provided it is effected within the six–month time limit fixed by r.7.5(2) (*Ashley v Tesco Stores* [2015] EWCA Civ 414, January 15, 2015, CA, unrep.). See further para.6.40.4 below.

Application of r.6.15 to service of other documents in proceedings

Add new paragraphs at end:

6.15.6   In *Dunbar Assets Plc v BCP Premier Ltd* [2015] EWHC 10 (Ch), unrep. the parties entered into an agreement by consent order in relation to pre–action protocol steps, and claimant undertook to serve claim form by a date 4 days before expiry of its validity. On the date for service claimant emailed a copy of the claim form to defendant. It was later conceded that was not good service and the claimant applied for an extension of time for serving the claim form under r.7.6(3) and/or relief from sanction, but also relying on r.6.15. Allowing defendant's appeal from decision of Deputy Master it was held that the claimant, under the terms of the consent order, had agreed to serve the claim form properly in accordance with the rules, had plenty of time in which to do so, and had provided no explanation whatsoever for not doing so. In the circumstances there was no "good reason" to permit as alternative service the "steps already taken" by claimant to bring the claim form to the attention of defendant.

In *Kaki v (1) National Private Air Transport Co (2) National Air Service Ltd CA* (2015) (Civ Div) May 13, 2015 (unrep.) (Case No.A3/2014/1912) the defendant Saudi company appealed against a decision ([2014] EWHC 1947 (Comm)) that the steps taken by the claimant to bring its claim form to the appellant's attention constituted good service under CPR r.6.15(2). In determining whether retrospectively to validate steps taken by a claimant as good alternative service under CPR r.6.15(2), the court had only to decide whether there was a good reason to do so: if the court found a good reason, there was no further discretion not to deem the service good. The fact that a r.6.15(2) application had been made after the time limit for service had expired was only one factor to take into account, and did not require any more rigorous or robust an approach.

In *R. (Lalu Hanuman) v University of East Anglia* (2015) QBD (Admin) May 18, 2015 (unrep.) (Case Nos CO/3442/2009, CO/15250/2009) the court retrospectively ordered service by alternative method under CPR r.6.27 holding that the debtor's refusal to accept service by email was unreasonable as he was residing in Barbados and had refused to provide an alternative address for service in the UK.

Interpretation

Rule 6.31(d) as reproduced in the White Book 2015 Main Work contained some errors; please delete and substitute with the following version:

(d) "the Judgments Regulation" means Regulation (EU) **6.31**
No.1215/2012 of the European Parliament and of the Council of 12 December 2012 on jurisdiction and the recognition and enforcement of judgments in civil and commercial matters (recast), as amended from time to time and as applied pursuant to the Agreement made on 19 October 2005 between the European Community and the Kingdom of Denmark on jurisdiction and the recognition and enforcement of judgments in civil and commercial matters;
(For application of the recast Judgments Regulation to Denmark, see also the Official Journal of the European Union at OJ L79, 21.3.2013, p.4)

Service of the claim form where the permission of the court is not required—out of the United Kingdom[1]

Rule 6.33 as reproduced in the White Book 2015 Main Work contained some errors; please delete and substitute with the following version:

6.33—(1) The claimant may serve the claim form on the defendant **6.33**
out of the United Kingdom where each claim against the defendant to be served and included in the claim form is a claim which the court has power to determine under the 1982 Act or the Lugano Convention and—
        (a) no proceedings between the parties concerning the same

---

[1] Introduced by the Civil Procedure (Amendment) Rules 2008 (SI 2008/2178). Amended by the Civil Jurisdiction and Judgments Regulations 2009 (SI 2009/3131) and the Civil Procedure (Amendment No.7) Rules 2014 (SI 2014/2948).

claim are pending in the courts of any other part of the United Kingdom or any other Convention territory; and

    (b) (i) the defendant is domiciled in the United Kingdom or in any Convention territory;

      (ii) the proceedings are within article 16 of Schedule 1 to the 1982 Act or article 22 of the Lugano Convention; or

      (iii) the defendant is a party to an agreement conferring jurisdiction, within article 17 of Schedule 1 or article 23 of the Lugano Convention.

(2) The claimant may serve the claim form on a defendant out of the United Kingdom where each claim made against the defendant to be served and included in the claim form is a claim which the court has power to determine under the Judgments Regulation and—

    (a) subject to paragraph (2A) no proceedings between the parties concerning the same claim are pending in the courts of any other part of the United Kingdom or any other Member State; and

    (b) (i) the defendant is domiciled in the United Kingdom or in any Member State;

      (ii) the defendant is not a consumer, but is a party to a consumer contract within article 17 of the Judgments Regulation;

      (iii) the defendant is an employer and a party to a contract of employment within article 20 of the Judgments Regulation;

      (iv) the proceedings are within article 24 of the Judgments Regulation; or

      (v) the defendant is a party to an agreement conferring jurisdiction within article 25 of the Judgments Regulation.

(2A) Paragraph (2)(a) does not apply if the jurisdiction conferred by the agreement referred to in paragraph (2)(b)(v) is exclusive.

(3) The claimant may serve the claim form on a defendant out of the United Kingdom where each claim made against the defendant to be served and included in the claim form is a claim which the court has power to determine other than under the 1982 Act or the Lugano Convention or the Judgments Regulation, notwithstanding that—

    (a) the person against whom the claim is made is not within the jurisdiction; or

    (b) the facts giving rise to the claim did not occur within the jurisdiction.

Delete paragraph 6.33.4 and substitute:

Rule 6.33(2)

6.33.4   Rule 6.33(2) states that a claim may be served out of the jurisdiction on a defendant without the permission of the court provided that each claim against that defendant is a claim which by virtue of the recast Judgments Regulation the court has the power to determine. A claimant may take advantage of this rule and serve the defendant out of the jurisdiction without first obtaining the permission of the court provided the conditions set out in r.6.33(2) are satisfied. The recast Judgments Regulation is directly applicable in the United Kingdom and, subject to certain conditions, confers jurisdiction on the English courts.

The conditions as stated in r.6.33(2) were amended in a significant respect with effect from January 10, 2015, by the Civil Procedure (Amendment No.7) Rules 2014 (SI 2014/2948) r.4(3), in particular by the insertion of para.(2A), to which the condition stated in para.(2)(a) is made subject. The effect is that the permission of the court to serve out is not required where the defendant is party to an agreement within art.25 conferring exclusive jurisdiction on the English court, even though proceedings between the parties concerning the same claim are pending in the courts of any other Member State. That amendment reflects differences between the terms of the original and recast Judgments Regulation relating to exceptions to the lis pendens rule. See further para.6.33.26 below.

"Member State" means every Member State of the EU.

Exclusion of arbitration

At the end of the second paragraph, add:

Most recently, the European Court of Justice has held that an anti–suit injunction **6.33.8.1** issued by an arbitral tribunal is not incompatible with the recast Brussels Regulation since arbitrators are not bound by the principle of mutual trust that underpins the Regulation: see *Gazprom* (C536/13) judgment of May 15, 2015.

The basic jurisdictional regime

At the end of the eighth paragraph ending "[2011] 1 Lloyd's Rep. 510.", add:

Nor on the jurisdiction of an arbitration tribunal to order an anti–suit injunction: **6.33.10** see *Gazprom* (C536/13), judgment of May 15, 2015.

Matters relating to tort, delict or quasi–delict

At the end of the twelfth paragraph ending "of the court seised.", add:

In *Kolassa v Barclays Bank Plc* (C–375/14) [2015] I.L.Pr, the European Court of **6.33.14** Justice held that when considering whether it had international jurisdiction under the Judgments Regulation, it was not necessary to undertake a comprehensive review of facts that went both to jurisdiction and the merits. However, it was permissible for a court to take into account all information available to it, including, where appropriate, the allegations made by the defendant.

Jurisdiction agreements

In the fourth paragraph, after "[2013] 1 B.C.L.C. 73." add:

When considering whether two separate contracts with competing dispute resolu- **6.33.26** tion clauses constitute a single overarching agreement, the "one stop, one jurisdiction presumption" in *Fiona Trust & Holding Corp v Privalov* [2007] UKHL 40; [2007] 4 All E.R. 951 is a useful starting–point but is not to be treated as giving rise to a presumption: see *Trust Risk Group SpA v Amtrust Europe Limited* [2015] EWCA Civ 437, judgment of April 30, 2015.

Restraint of foreign proceedings

At the end of the twelfth paragraph ending "2 All E.R. (Comm) 12", add:

, nor the grant of an anti–suit injunction by an arbitral tribunal: see *Gazprom* (C536/ **6.37.23** 13), judgment of May 15, 2015.

Paragraph 3.1(3) of 6BPD: "necessary or proper party" where a claim is made against someone on whom the claim form has been or will be served

At the end of the first paragraph, add:

In addition to satisfying the "necessary and proper person" criterion under **6.37.28** paragraph 3.1(3)(b), under paragraph 3.1(3)(a), a Claimant must demonstrate not only that there is "a real issue" but that there is an issue which " is reasonable for the Court to try: see *Erste Group Bank AG (London) v JSC (VMZ Red October)* [2015] EWCA Civ 379.

Service on a party in Scotland or Northern Ireland

Add new paragraph at end:

6.40.4   Rule 7.5 states that, where a claim form is to be served out of the jurisdiction, it must be served in accordance with Section IV of Part 6 within six months of the date of issue, and, in Section IV, r.6.40(2) states that where service is to be effected on party in Scotland and Northern Ireland, it must be served "by a method permitted by" Section II or III of Part 6. In *Ashley v Tesco Stores* [2015] EWCA Civ 414, January 15, 2015, CA, unrep., where the claimant (C) chose to effect service on a Scottish company (D) under the Companies Act s.1139(1) (see para.6.3.8 above) by posting the claim form to it at its registered office in Scotland four months after issue but within six months thereof, the Court of Appeal held that this was valid service out of the jurisdiction by a method permitted by Section II, rejecting the submission that, in the circumstances, C should have effected service within the jurisdiction at D's place of business therein as permitted by r.6.9, and should have done so within four months of issue.

PRACTICE DIRECTION 6B—SERVICE OUT OF THE JURISDICTION

Service out of the jurisdiction where permission is required

Claims about trusts etc.

Delete paragraph 3.1(12) and substitute:

6BPD.3   (12) A claim is made in respect of a trust which is created by the operation of a statute, or by a written instrument, or created orally and evidenced in writing, and which is governed by the law of England and Wales.

(12A) A claim is made in respect of a trust which is created by the operation of a statute, or by a written instrument, or created orally and evidenced in writing, and which provides that jurisdiction in respect of such a claim shall be conferred upon the courts of England and Wales.

PART 7

HOW TO START PROCEEDINGS—THE CLAIM FORM

Pre–action protocols

Add new paragraph at end:

7.0.2   That the Pre–action Conduct protocol has been complied with should be stated in the claim form or particulars of claim. See Practice Direction—Pre-Action Conduct para.9.7. See para.C1–008 below.

Related sources

Add new entry at end:

7.0.5   • Practice Direction—Pre–action Conduct.

Starting a claim in the County Court Money Claims Centre

Delete the third paragraph starting "In April 2012 HMCTS issued" and substitute:

7.2.2   In April 2012 HMCTS issued the following guidance in relation to the issue, close to the expiry of the limitation period, of money claims which, pursuant to 7APD.4A are to be issued at the County Court Money Claims Centre.

Delete paragraph 7.12.1 and substitute:

Practice direction

7.12.1   Practice Direction 5C (Electronic Working Scheme) was made under this rule (and r.5.5 (Filing and sending documents)), but in the circumstances explained in para.5.0.2 above was revoked with effect from October 1, 2014. Practice Direction 51J (Electronic Working Pilot Scheme), see para.51JPD.1 and following below, was also made under this rule and came into effect on April 27, 2015, in relation to claims brought in the TCC at the RCJ; see further para.5.0.2.1 above and para.51.2.12 below.

PART 12

DEFAULT JUDGMENT

Add new paragraph 12.11.2:

In *Thevarajah v Riordan* [2015] EWCA Civ 41 the Court of Appeal held that where a **12.11.2** defence and counterclaim had been struck out and the defendants had been debarred from defending the claimant's claim for breach of an unless order and the claim had been listed for a disposal hearing, the claimant could rely on the defence as indicating the ambit of the dispute between the parties without the need to prove matters which had been admitted or not disputed in the defence and counterclaim.

PART 13

SETTING ASIDE OR VARYING DEFAULT JUDGMENT

Rule 13.3(1)(b) "some other good reason"

Delete the third paragraph beginning "There were differing" and substitute:

The failure to serve a response pack could potentially constitute "some other good **13.3.2** reason" for the court to exercise its discretion to set judgment aside (*Ahmet Erol v Global Fashion Links Ltd* [2014] EWHC 4687 (IPEC)). There are differing decisions as to whether such failure was regarded, in the circumstances of the case, as sufficient for the court to exercise its discretion: see *Gulf International Bank B.S.C v Ektitab Holding Company K.S.C.C.* [2010] EWHC B30 (Comm) November 15, 2010, unrep. and *Henriksen v Pires* [2011] EWCA Civ 1720 (see above para.3.3.1).

PART 14

ADMISSIONS

Rule 14.1A

Add new paragraph at end:

In *Moore v Worcestershire NHS Trust* [2015] EWHC 1209 (QB) it was held that on an **14.1A.2** application to withdraw a pre–action admission and set aside a default judgment, the court should be aware of and consider the case against the background of the revitalised robustness of approach enunciated by the Court of Appeal in *Mitchell v News Group Newspapers Ltd* [2013] EWCA Civ 1537; [2014] 1 W.L.R. 795 and *Denton v TH White Ltd* [2014] EWCA Civ 906; [2014] 1 W.L.R 3926 but that an application to withdraw a pre–action admission did not necessarily import the full factors relevant to an application for relief from sanctions under CPR r.3.9.

PART 15

DEFENCE AND REPLY

Effect of rule

Add new paragraph at end:

The service of amended particulars of claim does not, by itself, cause the period for **15.4.1** filing a defence to begin again (*Singh v Thoree* [2015] EWHC 1305 (QB) William Davis J., noted in para.3.9.5, above).

PART 16

STATEMENTS OF CASE

Editorial introduction

Delete the third paragraph and substitute:

16.0.1   Part 16 and the Practice Direction supplementing it offers little guidance on drafting statements of case and contain no precedents or specimens. Various specimen forms of particulars of claim and defence have been prescribed for use in possession claims: the parties to such claims are required to use the appropriate forms (Practice Direction supplementing Pt 55, para.1.5, see para.55APD.1. Useful guidance on drafting statements of case is set out in Appendix 2 of the Chancery Guide (see Vol.2, para.1A–219), para.5.7 of the Queen's Bench Guide (see Vol.2, para.1B–29) and Appendix 4 of the Commercial Court Guide (see Vol.2, para.2A–161). Further guidance and precedents may also be found in text books and other works (for example Jackson and Powell, *Professional Liability Precedents*, Sweet & Maxwell, looseleaf).

In proceedings in which the Commercial Court Guide applies, statements of case must not be longer than 25 pages unless the court has given permission for a longer document (Commercial Court Guide, Appendix 4, para.17 (see Vol.2, para.2A–161). In *Tchenguiz v Grant Thornton UK LLP* [2015] EWHC 405 (Comm), Leggatt J., the claimants flagrantly failed to comply with the principles set out in the Guide by serving particulars of claim which were 94 pages long; on an application for retrospective permission to serve particulars of claim exceeding 25 pages the offending document was struck out, the costs of drafting it were disallowed and the claimants were ordered to serve compliant particulars of claim.

Particulars of claim served separately from the claim form

16.4.5 *Delete the second paragraph starting "Where particulars of claim".*

Add new paragraphs at end:

Where particulars of claim are not contained in or served with the claim form, the claimant must later file a copy of them in the appropriate court office.

In claims to which Practice Direction 7C or Practice Direction 7E apply, that is to say claims issued in the Production Centre or started using Money Claim Online, the place for filing copy particulars is the court to which the claim is sent or transferred and the deadline for doing so is seven days from the date the centre in question served a notice that the proceedings have been sent or transferred elsewhere (Practice Direction 7C, para.5.2(3) and Practice Direction 7E, para.6.3). In these cases there is no requirement to file a copy of the particulars unless and until the centre serves such a notice or serves an order requiring them to be filed (Practice Direction 7C, para.5.2(4) and Practice Direction 7E, para.6.4).

In all other cases, if the particulars of claim are not contained in or served with the claim form, the place for filing copy particulars is the court office which issued the claim and the deadline for doing so is seven days from the date of service on the defendant (r.7.4(3)).

PART 17

AMENDMENTS TO STATEMENTS OF CASE

Effect of rule

In the last paragraph, for "San Vicente v Secretary of State for Communities & Local Government [2013] EWCA Civ 817, July 5, 2013, CA" substitute:

17.4.1   San Vicente v Secretary of State for Communities & Local Government [2013] EWCA Civ 817; [2014] 1 W.L.R. 966, July 5, 2013, CA

Adding or substituting new cause of action (r.17.4(2))

Add at end:

17.4.4   An admirably brief summary of these cases is given in the judgment of Stephen

Morris QC, sitting as a Deputy High Court Judge, in *Diamandis v Wills* [2015] EWHC 312 (Ch), paras 43 to 49.

Issue (1): outside the limitation period?

Delete "Mercer Ltd v Ballinger EWCA Civ 996; [2014] 1 W.L.R.3597" and substitute:

Bellinger v Mercer Ltd [2014] EWCA Civ 996; [2014] 1 W.L.R. 3597   **17.4.4.1**

PART 19

PARTIES AND GROUP LITIGATION

"connected issues" (r.19.2(2)(b))

Add new paragraph at end:

In *XYZ v Various Companies, sub. nom. PIP Breast Implant Litigation* [2014] EWHC **19.2.4** 4056 (QB) claims were made against alleged tortfeasors some of whom took third party proceedings against their insurers. One of the alleged tortfeasors, A, a dormant company without assets, did not take any proceedings against its insurer, B. In the hope of facilitating the settlement of the whole proceedings, directions were obtained which were intended to determine the scope of the insurers' liability to the alleged tortfeasors other than A should the claims for compensation be successful. In the absence of any proceedings between A and its insurer, B, one of the other insurers sought to join B as a party to the proceedings, seeking a declaration as to the scope of the A's insurance. The applicant wished to establish in advance how much money would be available from B should the claims for compensation be successful. Refusing the application, Thirlwall J. held (i) the matters currently raised in these proceedings were limited to issues as between parties seeking compensation and their alleged tortfeasors, and issues as between the alleged tortfeasors and the insurers who had already been joined; (ii) as to r.19.2(2)(a), all matters in dispute between the existing parties could be determined without joining B as a new party; and (iii) as to r.19.2(2)(b), issues as between the insurers were not connected to any of the matters currently raised in these proceedings. A's insurance position with B was quite separate from A's liability, if any, to other parties.

Delete paragraph 19.3.2 and substitute:

Probate proceedings

For a definition of the terms "probate claim" and "probate counterclaim" see **19.3.2** r.57.1(2) and r. 57.9(1), respectively. Rule 57.13 makes provision about joinder of parties and about the substitution and removal of personal representatives. See also Practice Direction 57A, paras 4 and 12.

Exercise of discretion under r.19.5

Add new paragraph at end:

In *American Leisure Group Ltd v Olswang LLP* [2015] EWHC 629 (Ch), the master **19.5.11** held that the court did have jurisdiction under r.19.5(3)(a) to substitute a new party for a party named in the claim form by mistake, but that, on grounds of delay, the application should be dismissed. On appeal to HH Judge Walden–Smith, these decisions were upheld; the decision as to delay was an exercise of discretion which the master was entitled to make. The claim form had been issued a few days before the expiry of a six–year limitation period, the particulars of claim had been served just within the 4 month period allowed, there had been no pre–action contact with the defendant and the claimant had been slow applying for an order of substitution until just a few days before the hearing of the defendant's application to strike out.

Delete paragraph 19.8.1 and substitute:

Death of a party (r.19.8(1))

The general rule of joinder (r.19.2) applies where a party to proceedings has died **19.8.1** and a formal grant of representation (whether probate or letters of administration) is taken out in respect of his estate. Rule 19.8(1) applies where a party to proceedings (whether claimant or defendant) has died and that person has no personal representative. In such a case the court may order (a) the claim is to proceed in the absence of anyone representing the deceased party's estate, or (b) a person to be appointed to represent the estate of the deceased. These orders have the effect of making the deceased's estate bound by any rulings which the court may make in the proceedings (r.19.8(5)). In *Berti v Steele Raymond* [2001] EWCA Civ 2079 Robert Walker L.J. stated:

> "it is apparent from the rule [r.19.8] as a whole that it gives the court quite wide powers to dispense with the need for a formal grant of probate or letters of administration after the death of a party. It seems to recognise that, especially with relatively small claims, the need for a formal grant may be disproportionate and cause unnecessary delay and expense."

In that case the person named as the debtor in a bankruptcy petition died after the petition had been served upon him but before it had been heard. The Court of Appeal made an order under r.19.8(1) permitting the deceased's son to represent the estate in order to dispute the debt upon which the petition was based.

The court may direct that notice of an application under r.19.8 should be given to any person who has an interest in the claim, (r.19.8(4)). This sometimes brings to the court's notice the fact that someone is intending to take out a formal grant of representation. Orders to proceed in the absence of anyone to represent the deceased's estate are not commonly made. It may be appropriate if there are other parties to the proceedings in the same interest as the deceased and if the delay and expense of appointing a representative would be disproportionate. In *Ballard v Milner* [1895] W.N. 14, Chitty J. proceeded in the absence of a representative of the estate of a deceased person in an action which was then over 100 years old and efforts to identify a representative had failed.

The best person for the court to appoint under r.19.8(1) is the person most likely to have a right to apply for a formal grant of representation. However, an appointment under r.19.8(1) is for the purposes only of the proceedings in which the order is made: it does not grant to or impose upon the appointee all the rights and obligations which a formal grant of representation would. An order under r.19.8(1) is made in order to facilitate the continuance of proceedings so as to determine the rights and obligations of the parties to those proceedings. Whilst any remedies granted in the proceedings may be enforceable as between other parties, there is no person by whom or against whom they can be enforced in so far as the deceased's estate is concerned unless and until a formal grant of representation is taken out (see, for example, *Richerson (No.2), Re* [1893] 3 Ch. 146). As to the rights of a creditor of a deceased's estate to apply for a formal grant of representation, see the Non–Contentious Probate Rules 1987, r.20(f) and r.22(3).

Death of defendant (r.19.8(2) and (3))

At the end of the first paragraph, add:

19.8.3 Orders under this sub–rule are frequently made in respect of road accident claims brought against a deceased driver (see further, para.19.8A.2, below).

Claim form and application for permission to continue

In the third paragraph, for the text after "B.C.C. 700" to the end substitute:

19.9A.1 (bringing an "unfair prejudice" petition under Companies Act 2006, s.994 was inappropriate where the company was not trading and its shares had no value); *Cullen Investments Ltd v Brown* [2015] EWHC 473 (Ch) Mark Anderson QC (derivative action sought as a precautionary response to the defendant's defence in a personal action which denied that he owed relevant duties to anyone other than the company).

PART 21

CHILDREN AND PROTECTED PARTIES

Effect of rule

In the sixth paragraph, for "(being a designated money claim)" substitute:

21.10.2 (being a money claim)

Add new paragraphs at end:

In *JX MX v Dartford and Gravesham NHS Trust* [2015] EWCA Civ 96, with the Personal Injury Bar Association and the Press Association as interveners, the Court of Appeal gave guidance on anonymity orders in relation to applications by children and protected parties for approval of settlements for personal injury damages. The court stated that in dealing with such applications a court should recognise that it was dealing with private business, albeit in open court. Unless it was judged unnecessary, an anonymity order should normally be made without the need for a formal application. The court recognised that the public and the press have a legitimate interest both in observing the proceedings and making and receiving a report of them. Accordingly, the press should be given an opportunity to make submissions before any order is made restricting publication of a report of the proceedings, but for obvious reasons it will be unnecessary to notify the press formally that an application for an anonymity order will be made. If the press or any other party wishes to contend that an anonymity order should not be made, it will normally be necessary for it to file and serve on the claimant a statement setting out the nature of its case.

The Court of Appeal listed the principles which should apply:

[1] the hearing should be listed for hearing in public under the name in which the proceedings were issued, unless by the time of the hearing an anonymity order has already been made;

[2] because the hearing will be held in open court the press and members of the public will have a right to be present and to observe the proceedings;

[3] the Press will be free to report the proceedings, subject only to any order made by the judge restricting publication of the name and address of the claimant, his or her litigation friend (and, if different, the names and addresses of his or her parents) and restricting access by non–parties to documents in the court record other than those which have been anonymised (an "anonymity order");

[4] the judge should invite submissions from the parties and the press before making an anonymity order;

[5] unless satisfied after hearing argument that it is not necessary to do so, the judge should make an anonymity order for the protection of the claimant and his or her family;

[6] if the judge concludes that it is unnecessary to make an anonymity order, he should give a short judgment setting out his reasons for coming to that conclusion;

[7] the judge should normally give a brief judgment on the application (taking into account any anonymity order) explaining the circumstances giving rise to the claim and the reasons for his decision to grant or withhold approval and should make a copy available to the press on request as soon as possible after the hearing.

In the circumstances, the Court of Appeal held that the judge had been wrong to refuse to make an anonymity order.

In reality, with most approval hearings it is likely that the press will not have had notice of the hearing and that the press will not be in attendance. It is submitted that every anonymity order should give a non–party the right to apply to set aside the anonymity order and that the application should not be required to be made within any time limit. This gives non–parties an effective means of enforcing their rights under art.10; see *CVB* (above).

Expenses incurred by a litigation friend

Delete rule 21.12(1A) and substitute:

21.12—(1A) Costs recoverable under this rule are limited to—   21.12

(a) costs incurred by or on behalf of a child and which have been assessed by way of detailed assessment pursuant to rule 46.4(2); or

(b) costs incurred by or on behalf of a child by way of success fee under a conditional fee agreement or sum payable under a damages based agreement in a claim for damages for personal injury where the damages agreed or ordered to be paid do not exceed £25,000, where such costs have been assessed summarily pursuant to rule 46.4(5).

Delete paragraph 21.12.1 and substitute:

Note

21.12.1   This rule is supplemented by para.11 of Practice Direction 21 (see para.21PD.11 below). The rule was amended by the Civil Procedure (Amendment No.2) Rules 2015 (SI 2015/670) r.11, and the Civil Procedure (Amendment No.8) Rules 2014 (SI 2014/3299) r.5, which in combination inserted paras (1A), (7) and (8) and made consequential amendments elsewhere in the rule. These amendments came into effect on April 6, 2015, and were made for the purpose of addressing a growth in the number of applications at approval hearings for payment out of the child or protected party's damages to meet the success fee provided for in the conditional fee agreement or entered into between the litigation friend and the solicitor for the child or protected party.

PART 23

General Rules about Applications for Court Orders

Applications by parties in contempt

In the first paragraph, after "Motorola Credit Corp v Uzan (No.2), op cit, at [48])." add:

23.0.18   The relevant authorities were again reviewed in *JSC BTA Bank v Ablyazov* [2015] EWCA Civ 70, February 10, 2015, CA, unrep., where the Court of Appeal stated that the question whether to decline to hear a contemnor (a course which will almost invariably lead, as the case may be, to his application or his appeal being dismissed) is to be determined by reference to how, in the circumstances of the individual case, the interests of justice will best be served. As it is a strong thing for a court to refuse to hear a party it is a step which is only to be justified by grave considerations of public policy and which a court will take only when the contempt itself impedes the course of justice (ibid).

Application "totally without merit"

After the third paragraph, add as a new paragraph:

23.12.2   In a case where an extended civil restraint order (ECRO) imposed on a party (X) for two years had expired, and subsequently two further applications made by X were certified as TWM, it was held that in determining whether a further ECRO should be imposed on X the court was not limited to considering solely the applications made by X since the expiry of the first ECRO (*Society of Lloyd's v Noel* [2015] EWHC 734 (QB), March 20, 2015, unrep. (Lewis J.)). See further commentary following r.3.11.

PART 25

Interim Remedies and Security for Costs

Powers of Masters and district judges in relation to interim remedies

At the end of the third paragraph, add:

25.0.7   On June 12, 2015, the Chancellor issued additional guidance for Masters concerning the grant of injunctions and other relief in the Chancery Division.

Undertaking by defendant in lieu of injunction

Add at end:

In *Todaysure Matthews Ltd v Marketing Ways Services Ltd* [2015] EWHC 64 (Comm), **25.1.14.1**
January 21, 2015, unrep. (Teare J.), the claimant obtained an ex parte injunction and
the defendant gave undertakings effectively consenting to its continuation, unaware (as
it had not been disclosed to the court or the defendant) that the claimant had also applied for an injunction in America, which rendered the English injunction less
necessary. When the defendant learned, it applied to be released from its undertakings, but was not so released on the claimant's promise to withdraw the American
injunction, thus reinstating the consensual basis of the consent order.

Example of order to restrain disposal of assets

At the end of the second paragraph, add:

The latter form contains (at para.7(c)) a provision designed to cover interests in as- **25.1.25.6**
sets held by third parties under a trust or similar arrangement, which was the subject
of interpretation and analysis in *JSC Mezhdunarodniy Promyshlenniy Bank v Pugachev*
[2015] EWCA Civ 139, February 27, 2015, CA, unrep., at [23–25].

Term requiring respondent to provide information about assets

At the end of the second paragraph, before the full stop, add:

and para.25.1.26below (Order to provide information about property or assets **25.1.25.7**
(r.25.1(1)(g)))

Order to provide information about property or assets (r.25.1(1)(g))

In the first paragraph, for the sentence beginning "This interim remedy" substitute:

This interim remedy complements that stated in r.25.1(1)(f) and is restricted to "in- **25.1.26**
formation about relevant property or assets which are or may be the subject of an application for a freezing injunction".

In the third paragraph, for the last two sentences beginning "A reasonable possibility" substitute:

In *JSC Mezhdunarodniy Promyshlenniy Bank v Pugachev* [2015] EWCA Civ 139, February 27, 2015, CA, unrep., a defendant against whom a freezing order had been made
had disclosed the existence of several New Zealand trusts, and the claimant applied
under r.25.1(1)(g) for provision of information about the trusts and their assets. The
Court of Appeal at [49–52] held that the threshold for an application for such ancillary
order is that there must be "some credible material" or a reasonable possibility based
on credible evidence, and that it is not necessary for the applicant to show that a freezing order application in respect of such property would succeed. In *JSC BTA Bank v
Solodchenko* [2010] EWCA Civ 1436; [2011] 1 W.L.R. 888, CA, at [39] (per Patten L.J.)
it was explained that, in many cases, the order provides to the claimant an opportunity
of investigating the truth of the claim that assets are held on trust, and if it cannot be
shown to be untrue, they are then released from the injunction and its accompanying
disclosure obligations.

Applicant's disclosure duties where application made without notice

At the end of the sixth paragraph (ending "on tenants affected"), add:

In *Boreh v Republic of Djibouti* [2015] EWHC 769 (Comm), March 23, 2015, unrep. **25.3.5**
(Flaux J.), a case where it was found that the court had been deliberately misled, the
judge at [231–239] confirmed that where the claimant, by failing to make full and
frank disclosure or other misconduct, is alleged not to have come to equity with clean
hands, so that the setting aside of the injunction is sought, there needs to be "an immediate and necessary relation" between the misconduct and the equity sued for (i.e.
the injunction), which needs to be assessed by the judge.

Ideal time for applying

After the second paragraph, add as new paragraphs:

Where an application was made only three months before the date fixed for the **25.12.6**
trial, security was limited to future costs (*Warren v Marsden* [2014] EWHC 4410
(Comm)).

Where an applicant delayed his application for some three months (pending the
resolution of a jurisdiction dispute made by another defendant) the master exercised
her discretion against awarding security for costs and this was upheld on appeal: the

decision as to delay was an exercise of discretion which the master was entitled to make; the later that an application for security is made, the smaller is the opportunity for the claimant to consider his choice of putting up security in order to continue his claim or withdrawing it in order to avoid further expense (In the matter of *Bennet Invest Ltd*, 11 May 2015, (Ch) Richard Millett QC, unrep.).

Discretionary power to order security for costs

In the fourth paragraph, for the words "dismissed (and see further" to the end substitute:

25.13.1   dismissed. However, an ATE insurance policy may not amount to adequate security if the proper law of the policy does not confer upon the defendant, rights such as those conferred by the Third Parties (Rights against Insurers) Act 1930 in the event of the claimant's insolvency (*Harlequin Property (SVG) Ltd v Wilkins Kennedy (a firm)* [2015] EWHC 1122 (TCC), Coulson J.; and see further *Belco Trading Ltd v Kondo* [2008] EWCA Civ 205, noted in para.25.12.8, above).

Discretionary factors where both claims and counterclaims are raised

Add new paragraph at end:

25.13.1.1   The principle of *B.J. Crabtree (Insulation) v GPT Communications Systems* (1990) 59 B.L.R. 43, CA has also been applied to an overlap of claims brought by different co–claimants (a single purpose company and an individual resident in the UK in respect of whom no ground for security could be established (*Hello Quo the Movie Ltd v Duroc Media* [2014] EWHC 4622(Ch), Nicholas Strauss QC). However, on this point, see further, below, para.25.13.10 (Foreign and English co–claimants).

PRACTICE DIRECTION 25A—INTERIM INJUNCTIONS

Delete paragraph 25APD.10 and substitute:

Editorial note

25APD.10   The following forms which are annexed to this PD can be found in the Miscellaneous Forms section of the *Civil Procedure Forms Volume*:
- **F.I. Draft Freezing Injunction**
- **S.O. Draft Search Order**

See also App.5 of the Admiralty and Commercial Courts Guide, Section 2A, Commercial Court, Vol.2, para.2A–162.

PART 26

CASE MANAGEMENT—PRELIMINARY STAGE

Each party must file the completed questionnaire no later than the date specified

26.3.3   *In the first paragraph, delete "r.26.5(5) and".*

Add new paragraph at end:

Rule 26.7A sets out the procedure to be followed where a party fails to file a directions questionnaire in relation to a money claim issued in the County Court in a case which has become defended but has not yet been sent to a hearing centre. In such cases the court will serve a further notice under r.26.3(7A)(a) and in default of compliance the defaulting party's statement of case is struck out automatically. Rule 26.3(8) provides a more flexible approach but is expressly stated to apply only to "a claim to which rule 26.2 applies", i.e. proceedings in the High Court where the claim is for a specified amount of money, where the defendant is an individual, issued in a court which is not the defendant's home court and which has not been transferred to another defendant's home court. Thus r.26.3 does not contain any specific powers or indicate the approach to be taken if a party fails to return a directions questionnaire in a case to which neither r.26.2 nor r.26.2A applies. There would seem to be no reason in principle, however, why in any such case the court should not make such order as it considers appropriate, including one or other of the orders listed in r.26.3(8)(a)–(d).

PART 29

THE MULTI-TRACK

Fixing the trial date

Delete paragraph 29.2.6 and substitute:

29.2.6   Current practice in most courts is for directions to be given at an early stage in the proceedings which identify the likely date for trial should the claim proceed that far. In a Part 7 claim in London to which the Queen's Bench Guide or the Chancery Guide applies, the order made on the first case management conference is likely to specify the period in which the trial will be heard (the "trial window", a period of several months or coinciding with a Law Term) and will specify a date by which one party (usually the claimant) must make an appointment to attend on the relevant listing officer to fix a trial date within that trial window; notice of that appointment must then be given to the other parties (see generally Chancery Guide paras 6.7 to 6.11 (see Vol.2, para.1A–53): Queen's Bench Guide para.7.4 (see Vol.2, para.1B–46) and compare paras D8.7, D8.10 and D16 and D17 of the Admiralty and Commercial Court Guide (see Vol.2, paras 2A–68, 2A–76, 2A–77) and para.5.4.2 of the Technology and Construction Court Guide (see Vol.2, para.2C–40)).

In a Part 7 claim in London to which the Chancery Guide applies, the master will set the trial window having regard to the list of current trial windows published on the Justice website (para.6.8 of the Guide, see Vol.2, para.1A–53). In a Part 7 claim in London to which the Queen's Bench Guide applies, the master will set the trial window having regard to the targets set out in para.9.8.3 of the Guide (see Vol.2, para.1B–69). In each case, which trial window, or which target applies, depends upon the estimated length of trial. Target dates which are even shorter are provided for some cases governed by the Practice Direction 3D (Mesothelioma Claims) as to which see para.3DPD.7, above.

Appeals from the decisions made by listing officers lie to the Judge in charge of the relevant list (Chancery Guide, para.6.10 (see Vol.2, para.1A–53) and the Queen's Bench Guide para.9.4.10 (see Vol.2, para.1B–65).

The Queen's Bench Guide, para.9.7.1 states that once a fixed date for trial has been given, the parties are duty–bound to keep the listing officer informed as to any negotiations, settlement or withdrawal which may affect the estimated length of the hearing (see Vol.2, para.1B–68). The Chancery Guide, para.6.13, is in similar terms save that the duty is there said to fall upon the solicitors to the parties (see Vol.2, para.1A–55). Moreover, para.6.14 of the Chancery Guide requires notice to be given to the listing officer seven days before the fixed date stating whether there has been any variation in the estimate of duration; this notice is to be given by the claimant's solicitor or, if the claimant is a litigant in person, by the solicitor for the first named defendant who has instructed a solicitor.

Once a fixed date for trial in London has been given, any application to vacate the listing will be dealt with by the judge nominated by the relevant Division for that purpose (Chancery Guide, para.6.11 (see Vol.2, para.1A–53) and the Queen's Bench Guide para.9.7 (see Vol.2, para.1B–68).

Add new paragraph 29.2.7:

Directions for a speedy trial

29.2.7   In several cases each year applications are made for directions for a speedy trial (also called directions for an expedited trial, or directions for expedition). Such directions are most frequently sought in patent and trademark cases, employment law cases and cases in which an interim injunction is sought. However the categories of cases which can be expedited are not closed and the reasons for expedition are many and varied (*Petter v EMC Europe Ltd* [2015 EWCA Civ 480). Four factors to be considered were set out in the judgment of Neuberger L.J. (as he then was) in *WL Gore & Associates GMBH v Geox Spa* [2008] EWCA Civ 622, namely (1) good reason, (2) the level of interference with the administration of justice, (3) the prejudice to the other side and (4) other special factors.

As to (1), good reason (see above), the application will not be granted unless the applicant can show that his case, objectively viewed, has real and pressing urgency. This may arise from serious uncompensatable damage which the grant, or the refusal, of an interim injunction will cause (*WL Gore & Associates GMBH*, above; *OTS Logistics Belgium NV v Ocean Express Ltd* [2010] EWHC 3202 (QB)), in an employment dispute, the pressure upon an ex–employee who urgently needs to know whether working for a new employer will lead to him having to pay heavy damages to his former employer (*Petter*, above), issues as to freedom of expression (*EDO Technology Ltd v Campaign to Smash EDO* [2006] EWHC 598 (QB)) or important issues of public interest *Intervet (UK) Ltd v Merial* [2009] EWHC 1065 (Pat), obiter). However, a claimant's desire to obtain final judgment early so as to accelerate enforcement was held not to justify a speedy trial even where protection by means of a freezing order was not available (*Daltel Europe Ltd (in Liquidation) v Makki* [2004] EWHC 1631 (Ch)).

As to (2), the level of interference with the administration of justice (see above), the court must take into account its own available resources and the interests of parties to other cases (cf. r.1.1(2)(e)). The court will always have regard to information supplied by the listing officers and thus intending applicants for directions for a speedy trial often seek their guidance in advance. However, speedy trial directions will not be made simply because the listing officer states that no other case would be delayed because of them: although prejudice to a particular litigant cannot be identified, common sense suggests that someone would be disadvantaged if others are permitted to jump the queue (*JW Spear & Sons Ltd v Mattel Inc* [2012] EWHC 1374 (Ch)). The court exercises its discretion to expedite proceedings against the backdrop that the courts are busy and that expediting one case will often slow the progress of others (*Petter*, above).

As to (3), the prejudice to the other side (see above), the court will have regard to the burdens that may be placed upon opponents, for example, having to identify and proof witnesses, and having to instruct and receive reports from expert witnesses, whilst also making sure the witnesses chosen will be available for the trial. In some cases it may be appropriate to include in the directions a right for the opponents to apply for a refixing of the hearing date on proof that it has caused unfair prejudice (*WL Gore & Associates GMBH*, above).

As to (4), other special factors (see above), the applicant's failure to proceed with expedition earlier, or to seek directions for a speedy trial at the first available opportunity, may sometimes disentitle it to the relief claimed (*Teva UK Ltd v Boehringer Ingelheim International GmbH* [2014] EWHC 3186 (Pat) at [62]) but this is not always the case (*Daltel Europe Ltd (in Liquidation)* above at [19]; (*WL Gore & Associates GMBH*, above).

The application for a speedy trial should be made as soon as practicable (see factor (4), above). In the Commercial Court the application should normally be made to the Judge in Charge of the Commercial List, on notice to all parties, after issue and service of the claim form but before service of particulars of claim (Admiralty and Commercial Court Guide, para J1.2; see Vol.2, para.2A–107). A party whose application for a speedy trial is successful is duty–bound to work diligently towards achieving a speedy trial (*EDO Technology Ltd v Campaign to Smash EDO* [2006] EWHC 598 (QB) at [68] (interim injunction lifted when, because of the applicant's delay, the early trial date was lost; and see further, para.3.9.6.6 above).

Timetable for pre–trial check lists

Delete the last paragraph and substitute:

29.6.2   Question E in the pre–trial checklist asks whether the estimate of the time needed for trial changed, if so what it now is, and whether this revised estimate has been agreed with other parties. Whilst the giving of an accurate estimate has always been important it is now more important still for all trials in the Chancery Division in London. A Practice Note issued on April 28, 2015 by Sir Terence Etherton, Chancellor of the High Court, states that all such trials are in future to be conducted on a fixed–end basis. That means that each trial will, save in exceptional circumstances, be required to be completed within the period allotted to it. Thus, for example, if the estimate given does not make a realistic allowance for pre–reading by the judge, the time available in Court will be shortened correspondingly (and see further, Practice Note: Fixed–end trials, see para.B18–001, below).

Filing costs estimates

For the sentence "This statement appears to be of no effect." substitute:

29.6.3   This statement appears to be of no effect except for cases commenced before April 2013.

Pre–trial review

At the end of the first paragraph, before the full stop, add:

29.7.1   , if the case is proceeding in the Queen's Bench Division (Queen's Bench Guide para.7.5.1 (see Vol.2, para.1B–47)), or five days if the case is proceeding in the Chancery Division (Practice Note: Fixed–end trials, see para.B18–001, below)

PART 30

TRANSFER

Related sources

Add at end:

- Chancery Masters' Guidelines for the Transfer of Claims (May 20, 2015) **30.0.2**
  (para.B20–001)

Add new paragraph 30.3.1.1:

Chancery Masters' Guidelines for the Transfer of Claims (May 20, 2015)

This document provides informal guidance for Chancery Masters concerning the **30.3.1.1** transfer of claims out of the Chancery Division in London (for text see para.B20–001 below). The guidance relates to transfers of claims to (a) a Chancery District Registry outside London; (b) the County Court; (c) another Division of the High Court. The Guidelines incorporate references to Practice Direction 29 (The Multi–Track) paras 2.1 to 2.6 (Case management in the Royal Courts of Justice) (see para.29PD.2 above) and to para.(2) of r.30.3 (Criteria for transfer order) (see para.30.3 below) and include the texts of those provisions in Appendixes. The objective of these Guidelines is to ensure that only cases which may properly be regarded as being suitable for management and trial in the Chancery Division of the High Court in London are retained there. All other claims should be transferred out. It would seem that guidance given in Ch.10 of the Chancery Guide (Vol.2 para.1A–135) is to be read together with these Guidelines.

PART 31

DISCLOSURE AND INSPECTION OF DOCUMENTS

Disclosure statement

Delete the last paragraph and substitute:

Arrow Trading was approved by the Court of Appeal in *HRH Prince Abdulaziz Bin* **31.10.5** *Mishal Bin Abdulaziz Al Saud v Apex Global Management Ltd* [2014] EWCA Civ 1106; upheld [2014] UKSC 64. In that case a prince in the Saudi Royal Family claimed that he was bound by a protocol which prevented him from participating in litigation personally or from signing court documents. The court had made an order requiring personal signature of the disclosure statement, an unless order enforcing that personal signature order, and ultimately struck out the prince's counterclaim for failure to comply with these orders. The Court of Appeal and Supreme Court upheld those decisions. The Supreme Court noted that the standard form of disclosure by a party requires personal signing by the party, and that the court can permit a departure from this when good reasons are made out.

Rule 31.16(3)(a), (b) and (d)

Add new paragraph at end:

Pre–action disclosure under CPR r.31.16 extends to documents relating to issues as **31.16.4** to quantum: *Big Bus Company Ltd v Ticketogo Ltd* [2015] EWHC 1094 (Pat). That was not undermined by the fact that the court could and would normally exercise its discretion in favour of staged disclosure. In the instant case pre–action disclosure of documents relevant to quantum included documents relevant to damages payable on an inquiry as to damages. It was irrelevant that, in theory, Ticketogo might elect for an account of profits. The court had to consider the issues that were likely to arise and in the circumstances it was more likely that Ticketogo would elect an inquiry as to damages than an account of profits.

"The court may make an order . . ."

Add new paragraph at end:

CPR r.31.17 may be used to order disclosure for the purposes of identifying an un- **31.17.2.1** known party: *Kerner v WX* [2015] EWHC 1247(QB). The court would balance the interests of the applicant in the fair disposal of the litigation against the rights, including the rights under art.8 of the European Convention of Human Rights, of those whose identities might be disclosed pursuant to such an order. There was ample scope for deciding, in an appropriate case, that disclosure would represent an unnecessary and disproportionate intrusion into personal privacy, or should not be ordered for some other reason.

Subsequent use of disclosed documents

At the end of the penultimate paragraph, ending ", para 22" add:

31.22.1   Also see *Rawlinson and Hunter Trustees SA v Serious Fraud Office* [2015] EWHC 266 (Comm).

PART 34

WITNESSES, DEPOSITIONS AND EVIDENCE FOR FOREIGN COURTS

Applications

For the sentence beginning "Note that it is the Court" to the end of the paragraph, substitute:

34.21.26   Note that it is the court where the proceedings are taking pace which orders the issue of a request which then sends the request (in Form A, unsigned) directly to the designated court; see para.10.1 and 10.4 of the Practice Direction at 34APD.10 and art.2 of the Taking of Evidence Regulation. Accordingly, a county court may order the issue of a request. Where the person to be examined is not in a Regulation State, only the High Court may order the issue of a letter of request; see r.34.13(1A). The designated court then signs the request and transmits directly to the requested court. A list of designated courts is at Annex A to 34APD.

PART 35

EXPERTS AND ASSESSORS

Delete paragraph 35.0.2 and substitute:

Guidance for Instruction of Experts in Civil Claims

35.0.2   The Guidance replaces the Protocol for Instruction of Experts and was posted on the Civil Justice Council website in August 2014 having been amended and approved by the Civil Procedure Rule Committee and the Master of the Rolls. It came into effect in December 2014. The Guidance is no longer annexed to the CPR, but as stand alone guidance can be found in Part 11 of the White Book.

Expert evidence in small claims

In the last paragraph, for "£200" substitute:

35.0.3   £750

Expert evidence at trial

Add new paragraph at end:

35.0.5   In *Homebase Ltd v Jeyakanthan Rengasamy* 2015 EWHC 68 QB the court held that the first instance judge was wrong not to allow oral liability expert evidence in a low value multi–track personal injury claim when the experts in their joint statement continued to disagree about how the accident happened.

Effect of rule

Add new paragraph at end:

35.1.1   In *Allen v Cornwall Council* 2015 EWHC Civ 1461 QB the High Court refused the Defendant permission to appeal the decision of a District Judge to permit the Claimant to rely upon an expert in cycling skills and safety in a personal injury claim arising from an accident in which the cyclist came off his bike where the verge had encroached onto the busy country road, because it was an unusual type of accident, the Defendant was alleging contributory negligence, the expert was known to have particular expertise, the decision would not prevent the Defendant from applying later for their own expert, nor would it bind the trial judge in any way, and particularly because it was a case management decision where the decision had been exercised reasonably.

PART 36

OFFERS TO SETTLE

Before rule 36.2 add the rule group heading "GENERAL".

Before rule 36.5 add the rule group heading "MAKING OFFERS".

Before rule 36.8 add the rule group heading "CLARIFYING, WITHDRAWING AND CHANGING THE TERMS OF OFFERS".

Before rule 36.11 add the rule group heading "ACCEPTING OFFERS".

Before rule 36.16 add the rule group heading "UNACCEPTED OFFERS".

Costs consequences following judgment

The table in rule 36.17(4)(d)(ii) as reproduced in the White Book 2015 Main Work contained an error; please delete and substitute with the following version:

Amount awarded by the court	Prescribed percentage	36.17
Up to £500,000	10% of the amount awarded	
Above £500,000	10% of the first £500,000 and (subject to the limit of £75,000) 5% of any amount above that figure.	

Order for "an additional amount" (r.36.17(4)(d))

Add new paragraph at end:

    See *Cashman v Mid Essex Hospital Services NHS Trust* [2015] EWHC 1312 (QB); **36.17.7** [2015] All E.R. (D) 104 (May), decided under the former Part 36 14(3)(d), in respect additional amounts in Part 36 offers in the context of detailed costs assessments.

Before rule 36.18 add the rule group heading "PERSONAL INJURY CLAIMS".

Before rule 36.23 add the rule group heading "MISCELLANEOUS".

Cost consequences following judgment

In rule 36.29(2) for "will" substitute:

must   **36.29**

In rule 36.29(3) for "will" substitute:

must

In rule 36.29(4) for "will" substitute:

must

PRACTICE DIRECTION 36B SUPPLEMENTING PART 36

Delete Practice Direction 36B.

PART 39

MISCELLANEOUS PROVISIONS RELATING TO HEARINGS

Add new paragraph 39.0.6:

Recording of hearings

39.0.6   Paragraph 6 of Practice Direction 39A contains provisions about the recording of hearings (see para.39APD.6 below). On February 14, 2014, the Lord Chief Justice issued *Practice Direction (Audio Recordings of Proceedings: Access)* [2014] 1 W.L.R. 632, Sen Cts, for the purpose of clarifying the practice and procedure governing access to CD or digital audio recordings of civil and family proceedings in all courts in England and Wales; for text of this practice direction, which should be read with para.6 of PD 39A, see para.B19–001 below.

Order following a hearing in private

For "CPR 39APD32 para.1.13" substitute:
39.2.7.1   CPR 39APD para.1.13

Add new paragraph 39.2.10.1:

Practice Direction (Committal for Contempt: Open Court)

39.2.10.1   The PD requires the Court (see para.8 and para.10) to (a) give advance warning to the national media if it is considering taking the unusual step of hearing a committal application in private and (b) to give a judgment in open court, after hearing submissions, setting out the reasons why it is considered appropriate to depart for the general rule that the hearing should be in public. This is a welcome restatement of the fundamental principle that all hearings should take place in public and of the need to take great care before derogating from that principle (see also para.3 and para.4).

Paragraph 13 of the PD requires the Court to take certain further steps at the conclusion of a contempt hearing. These include notifying both the national media and the Judicial Office of the name of the contemnor, in general terms the nature of the contempt and the punishment to be imposed. These requirements appear to apply only when (a) there has been a hearing and (b) a committal order (either immediate or suspended) is made.

Paragraph 13(2) provides that there are never any circumstances in which any one may be committed to custody or made subject to a suspended committal order without these matters being stated by the court sitting in public. This gives rise to a difficulty. Suspended committal orders are regularly made on paper (without a hearing) where a debtor has failed to attend an oral examination (see CPR r.71.8). Whilst it seems likely that para.13(2) was not intended to override the operation of CPR r.71, Judges may now be less likely to exercise their discretion to make a suspended committal order on paper.

Paragraphs 14 and 15 of the PD restate the requirement for a written judgment or a transcript to be provided to the parties.

For the full text see [2015] 1 WLR 2195 and para.B17–001. The Practice Direction is issued by the Lord Chief Justice in accordance with the procedure laid down in Part 1 of Schedule 2 ofthe Constitutional Reform Act 2005. As such the PD is not a part of the CPR and has not had the benefit of being scrutinised by the Civil Procedure Rules Committee.

PART 40

JUDGMENTS, ORDERS, SALE OF LAND ETC.

Handing down written judgments

Add new paragraph at end:
40.2.5   In *R. (Williams) v Secretary of State for Energy and Climate Change* [2015] EWHC 1202 (Admin), April 30, 2015, unrep. (Lindblom J.), a judge tried a judicial review claim on the merits and reserved judgment. Before handing down judgment the judge invited

the parties to make written submissions on the issue (not raised in the course of the hearing) whether the court had no jurisdiction to hear and determine the claim because the proceedings had been issued out of time, and after considering those submissions, handed down a judgment dismissing the claim on that ground. The judge declined the parties' invitation to state what his decision on the merits of the claim would have been had the court had jurisdiction to determine it.

Effect of Rule

After the third paragraph, add as a new paragraph:

A correction to an order cannot have retrospective effect where it would prejudice **40.7.1** those who relied on the order as it was originally drawn up (*R. (James) v Governor of Birmingham Prison* [2015] EWCA Civ 58, February 9, 2015, CA, where the order was a committal order, and the party prejudiced by a purported correction were the prison authorities).

Power to award interest

At the end of the first paragraph, add:

The fact that a single judgment is envisaged does not compel the conclusion that **40.8.2** interest can only run from the date upon which the court makes a final order identifying total liability for principal and interest; so, where judgment is given for a principal sum first, that judgment constitutes a final judgment for a quantified sum and would, itself, fall within s.17 (*Novoship (UK) Ltd v Mikhaylyuk* [2013] EWHC 89 (Comm); [2014] 1 All E.R. (Comm) 993 (Christopher Clarke J.)).

Interest rate on claims in foreign currency

Add at end:

In *Novoship (UK) Ltd v Mikhaylyuk* [2014] EWCA Civ 908; [2015] 1 W.L.R. 526, CA, **40.8.4** on an appeal by a judgment creditor against an award of interest on a judgment in a foreign currency at a commercial rate rather than at the Judgments Act rate of 8 per cent, the Court of Appeal rejected the submission that, given the way that the judgment rate had departed so clearly from commercial rates without any reduction being made to it, it must be taken that there was a legislative policy of providing more than ordinary financial compensation by the award of interest, which should accordingly inform the approach of the court in deciding the rate of interest on a judgment in a foreign currency. In doing so the Court held (1) that the underlying purpose of both the Judgments Act and s.44A of the 1970 Act is to provide compensation to the claimant for being kept out of its money, and not to provide for an enhanced rate that might act as a spur for prompt payment, and (2) that in the circumstances the judge was right to hold that the compensatory principle provided sufficient (even compelling) grounds for departing from the prescribed rate applicable to sterling judgments. See also, applying the compensatory principle to an award in a foreign currency, *Barnett v Creggy* [2015] EWHC 1316 (Ch), January 29, 2015, unrep. (David Richards J.).

Interest on costs orders in substantive proceedings

In the third paragraph, after ""from or until a certain date, including a date before judgment"." add:

Cases in which judges have seen fit to postpone the accrual of the Judgments Act **40.8.11** rate of interest on the interest on costs orders to a date after the order, and cases in which judges have declined to take that approach, were referred to *Excalibur Ventures LLC v Texas Keystone Inc* [2015] EWHC 566 (Comm), February 3, 2015, unrep. (Christopher Clarke L.J.) at para.7 (where an order for costs was made against the defendants on one date and against non–parties ten months later, and the judge rejected the submission that in relation to the latter order the higher rate could run from a date earlier than the later).

In the third paragraph, for "See further para.44.3.14 below" substitute:

See further para.44x.3.22 below

Default judgments

After the fourth paragraph, add as a new paragraph:

In a case where a claimant (C), having entered judgment by default against a char- **40.9.5** ity (D) in a claim for repayment of a loan, obtained a third party debt order against D's bank and a non–party (X) who was a member of D (but whose role in the management of its affairs was a matter of dispute) applied to set aside the judgment and the order, it was held at first instance that X did not have any interest capable of recognition by the law that was "directly affected", within the meaning of r.40.9 as properly understood, by the judgment obtained by C (*Abdelmamoud v Egyptian Association in Great Britain Ltd* [2015] EWHC 1013 (Ch), April 17, 2015, unrep. (Edward Murray)).

PART 44

GENERAL RULES ABOUT COSTS

Payment on account of costs (r.44.2(8))

44.2.15 *Delete the seventh paragraph starting "In exercising the discretion".*

After the eighth paragraph (ending "to no presumption"), add as a new paragraph:
   Where the court had ordered the defendants to pay the claimants' costs of and occasioned by the adjournment of the trial, it went on to order a payment on account of those costs even though the claim was funded by conditional fee agreements and the claimants had not yet "won". As is commonly the case the agreement contained a provision that the claimants would be liable to pay their solicitors if an order for payment on account was made in their favour and therefore there was no breach of the indemnity principle: *PIP Breast Implant Litigation, Re* [2015] EWHC 1151 (QB) (Thirlwall J.).

Delete the ninth paragraph (starting "Necessarily, the determination of "a reasonable sum" involves") and substitute:
   Necessarily, the determination of "a reasonable sum" involves the court in arriving at some estimation of the costs that the receiving party is likely to be awarded by the costs judge in the detailed assessment proceedings or as a result of a compromise of those proceedings. In a case of any complexity, the evidence and submissions arguably relevant to that exercise may be extensive. The court has to guard against the risk that it may be drawn into costly and time–consuming "satellite" litigation. There is no rule that the amount ordered to be paid on account should be the "irreducible minimum" of what may be awarded on detailed assessment (*Gollop v Pryke*, November 29, 2011, unrep. (Warren J.)). The relevant authorities were reviewed by Christopher Clarke L.J. in *Excalibur Ventures LLC v Texas Keystone Inc* [2015] EWHC 566 (Comm), February 3, 2015, unrep., where he concluded that what is "a reasonable sum on account of costs" will have to be an estimate dependent on the circumstances, the chief of which is that there will, by definition, have been no detailed assessment and thus an element of uncertainty, the extent of which may differ widely from case to case as to what will be allowed on detailed assessment. He explained (paras 23 and 24) that a reasonable sum would often be one that was an estimate of the likely level of recovery subject, as the costs claimants accept, to an appropriate margin to allow for error in the estimation. This can be done by taking the lowest figure in a likely range or making a deduction from a single estimated figure or perhaps from the lowest figure in the range if the range itself is not very broad. In determining whether to order any payment and its amount, account needs to be taken of all relevant factors including the likelihood (if it can be assessed) of the claimants being awarded the costs that they seek or a lesser and if so what proportion of them; the difficulty, if any, that may be faced in recovering those costs; the likelihood of a successful appeal; the means of the parties; the imminence of any assessment; any relevant delay and whether the paying party will have any difficulty in recovery in the case of any overpayment.
   The procedure contained in Section II of CPR Part 3 for the filing, exchange, and approval by the court of the costs budgets of parties (introduced as part of the costs reforms taking effect from April 1, 2013) significantly affects the approach of the court to orders for payments on account costs. The procedure is designed to control costs in proceedings to which it applies, to make the level of costs likely to be incurred by the parties predictable, and to restrict costs recoverable by parties to sums stated in approved budgets. In cases where the court has made a costs management order under r.3.15, the receiving party's budget, insofar as it has been agreed between the parties or approved by the court, may be a sensible starting position for determining the "rea-

sonable sum" to be paid on account under r.44.2(8). That is because, on detailed assessment, the court will not depart from an agreed or approved budget unless satisfied that there is good reason to do so (r.3.18(b)) (see *Thomas Pink Ltd v Victoria's Secret UK Ltd* [2014] EWHC 3258 (Ch), July 31, 2014, unrep. (Birss J.), where payment on account ordered in sum amounting to 90 per cent of the claimant's approved budget).

Failure to serve statement of costs

Add at end:

The court may mark the failure to serve a statement by disallowing some of the **44.4.2** costs that would otherwise have been allowed: *Simpson v MGN* [2015] EWHC 126 (QB) (Warby J.).

PART 45

FIXED COSTS

Add new paragraph 45.43.1:

The nature of the claimant

A claimant will not lose the protection of the rules because it is a public authority. It **45.43.1** was not appropriate to refer to the Convention to place a gloss on the ordinary and natural meaning of "claimant" in PD 45: *HS2 Action Alliance & London Borough of Hillingdon v Secretary of State for Transport* [2015] EWCA Civ 203.

PART 46

COSTS—SPECIAL CASES

Costs where money is payable by or to a child or protected party

In rule 46.4(3), add before "Practice Direction 46":

paragraph (5) or in   **46.4**

Add new rule 46.4(5):

(5) Where the costs payable comprise only the success fee claimed by the child's or protected party's legal representative under a conditional fee agreement or the balance of any payment under a damages based agreement, the court may direct that—

> **(a) the assessment procedure referred to in rule 46.10 and paragraph 6 of Practice Direction 46 shall not apply; and**
>
> **(b) such costs be assessed summarily.**

Editorial note

After the second paragraph, add as a new paragraph:

However where the costs payable consist only of a success fee or a payment due **46.4.1** under a damages based agreement to the child's or protected party's solicitor, the court may direct that such costs be assessed summarily rather than by detailed assessment.

Editorial note

Add new paragraph at end:

In *Conlon v Royal Sun Alliance Insurance PLC* [2015] EWCA Civ 92 the Court of Ap- **46.13.1** peal assumed that the words "unless the court orders otherwise" in r.46.13(2) enabled it to backdate the re–allocation for costs purposes if it were satisfied that there were good reasons for doing so.

Add new Section V to Part 46:

V. Costs in Claims for Judicial Review

Claims for judicial review: costs against interveners

46.15   **46.15—(1) In this rule the terms "intervener" and "relevant party" have the same meaning as in section 87 of the Criminal Justice and Courts Act 2015 ("the 2015 Act").**

(2) A relevant party may apply to the court for an order for an intervener to pay costs in accordance with section 87 of the 2015 Act.

(Section 87 of the 2015 Act applies to judicial review proceedings in the High Court and Court of Appeal.)

(Rule 54.17 makes provision for any person to be able to apply for permission to file evidence or make representations at the hearing of a judicial review.)

Add new paragraph 46.15.1:

Editorial note

46.15.1   Rule 46.15 is simply a signpost to s.87 of the Criminal Justice and Courts Act 2015 (see para.9A–1311), which provides for the payment of costs by those who intervene in judicial review proceedings in the High Court or Court of Appeal. Provided that one of the four conditions in s.87(6) has been met, on an application by a "relevant party" the court must order the intervener to pay the costs that the court considers have been incurred by that party as a result of the intervener's involvement in that stage of the proceedings. "Relevant party" is defined widely by s.87(10) to include not only applicants and defendants (and appellants and respondents on appeal) but also any other person directly affected by the proceedings and upon whom the application for judicial review or for leave to apply has been served. "Intervener" is defined as a person who is granted permission to file evidence or make representations in judicial review proceedings but who is not a relevant party. The four conditions in s.87(6) are:

    (a) the intervener has acted, in substance, as the sole or principal applicant, defendant, appellant or respondent;

    (b) the intervener's evidence and representations, taken as a whole, have not been of significant assistance to the court;

    (c) a significant part of the intervener's evidence and representations relates to matters that it is not necessary for the court to consider in order to resolve the issues that are the subject of the stage in the proceedings;

    (d) the intervener has behaved unreasonably.

The court does not have to make a costs order against an intervener, even if one of the conditions is met, if there are exceptional circumstances that make it inappropriate to do so: s.87(7).

If an intervener becomes a relevant party, that person is to be treated as having been a relevant party, rather than an intervener, throughout: s.87(11).

A relevant party may not be ordered to pay an intervener's costs unless there are exceptional circumstances that make it appropriate to do so: s.87(3).

Rule 46.15 came into effect on the day on which s.87 of the 2015 Act came into force, that is to say, on April 13, 2015 (see SI 2015/778 art.3). Section 87 and r.46.15 do not apply to an application for judicial review where the claim form was filed before that date (ibid art.4, Sch.2 para.6, and SI 2015/670 r.12(1)).

Section 87(8) provides that in determining whether there are exceptional circumstances the court must have regard to criteria specified in rules of court. No rules have been made specifying such criteria.

PART 47

Procedure for Detailed Assessment of Costs and Default Provisions

Instructing distant solicitors

Add new paragraph at end:

Having decided that it was unreasonable to instruct solicitors in the City of London **47.14.9** in a personal injury claim which settled for £50,000, the next question was what type of firm should have been retained, not what type of firm would it have been reasonable for the claimant to instruct: *Kelly v Hays Plc* [2015] EWHC 735 (QB), February 19 2015, unrep. (Jeremy Baker J.).

PART 45

[Before April 1, 2013] Fixed Costs

Effect of rule

At the end of the third paragraph, add:

Where on the day fixed as the first day of the trial the court adjourned the case **45x.15.1** until 2pm the following day and the case then settled, the claim did not conclude at trial: *James v Ireland* [2015] EWHC 1259 (QB) (Slade J.).

Add new paragraph 45x.20.2:

The meaning of "employee"

A serving member of the armed services does not work under a contract of service, **45x.20.2** is not therefore an employee for the purposes of s.2(1) of the Employer's Liability (Compulsory Insurance) Act 1969 and so is not an employee for the purposes of section IV: *Broni v Ministry of Defence* [2015] EWHC 66 (QB) (Supperstone J.).

Claims falling with Section V

Add new paragraph at end:

However it has been held that noise–induced hearing loss is a disease for the **45x.23.2** purposes of section V and that, having regard to the legislative history, "disease" includes "any illness (whether physical or physiological), disorder, ailment, affliction, complaint, malady or derangement other than a physical or physiological injury solely caused by an accident or other similar single event": *Dalton v British Telecommunications Plc* [2015] EWHC 616 (QB) (Phillips J.).

PART 51

Transitional Arrangements and Pilot Schemes

Add new paragraph 51.2.12:

Electronic Working Pilot Scheme

By Update 79 (April 2015) Practice Direction 51J (Electronic Working Pilot Scheme) **51.2.12** was made under r.51.2 and supplements r.5.5 (Filing and sending documents), and r.7.12 (Electronic issue of claims) (see para.51JPD.1 and following below). It operates in the Technology and Construction Court in the High Court at the RCJ Rolls Building ("the Rolls Building TCC") from April 27, 2015, and applies to existing claims and claims started on or after that date. Where there is a conflict between provisions of this Practice Direction and the provisions of Practice Direction 5B (Electronic Communication and Filing of Documents) (para.5BPD.1 above), the former shall take precedence.

Add new paragraph 51.2.13:

The County Court Legal Advisers Pilot Scheme

51.2.13 By Update 79 (April 2015) Practice Direction 51K (The County Court Legal Advisers Pilot Scheme) was made under r.51.2 (see para.51JPD.1 and following below). It provides for a pilot scheme in respect of, and applies to, claims started in the County Court Business Centre and the County Court Money Claims Centre for a period of twelve months from October 1, 2015, to September 30, 2015.

Add new Practice Direction 51J:

PRACTICE DIRECTION 51J—ELECTRONIC WORKING PILOT SCHEME

51JPD.1 1.   General

1.1(1) This Practice Direction is made under rules 5.5, 7.12 and 51 of the Civil Procedure Rules ("CPR"). It provides for a pilot scheme ("Electronic Working") to—

(a) operate from 27 April 2015;

(b) operate in the Technology and Construction Court in the High Court at the Royal Courts of Justice, Rolls Building, London ("the Rolls Building TCC"); and

(c) apply to existing claims and claims started on or after 27 April 2015.

(2) Where the provisions of this Practice Direction conflict with the provisions of Practice Directions 5B or 5C this Practice Direction shall take precedence.

1.2(1) This Practice Direction provides for Electronic Working by which—

(a) proceedings may be started and all subsequent steps may be taken using Electronic Working; and

(b) proceedings which have not been started using Electronic Working, may be continued using Electronic Working after documents in paper format in those proceedings have been converted to PDF format and the proceedings shall then continue as if they had been started using Electronic Working.

(2) As an electronic system, the Electronic Working scheme will operate 24 hours a day all year round, including weekends and bank holidays. This will enable claim forms to be issued and documents to be filed in electronic format out of normal court office opening hours. However, there will be two exceptions to this—

(a) planned "down–time": as with all electronic systems, there will be some planned periods for system maintenance and upgrades when Electronic Working will not be available; and

(b) unplanned "down–time": in the event of unplanned periods during which Electronic Working will not be available due, for example, to a system failure or power outage.

1.3 The Electronic Working scheme will be subject to the following provisions of the CPR, unless specifically excluded or revised by this Practice Direction—

(a) Part 60 (Technology and Construction Court claims); and

(b) Part 62 (Arbitration claims).

(Litigants will need to give careful consideration to The Technology and Construction Court Guide.)

1.4 Electronic Working may be used to start and continue Part 7, Part 8, Part 20 and also Arbitration claims in the Rolls Building TCC.

1.5 Any form or document which is filed electronically—

(a) must not be filed in paper format unless this is required by a court order, rule, or practice direction;

(b) must consist of one copy only with no further copies unless required by a court order, rule or practice direction; and

(c) will receive an automated notification acknowledging that the form or document has been submitted and is now pending approval by the Court staff. This notification will contain the submission date and a submission number.

1.6(1) Persons wishing to use Electronic Working are required to register for an account on the Website by providing personal information such as name, email address, postal address and name of firm (if applicable).

(2) A claim form filed by a party using Electronic Working will be issued by the Rolls Building TCC and the claim will proceed in that court unless it is transferred to another court.

(3) If the claim which has been issued using Electronic Working is transferred from the Rolls Building TCC to another court it will no longer use Electronic Working and this Practice Direction shall not apply to the proceedings in relation to any step taken after the date of transfer.

(Paragraph 6 contains further provisions about the transfer of proceedings.)

1.7 Unless the court orders otherwise, any form or document filed by any party or issued by the Court using Electronic Working in the Rolls Building TCC, which is required to be served shall be served by the parties and not the Court.

1.8 All forms or documents filed at court using Electronic Working are to be in PDF format except that draft orders are to be filed in Word format and the court may direct that any forms or documents to be filed in another format.

1.9(1) Any form or document filed using Electronic Working must not exceed 10 (ten) megabytes or such other limit that may be specified by Her Majesty's Courts and Tribunals Service.

(2) In the event that any form or document exceeds the maximum limit in sub–paragraph (1), the party seeking to file the form or document shall contact the Registry for the Rolls Building TCC.

2. Security

Her Majesty's Courts and Tribunals Service will take such measures **51JPD.2** as it thinks fit to ensure the security of steps taken or information communicated or stored electronically. These may include requiring persons using Electronic Working to—

(a) enter an email address as their customer identification and/or password;

(b) provide personal information for identification purposes; and

(c) comply with any other security measures, as may from time to time be required before using Electronic Working.

3. Fees

51JPD.3 **3.1** Where any Rule or Practice Direction provides for a fee to be paid, a party filing a form or document using Electronic Working must pay the appropriate fee by an online method specified by Her Majesty's Courts and Tribunals Service.

3.2 In certain circumstances, a party may be entitled to a remission or part remission of fees. A party who wishes to apply for remission or part remission of fees cannot use Electronic Working to file forms and documents.

3.3(1) Any form or document filed using Electronic Working will be subject to an administrative validation to ensure that it is in the correct form and properly filed.

(2) Once validated and if the appropriate fee has been paid the form or document will, as appropriate, be issued and sealed by the Court and returned to the person filing it.

4. Filing forms and documents using Electronic Working

51JPD.4 **4.1** A party wishing to file any form or document using Electronic Working shall—

(a) access the website at https://efile.cefile–app.com ("the Website");

(b) register for an account or log on to an existing account;

(c) enter details of a new case or use the details of an existing case;

(d) upload the appropriate form or document; and

(e) pay the appropriate fee.

4.2(1) When a claim form is filed using Electronic Working then, subject to the validation referred to in paragraph 3.3, the claim form will be issued, sealed and returned in PDF format to the claimant for service.

(2) When following validation the court issues a claim form which has been filed using Electronic Working—

(a) the court will seal the claim form with the date on which the claim form was filed using Electronic Working and this shall be the issue date; and

(b) the court will keep a record of when claim forms were filed using Electronic Working.

(3) A claim form filed using Electronic Working out of normal court office opening hours will bear the date on which they are filed as the issue date.

(4) If a claim form fails the validation referred to in paragraph 3.3 it will be returned to the claimant together with notice of the reasons for failure.

4.3(1) When a party files a form or document using Electronic Working then, subject to the validation referred to in paragraph 3.3, the form or document will be filed when a party receives the automated notification acknowledging that the form or document has been submitted.

(2) The defendant may file forms and documents electronically through Electronic Working out of normal court office opening hours.

(3) A form or document filed out of normal court office opening hours will be treated as having been filed on the day on which the automated notification acknowledging that the form or document has been submitted is received by a party.

(Paragraph 1.2(2) contains provisions about system "down–time" which may prevent immediate filing of forms or documents.)

4.4 Part 22 and the Practice Direction supplementing that Part which requires certain forms and documents to be verified by a statement of truth shall apply to any forms or documents filed using Electronic Working.

5. Filing forms or documents in paper format

5.1 Proceedings issued after 27 April 2015 in the Rolls Building **51JPD.5** TCC will be stored by the court in PDF format as an electronic case file ("the Electronic Working Case File"). Any claims which are not started by using Electronic Working will be converted to PDF format and the provisions of paragraph 1.2(1)(b) shall apply to those proceedings.

5.2 Documents which the parties wish to file with the court may be lodged either by using Electronic Working or by lodging copies in paper format.

5.3 In the event that a party lodges a document in paper format the court will—

(a) where appropriate, seal the paper copy of the document;

(b) obtain payment of any fee due;

(c) request the party to provide the document in PDF format or scan the document into PDF format and store it on the Electronic Working Case File;

(d) any party may thereafter file any form or document using Electronic Working in accordance with paragraph 4.1.

6. Transfer of proceedings

6.1 If proceedings which have used Electronic Working are **51JPD.6** subsequently transferred to a court not operating Electronic Working the parties must ensure that a version of the court file in paper format is made available to that court.

6.2 If proceedings are transferred to the Rolls Building TCC all steps subsequent to the order transferring those proceedings may be taken using Electronic Working after documents in paper format in those proceedings have been converted to an electronic format pursuant to paragraph 1.2(1)(b).

7. Applications in proceedings

(1) Where a party to proceedings files an application for an order **51JPD.7** using Electronic Working and a hearing is required, the party filing the application shall lodge an application bundle with the court.

(2) The application bundle must—

    (a) be filed in electronic format and, unless ordered otherwise, also be filed as a paper copy;

    (b) contain the application notice and any evidence filed in the application, including exhibits together with such other documents as may be required by any rule, practice direction, order of the court or court guide; and

    (c) be filed in accordance with the time limits required by any applicable rule, practice direction, or order of the court or in the absence of such a requirement 3 (three) days before the hearing.

(3) The electronic copy of the application bundle must—

    (a) be filed using Electronic Working;

    (b) be formatted as one PDF document with bookmarks as appropriate for each document and with section headings within the document;

    (c) comply with the requirements of paragraph 1.9; and

    (d) be updated as required and filed in compliance with sub–paragraphs (a) to (c) above.

(4) The copy in paper format should be indexed and should correspond exactly to the electronic version of the bundle including sequential pagination.

8.   Case Management

51JPD.8   (1) Where—

    (a) a rule, practice direction, or order of the court requires—

      (i) the court to give case management or other directions, whether at a hearing or not;

      (ii) a bundle to be filed with the court in connection with case management or other directions; and

    (b) a party wishes to file the bundle using Electronic Working, the bundle must contain such documents as are required by any rule, practice direction, order of the court or court guide.

(2) The bundle must be filed, unless the court orders otherwise, in paper copy as well as electronic format.

(3) The electronic copy must—

    (a) be formatted as one PDF document with bookmarks as appropriate for each document and with section headings within the document;

    (c) comply with the requirements of paragraph 1.9; and

    (d) be updated as required and filed in compliance with sub–paragraphs (a) to (b) above.

(4) The paper copy should be indexed and should correspond exactly with the electronic version of the bundle with sequential pagination.

9.   Trial Bundles

51JPD.9   (1) The trial bundle must be filed with the court in paper format.

(2) An electronic version of the trial bundle must also be filed if the court so orders, in which case it must comply with the

requirements of paragraph 8(3) and the paper copy must comply with paragraph 8(4).

(3) The court will retain any electronic copy of the trial bundle for a period of two months after judgment has been delivered, after which it may be deleted.

(4) The time in paragraph 9(3) may be extended by order of the court at the request of a party or on the court's own initiative.

10. Inspecting the case record

10.1 The parties or their legal representatives shall be entitled to **51JPD.10** inspect an electronic record of the proceedings and obtain documents in the Electronic Working Case File.

(Rule 5.4B contains provisions about the supply to a party to the proceedings of documents from the court record.)

10.2 The Electronic Working Case File will be automatically updated.

10.3 Information concerning the availability of this facility will be communicated by Her Majesty's Courts and Tribunals Service on the Website.

11. Public kiosk service

11.1 A version of the Electronic Working Case File allowing access **51JPD.11** only to those documents which are available to non–parties will be made available through a public kiosk service.

(Rule 5.4C contains provisions about access to court documents by non–parties.)

11.2 Persons wishing to obtain copies of documents available to non–parties—

(a) may use the computer facilities provided by the public kiosk to search the court record for cases which have documents available to the public;

(b) complete the appropriate office copy request form; and

(c) must pay the appropriate fee.

11.3 Electronic copies of the documents will be sent by e–mail to an address supplied by the person applying for copies.

Add new Practice Direction 51K:

Editorial introduction

Please note that this Practice Direction does not come into force until October 1, **51KPD.0** 2015.

PRACTICE DIRECTION 51K—THE COUNTY COURT LEGAL ADVISERS PILOT SCHEME

1. Scope and interpretation

1.1 This Practice Direction is made under rule 51.2. It provides for **51KPD.1** a pilot scheme ("the County Court Legal Advisers Pilot Scheme") in respect of, and applies to, claims started at the County Court Business Centre ("CCBC") and the County Court Money Claims Centre ("CCMCC") for a period of 12 months from 1 October 2015 to 30 September 2016.

1.2 In this Practice Direction—

(a) "the County Court Business Centre" means the Production Centre and Money Claim Online;

(b) "legal adviser" means a court officer assigned to the County Court who is—

(i) a barrister; or

(ii) a solicitor,

who may exercise the jurisdiction of the County Court with regard to the matters set out in paragraph 2.1 and in the schedule to this Practice Direction, with the consent of the Designated Civil Judges for Northampton and Leicester Trial Centre, in respect of the CCBC, and Manchester Civil Justice Centre & Manchester Outer, in respect of the CCMCC, or their nominee.

2. Jurisdiction of the County Court that may be exercised by a legal adviser

51KPD.2 **2.1** A legal adviser may exercise the jurisdiction of the County Court with regard to the matters set out in the first column of the schedule to this Practice Direction, subject to the corresponding restrictions in the second column.

3. Reconsideration of a decision made by a legal adviser

51KPD.3 **3.1** Decisions of a legal adviser will be made without a hearing.

3.2 A party may request any decision of a legal adviser to be reconsidered by a District Judge.

3.3 A request must be filed within 14 days after the party is served with notice of the decision.

3.4 The request must include a summary of the issue and an explanation of why the reconsideration is sought.

3.5 Reconsideration will take place without a hearing.

Schedule

Jurisdiction of the County Court that may be exercised by a legal adviser

51KPD.4	**Work type**	**Restrictions on the exercise of jurisdiction and modifications of the Civil Procedure Rules**
	1. Order to rectify a procedural error pursuant to rule 3.10	Limited to those instances where the court serves a claim contrary to the claimant's instructions.
	2. Application to extend time for service of the claim form pursuant to rule 7.6	Limited to the first application, unless the claim would normally be allocated to the small claims track, and further limited to applications made within the period specified in rule 7.5 for service of the claim form.

Work type	Restrictions on the exercise of jurisdiction and modifications of the Civil Procedure Rules
3. Applications to amend a claimant's or defendant's address or details after service, pursuant to rule 17.1(2)	Limited to applications prior to the expiration of the relevant limitation period and claims which have been, or would normally be, allocated to the small claims track.
4. Application to amend the particulars of claim or the amount of the claim pursuant to rule 17.1(2)	Limited to— (a) applications received before a defence is filed; or (b) if an application is received after a defence is filed, claims which have been, or would normally be, allocated to the small claims track.
5. Application to add or substitute a party to the proceedings pursuant to rule 19.4	Limited to applications where all existing parties and the proposed new party agree to the addition or substitution and are in agreement that the application may be dealt with without a hearing.
6. Application to set aside default judgment, pursuant to rule 13.2	
7. Application to set aside default judgment, pursuant to rule 13.3	Limited to applications where— (a) all parties consent; and (b) the judgment is not satisfied.
8. Application to vary default judgment entered under Part 12, pursuant to rule 13.3	Limited to applications where— (a) the application relates to the time and rate of payment; and (b) all relevant parties consent.
9. Application to make a counterclaim after a defence has been filed, pursuant to rule 20.4(2)(b)	Limited to applications where all parties consent.

Work type	Restrictions on the exercise of jurisdiction and modifications of the Civil Procedure Rules
10. Application to extend time for complying with a notice of proposed allocation in accordance with rule 26.3(1)	Limited to one application per party, unless the claim has been provisionally allocated to the small claims track, and subject to the further limitation that time can be extended for a period not exceeding 28 days.
11. Application to stay proceedings pursuant to rule 26.4(2A) or to extend the period of a stay pursuant to rule 26.4(3)	Limited to one application and where all parties consent.
12. Application to remove a stay of proceedings made pursuant to rule 26.4(2A) or (3)	Limited to applications where all parties consent.
13. Applications for interim payments pursuant to rule 25.6	Limited to applications where all parties consent to the payment.
14. Entering and sealing an agreed judgment pursuant to rule 40.6(2) in any case where the requirements in Form EX224 are not met	
15. Applications for judgments or orders in terms agreed pursuant to rule 40.6(5)	
16. Application for an Order that a solicitor has ceased to act pursuant to rule 42.3	

PART 52

APPEALS

Add new paragraph 52.0.3.1:

Modification of Part 52 (Appeals to Court of Appeal)

52.0.3.1   Where an appeal lies to the Court of Appeal in proceedings to which the following CPR Parts apply, the rules in Part 52 (and supplementing practice directions) are modified as provided in those Parts (by the rules referred to in parentheses):

Part 76 (Proceedings Under the Prevention of Terrorism Act 2005) (r.76.16)

Part 79 (Proceedings Under the Counter–Terrorism Act 2008 and Part 1 of the Terrorist Asset–Freezing etc Act 2010) (r.79.14B)

Part 80 (Proceedings Under the Terrorism Prevention and Investigation Measures Act 2011) (r.80.12)

Part 82 (Closed Material Procedure) (r.82.32)

Part 88 (Proceedings Under the Counter–Terrorism and Security Act 2015) (r.88.15).

Requirement for permission

After the first paragraph, add as a new paragraph:

Where an applicant for permission to appeal is a party who has been committed for **52.3.1**
contempt of court and the contempt is unpurged the appeal court has power to refuse
to hear the application and to dismiss it accordingly, but that is a discretion to be
exercised with great caution (*JSC BTA Bank v Ablyazov* [2015] EWCA Civ 70, February
10, 2015, CA, unrep.); see further para.23.0.18 above.

Delete paragraph 52.3.4 and substitute:

When and where should the application for permission be made?

Rule 52.3 is made in exercise of the rule–making power granted by the Access to **52.3.4**
Justice Act 1999 s.54 (See Vol.1 para.9A–841). It applies to appeals generally, whether
to the Court of Appeal or to the High Court or to the County Court. It is supplemented
by provisions in Section 4 of Practice Direction 52A where detailed directions are
given as to which judges have power to grant permission to appeal in particular circumstances (see para.52APD.5 below).

Where permission is required, an application for permission may be made to the
lower court "at the hearing at which the decision to be appealed was made" or to the
appeal court (r.52.3(2)). Paragraph 4.1(a) of PD 52A states that, in the former event,
the lower court may adjourn the hearing to give a party an opportunity to apply for
permission to appeal. Where the lower court refuses an application for permission to
appeal a further application may be made to the appeal court (r.52.3(3)). Paragraph
4.1(b) of PD 52A states that, in the events of no application being made to the lower
court or of an application being made to that court and refused, an application for
permission to the appeal court may be made in accordance with r.52.4 (Appellant's
notice), which means, amongst other things, in accordance with the time limits imposed
by that rule.

Paragraph 4.1 of PD 52A came into its present form with effect from October 1,
2012. Its terms differ from those of the provision it replaced. In particular, contrary to
the position which prevailed before that date, there is nothing in para.4.1 (or in
r.52.3) which expressly or impliedly requires that, before applying to an appeal court
for permission to appeal, a party must first apply to the lower court for such
permission. This point was explained in *P v P* [2015] EWCA Civ 447, May 6, 2015,
CA, unrep., where the appeal context was an appeal from the decision of a Family
Division judge sitting at the RCJ to the Court of Appeal.

Commentary on r.52.3 in successive editions of the White Book since the 2000 edition has suggested that, although that rule in terms gives parties a choice to apply for
permission either to the lower court or to the appeal court, and expressly states that a
refusal in the lower court does not act as a bar to an application to the appeal court,
for several reasons a would–be appellant would generally be well–advised in the first
instance to apply for permission to the lower court for five reasons. The reasons are:

(a) The judge below is fully seized of the matter and so the application will take
    minimal time. Indeed the judge may have already decided that the case raises
    questions fit for appeal.
(b) An application at this stage involves neither party in additional costs.
(c) No harm is done if the application fails. The litigant enjoys two bites at the
    cherry.
(d) If the application succeeds and the litigant subsequently decides to appeal,
    they avoid the expensive and time–consuming permission stage in the appeal
    court.
(e) No harm is done if the application succeeds, but the litigant subsequently
    decides not to appeal.

That guidance was firmly endorsed by the Court of Appeal in the case of *T (A Child)*
(Contact: Alienation: Permission to Appeal), Re [2002] EWCA Civ 1736 at [12]–[13], and in
P v P at [68]. As a practical matter the guidance is more likely to be apposite in rela-
tion to appeals to the Court of Appeal than to other appellate contexts.

Where an application for permission is made to the lower court it is to be made "at
the hearing at which the decision to be appealed was made" which in effect means that
the application should be made to the judge whose decision is being challenged (and
not to some other judge of the lower court). The object is to discourage would–be appellants from delaying an application for permission to the lower court and to avoid

the inconveniences that might arise where the judge of that court is peripatetic or part–time. As noted above, para.4.1(a) of PD 52A states that the lower court may adjourn the hearing, that is to say, "the hearing at which the decision to be appealed was made", to give a party an opportunity to apply to it for permission to appeal. There is nothing in that provision to encourage the view that the court may order such adjournment retrospectively, a point that was arguable under relevant supplementing practice directions as they stood before October 1, 2012 (see *Balmoral Group Ltd v Borealis (UK) Ltd* [2006] EWHC 2228 (Comm), August 23, 2006, and *Multiplex Construction (UK) Ltd v Honeywell Control Systems Ltd* [2007] EWHC 236 (TCC), February 8, 2007, unrep.). If a judge hands down a reserved judgment in the absence of the parties and is aware that one party wishes to appeal, the judge should formally adjourn the hearing to enable that party to apply for permission to appeal (*Jackson v Marina Homes Ltd* [2007] EWCA Civ 1404, November 13, 2007, CA, unrep., at [8]).

If one ground of appeal is that the judge has failed to deal with a particular point, the judge should be given an opportunity to deal with that point at the hearing before the application for permission is made: see *English v Emery Reimbold & Strick Ltd* [2002] EWCA Civ 605; [2002] 1 W.L.R. 2409 at [25] and *S (Children), Re* [2007] EWCA Civ 694 at [23]–[25]. In *Greenwich Millennium Village Ltd v Essex Services Group Plc (formerly Essex Electrical Group Ltd)* [2014] EWCA Civ 960; [2014] 1 W.L.R. 3517, CA, the Court of Appeal explained that, where a judge of a lower court in refusing permission to appeal amplifies the reasons for his original decision, the appeal court in determining the appeal is entitled to take those additional reasons into account. These authorities and others are discussed further in the commentary following r.52.11, and in para.40.2.1.0.3 above.

How the appeal court deals with such applications

Add new paragraph at end:

52.3.6   Courts are entitled to give directions for the proper and efficient conduct of proceedings before them, including the conduct of applications for permission to appeal, and to impose sanctions on parties who fail to comply with their orders, including, in an appropriate case, the serious sanction of striking out of the proceedings, provided such powers are exercised fairly so as not to constitute a breach of art.6 of the Convention. In *Patel v Mussa* [2015] EWCA Civ 434, April 29, 2015, CA, unrep., where the application by a claimant (C) for permission to appeal from a decision of a district judge was struck out by a circuit judge for his failure to comply with directions given by the judge for the conduct of the application, the Court of Appeal dismissed C's appeal against the striking out. In doing so the Court observed that it had a "residual jurisdiction" to entertain an appeal against a judge's refusal of permission to appeal where the process by which the judge reached his decision was unfair and contravened art.6. However, resort to that jurisdiction may not be had where there are other adequate means by which remedy for breach of art. 6 may be obtained and compliance with the Human Rights Act 1998 s.9(1) ensured. In the case of a decision of the County Court a suitable remedy may be obtained by way of a claim for judicial review.

Statutory time limits for filing notice of appeal

Delete the second paragraph (starting "In relation to appeals under s.26(4) of the Extradition Act 2003") and substitute:

52.4.1.1   In relation to appeals under s.26(4) of the Extradition Act 2003, para.21.1(c) of PD52D stated that the appellant must serve a copy of the notice of appeal on the CPS, if they are not a party to the appeal, in addition to the persons to be served under r.52.4(3) "and in accordance with that rule". With effect from October 6, 2014, and subject to transitional provisions, rules of court for appeals to the High Court in extradition proceedings were included in Section 3 of Pt.17 in the Criminal Procedure Rules 2014 (SI 2014/1610) and by CPR Update 75 the whole of para.21.1 was omitted from PD52D. Cases dealing with the point that the court had no jurisdiction to extend the times limits for service of notices of appeal as required by para.21.1 are: *R. (Bajorek Sawczuk) v Poland* [2014] EWHC 1108 (Admin), March 21, 2014, unrep. (Collins J.); *Bugyo v Slovakia* [2014] EWHC 4230 (Admin), November 21, 2014, unrep. (Blake J.).

Point not raised below

After the second paragraph, add as a new paragraph:

    In *Walsham Chalet Park Ltd (t/a Dream Lodge Group) v Tallington Lakes Ltd* [2014] **52.8.2**
EWCA Civ 1607; [2015] C.P. Rep. 15, CA, the defendant (D) was granted permission
to appeal to the Court of Appeal against the decision of a judge at a CMC dismissing
D's application to strike out the claimant's claim under r.3.4 for their failure to comply
with court orders. At the hearing of the appeal, additional submissions made by D (in
person) to the effect that, by operation of r.32.10, C were debarred from calling any
witnesses at the trial were rejected by the Court on the grounds that they were not
made before the judge, it was not incumbent on the judge to take a point on r.32.10,
and it was plainly too late to advance such submissions for the first time on the appeal.

Scope of the rule

After the seventh paragraph, add as a new paragraph:

    In *Lawal v Circle 33 Housing Trust* [2014] EWCA Civ 1514; [2015] H.L.R. 9, CA, the **52.17.2**
Judge summarised the principles relevant to an application under r.52.17 as follows
(para.65).

    "First, the same approach applies whether the application is to re–open a refusal
of permission to appeal or to re–open a final judgment reached after full
argument. Second, r. 52.17(1) sets out the essential pre–requisites for invoking
the jurisdiction to re–open an appeal or a refusal of permission to appeal. More
generally, it is to be interpreted and applied in accordance with the principles
laid down in *Taylor v Lawrence*. Accordingly, third, the jurisdiction under r. 52.17
can only be invoked where it is demonstrated that the integrity of the earlier litigation process has been critically undermined. The paradigm case is where the
litigation process has been corrupted, such as by fraud or bias or where the
judge read the wrong papers. Those are not, however, the only instances for the
application of r. 52.17. The broad principle is that, for an appeal to be re–
opened, the injustice that would be perpetrated if the appeal is not reopened
must be so grave as to overbear the pressing claim of finality in litigation. Fourth,
it also follows that the fact that a wrong result was reached earlier, or that there
is fresh evidence, or that the amounts in issue are very large, or that the point in
issue is very important to one or more of the parties or is of general importance
is not of itself sufficient to displace the fundamental public importance of the
need for finality."

Add new paragraphs at end:

    In *Lawal v Circle 33 Housing Trust* [2014] EWCA Civ 1514; [2015] H.L.R. 9, CA, ten-
ants applied to the Court of Appeal for permission to appeal against a County Court
possession order, principally on ground that a defence based on art.8 of the Convention had not been properly considered. In dismissing the application at an oral hearing, the single lord justice proceeded under the false assumption that in the circumstances of the case it would be open to D to raise such defence at the enforcement
stage by asking for the warrant for possession to be rescinded or varied. D then made
a County Court application to vary or revoke the possession order under r.3.1(7), and
to prevent or suspend execution of the subsequent warrant of possession. At the trial
of that application D argued in full their art.8 defence and adduced evidence in support of it. The judge dismissed the application holding, amongst other things, that in
the circumstances of the case the procedural time limit in the Housing Act 1980
s.89(1) prevented the court from postponing possession, whether by suspending the
possession order or refusing execution of the warrant. D then applied to the Court of
Appeal for an order under r.52.17 re–opening their application for permission to appeal to the Court to enable their art. 8 ground of appeal therein to be reconsidered. D
submitting that only by re–opening the appeal could they (1) put themselves back into
a position in which they would be able to argue, before the grant of a possession order, that no such order should be made because it would infringe their art.8 rights,
and (2) overcome the time limitation on any stay or suspension of an order for possession by virtue of s.89(1) of the 1980 Act. The Court dismissed the application, holding
that the pre–conditions in r.52.17(1) were not satisfied. In doing so the Court conceded
that, had the single lord justice been aware that the County Court had no power to
entertain D's art.8 defence at the enforcement stage, she would have granted D
permission to appeal on that point, but pointed out that the criticism that she was
wrong not to do so is not enough to invoke the Court's jurisdiction under r.52.17.

    Amendments made to the Extradition Act 2003 by the Crime and Courts Act 2013
provided an "alternative effective remedy" in the form of a statutory appeal to the

High Court where at the end of extradition process an issue arises whether extradition would be compatible with the requested person's human rights (see *McIntyre v United States* [2014] EWHC 1886; [2015] 1 W.L.R. 507, DC, and cases referred to there). Previously a requested person's remedy in this respect lay in an application under r. 52.17 to re–open the final appeal in the process. With effect from October 6, 2014, and subject to transitional provisions, rules of court for appeals to the High Court in extradition proceedings were included in Section 3 of Pt 17 in the Criminal Procedure Rules 2014 (SI 2014/1610). In those Rules, r.17.27 (Reopening the determination of an appeal) applies where a party wants the Court "to reopen a decision of that court which determines an appeal or an application for permission to appeal".

PRACTICE DIRECTION 52C—APPEALS TO THE COURT OF APPEAL

Delete paragraph 19 and substitute:

Respondents actions when served with the appellant's notice

52CPD.19 **19**(1) (a) If the appellant seeks permission to appeal a respondent is permitted, and is encouraged, within 14 days of service of the appellant's notice or skeleton argument if later to file and serve upon the appellant and any other respondent a brief statement of any reasons why permission should be refused, in whole or in part.

(b) The statement should be not more than 3 pages long, and should be directed to the relevant threshold test for the grant of permission to appeal. The statement must also comply with paragraph 31(1)(b).

(c) The statement should identify issues to which the appeal should be limited, and any conditions to which the appeal should be subject (see Rule 52.3(7)).

(2) (a) If the appellant makes any application in addition to an application for permission to appeal (such as a stay of execution, an injunction pending appeal or an extension of time for appeal) a respondent should include in its written statement under paragraph 19(1)(a) any reasons why that application should be refused or granted only on terms.

(b) If, exceptionally, a respondent wishes to rely upon evidence for that purpose its evidence should be included in its written statement, supported by a statement of truth, or filed and served upon the appellant and any other respondent at the same time as its written statement under paragraph 19(1)(a).

(3) Unless the court directs otherwise, a respondent need take no further steps when served with an appellant's notice prior to being notified that permission to appeal has been granted.

Respondent's costs of permission applications

Delete paragraph 20(1) and substitute:

52CPD.20 **20**(1) There will normally be no order for the recovery of the costs of a respondent's written statement. In most cases an application for permission to appeal will be determined without the need for the respondent to attend a hearing. In such circumstances an order for costs will not normally be made in favour of a respondent who voluntarily attends a hearing.

PART 53

DEFAMATION CLAIMS

Editorial introduction

At the end of the second paragraph, add:

It is unfortunate that to date (June 2015) the Practice Direction to Part 53 has still **53.0.1** not been amended to reflect the changes made by the Defamation Act 2013. For example, para.2.7 fails to make any mention of the new statutory defence of publication on a matter of interest (Defamation Act 2013 s.4) , which replaces the *Reynolds* defence.

PRACTICE DIRECTION 53—DEFAMATION CLAIMS

Add new paragraph 53PD.17.1

It is unfortunate that this Practice Direction has still not been brought up to date to **53PD.17.1** reflect the changes made by the 2013 Act. (Note the observations of Warby J. in *Barron v Vines* [2015] EWHC 1161 (QB) at [17]). As far as paragraph 2.7 is concerned, those changes relate primarily to the abolition of the form of common law privilege known as *Reynolds* privilege for causes of action which accrued on or after January 1, 2014, and its replacement with a new statutory defence of publication on a matter of public interest: Defamation Act 2013 s.4. The old common law *Reynolds* privilege lingers on in defences to claims where the cause of action accrued before January 1, 2014. The pleading requirements for *Reynolds* privilege are fully set out in the main 2015 volume of this work.

Classical duty/interest qualified privilege is unaffected by the changes made by the 2013 Act.

The new s.4 defence of publication on a matter of public interest requires that the court should, in determining whether the statement complained of was or formed part of a statement on a matter of public interest, and whether the defendant reasonably believed that publishing the statement was in the public interest, have regard to all the circumstances of the case. It therefore seems likely that all the matters treated as relevant for the purposes of *Reynolds* privilege will continue to be important. Those would include such matters as the seriousness of the allegation, the extent to which it was a matter of public interest or concern, the source and status of the information, the steps taken to verify it, the urgency of the matter, and the steps taken to obtain and print the claimant's side of the story. Of course, the terms of s.4 itself oblige the pleader to set out the facts giving rise to the contention that the statement complained of was or formed part of a statement on a matter of public interest, and that the defendant believed on reasonable grounds that publishing the statement was in the public interest.

Malice

Delete the second paragraph beginning "Malice has been thought" and substitute:

Malice is almost certainly a dead letter in *Reynolds* privilege, for reasons stated in **53PD.22** earlier editions of this work. But *Reynolds* privilege itself is now moribund: it was abolished by Defamation Act 2013 s.4, and only appears as a defence to claims that accrued before January 1, 2014. However, the pleader faced with a *Reynolds* defence must of course set out in his Reply his full case as to why the defence should not succeed, which will usually include all facts relied on to show that the journalism which produced the article or programme was careless or otherwise not responsible.

In the third paragraph, delete the first sentence and substitute:

Similarly, the claimant faced with the new statutory defence of publication on a matter of public interest would be wise to set out in his reply all the circumstances which go to show that the words complained of were not a statement on a matter of public interest, and/or that the defendant did not reasonably believe that publication was in the public interest.

The section 3 procedure

In the first paragraph, at the end of the sentence ending "[2010] E.M.L.R. 11" add:

; *Murray v Associated Newspapers Ltd* [2015] EWCA Civ 488 **53PD.29**

In the first paragraph, in the sentence beginning "An application to make" for the "Murray v Associated Newspapers Ltd [2014] EWHC 1170 (QB); [2015] E.M.L.R. 23" case substitute:

    Murray v Associated Newspapers Ltd, above

Ruling on meaning

Add at end:

53PD.32   In *Rufus v Elliott* [2015] EWCA Civ 121; [2015] E.M.L.R. 16, a pre–2013 Act case, the claimant would not agree to the defendant's proposal that the actual meaning should be determined by the judge, so the issue of capability had to go to the Court of Appeal and the issue of the actual meaning had then to be remitted to the judge: see [28].

Procedure

Delete the first paragraph and substitute:

53PD.43   Statements in open court are made where a party wishes to accept a Pt 36 offer, where a claimant has accepted an offer of amends and wishes to make a unilateral statement (see *Winslet v Associated Newspapers Ltd* [2009] EWHC 2735 (QB), [2010] E.M.L.R.. 11 and *Murray v Associated Newspapers Ltd* [2015] EWCA Civ 488), and where the action has settled and (generally) one of the terms of settlement provides for a bilateral statement to be made in agreed terms. The normal practice is for the applicant to issue an application notice under CPR Pt 23 seeking permission to make a statement in terms approved by the court. The practice is now to make the application not to the judge but to the Senior Master, but the judge retains the right to approve the statement, since it is read in the judge's court. Permission is required for the making of a statement in open court so that the judge can ensure that the court's process, or the forum it provides, is not abused: *CTB v News Group Newspapers Ltd* (above) at [26]. In the case of an agreed statement, if the Senior Master gives permission, the order is sealed and a setting down number is obtained from the Clerk of the Lists. A date convenient for both parties is arranged between counsel's clerks or between solicitors, and the signed statement is released to the judge for mention. It is unusual for a bilateral statement to be refused by the court, but the court will refuse permission if informed that one of the parties proposing to join in the statement believes that it is false:

> "It is one thing for the court to be unable to guarantee that all its judgments or verdicts are the whole truth. It is quite another for the court to permit itself to be used for the making of a statement that the maker is at the same time declaring he believes to be untrue" (per Tugendhat J., *Adelson v Associated Newspapers Ltd (No.3)* [2008] EWHC 278 (QB) [67], [70]).

Where a statement is opposed

In the second paragraph, after the second sentence ending "(ibid)." add:

53PD.44   A claimant who has reached a bona fide settlement can normally expect to be given permission to make a unilateral statement unless that would give rise to unfairness to the other party: *Murray v Associated Newspapers Ltd* [2015] EWCA Civ 488. A statement in open court, whether unilateral or joint, must be fair and proportionate, should not misrepresent a party's case or the nature of the settlement reached, and must bear in mind the interests of third parties. The court is unlikely to intervene in the absence of any real or substantial unfairness to the objecting party or a third party, and 'nit–picks' are to be discouraged: *Murray*, above.

In the last paragraph, for "Murray v Associated Newspapers Ltd [2014] EWHC 1170 (QB); [2014] E.M.L.R. 23" substitute:

    Murray v Associated Newspapers Ltd [2014] EWHC 1170 (QB); [2015] EWCA Civ 488; [2014] E.M.L.R. 23

Offer of amends

In the first sentence, for "A statement may" substitute:

53PD.45   As explained above, a statement may

After "[2010] E.M.L.R. 11" add:

    ; *Murray v Associated Newspapers Ltd* [2015] EWCA Civ 488

PART 54

JUDICIAL REVIEW AND STATUTORY REVIEW

Editorial introduction

Add at end, as a new paragraph:

In Part 4 of the Criminal Justice and Courts Act 2015, sections 84 to 90 make pro- **54.0.1**
vision about the refusal by the High Court and the Upper Tribunal of relief in judicial
review proceedings, and about funding and costs in relation to such proceedings. (The
other sections in Part 4 (ss.91 and 92) make provision about the procedure for certain
planning proceedings.) Sub–sections (1) to (3) of s.84 amend SCA 1981 s.31 to provide
that the High Court must refuse permission to apply for judicial review, or refuse a
remedy, when it appears to the Court to be highly likely that the outcome for the
claimant would not have been substantially different if the conduct complained of had
not occurred, unless it is appropriate to do so for reasons of exceptional public interest.
Those amendments came into effect on April 13, 2015, but do not apply to an application for judicial review where the claim form was filed before that date (see SI 2015/
778 arts 3 & 4). (For text of s.31 as amended, see Vol.2 para.9A–101.)

When brought into force, sub–section (1) of s.85 will amend SCA 1981 s.31(3) to
provide that no application for judicial review may be made unless the claimant
provides any information about the financing of the claim which is required under any
rules of court. Section 87 deals with interveners, defined as persons who were granted
permission to file evidence or make representations in judicial review proceedings and
were not, at that time, parties (see para.9A–1311 below). That section came into force
on April 13, 2015, subject to the same transitional provision as applied to s.84(1) to (3)
(see SI 2015/778 arts 3 & 4). The section states that a party may not be ordered to pay
an intervener's costs unless there are exceptional circumstances making it appropriate
to do so. There are also provisions in the section governing the circumstances in which
interveners can be made to pay costs incurred by other parties. There are provisions
in ss.88 to 90 dealing with orders limiting or removing the liability of a party to pay
costs (these are currently known as protective costs orders, although they are referred
to in the 2015 Act as cost–capping orders) (see paras 9A–1312 to 9A–1314 below). The
Civil Procedure (Amendment No.2) Rules 2015 (SI 2015/670) amended CPR rr.54.8
and 54.11 to make provision for changes consequent upon ss.84(1) to (3) and 87 of the
2015 Act. Those amendments do not apply to an application for judicial review where
the claim form was filed before April 13, 2015.

Delete paragraph 54.0.3 and substitute:

Pre–action Protocol

A revised pre–action protocol has been adopted with effect from 6 April 2015. **54.0.3**

Time limit for filing claim form

*In rule 54.5(A1) delete the definitions of "decision governed by the Public Contracts Regulations
2006" and "economic operator" and substitute:*

> "decision governed by the Public Contracts Regulations 2015" means any de- **54.5**
> cision the legality of which is or may be affected by a duty owed to an
> economic operator by virtue of regulations 89 or 90 of those Regula-
> tions (and for this purpose it does not matter that the claimant is not an
> economic operator); and
>
> "economic operator" has the same meaning as in regulation 2(1) of the Public
> Contracts Regulations 2015.

Delete rule 54.5(6) and substitute:

**54.5—(6) Where the application for judicial review relates to a
decision governed by the Public Contracts Regulations 2015, the
claim form must be filed within the time within which an economic
operator would have been required by regulation 92 of those
Regulations (and disregarding the rest of that regulation) to start
any proceedings under those Regulations in respect of that
decision.**

Acknowledgment of service

After rule 54.8(4)(a)(i), add new rule 54.8(4)(a)(ia):

54.8   **(a) (ia) where the person filing it intends to contest the application for permission on the basis that it is highly likely that the outcome for the claimant would not have been substantially different if the conduct complained of had not occurred, set out a summary of the grounds for doing so; and**

Add after rule 54.8(5):

(Section 31(3C) of the Senior Courts Act 1981 requires the court, where it is asked to do so by the defendant, to consider whether the outcome for the claimant would have been substantially different if the conduct complained of had not occurred.)

Content

Add at end, as a new paragraph:

54.8.2   In r.54.8(4), para.(ai) was inserted by the Civil Procedure (Amendment No.2) Rules 2015 (SI 2015/670) r.9 and provides for the defendant to set out a summary of the grounds upon which the defendant contends that it is highly likely that the outcome for the claimant would not have been substantially different if the conduct complained of had not occurred. The court must consider that issue and, if it considers that is the position, must refuse permission to apply for judicial review: see SCA 1981 s.31(3C). Paragraph (ia) of r.54.8(4) came into effect on the day on which s.87 of the 2015 Act came into force, that is to say, on April 13, 2015 (see SI 2015/778 art.3). Section 87 and para.(ai) of r.54.8(4) do not apply to an application for judicial review where the claim form was filed before that date (ibid art.4, Sch.2 para.6, and SI 2015/670 r.12(2)).

Service of order giving or refusing permission

After rule 54.11(a), add a new rule 54.11(ai):

54.11   **(ai) any certificate (if not included in the order) that permission has been granted for reasons of exceptional public interest in accordance with section 31(3F) of the Senior Courts Act 1981; and**

Add new rule 54.11A:

Permission decision where court requires a hearing

54.11A   **54.11A—(1) This rule applies where the court wishes to hear submissions on—**

        (a) whether it is highly likely that the outcome for the claimant would not have been substantially different if the conduct complained of had not occurred; and if so

        (b) whether there are reasons of exceptional public interest which make it nevertheless appropriate to give permission.

(2) The court may direct a hearing to determine whether to give permission.

(3) The claimant, defendant and any other person who has filed an acknowledgment of service must be given at least 2 days' notice of the hearing date.

(4) The court may give directions requiring the proceedings to be heard by a Divisional Court.

(5) The court must give its reasons for giving or refusing permission.

Add new paragraph 54.11A.1:

Editorial note

Rule 54.11A provides that the court may direct an oral hearing where the court **54.11A.1** wishes to hear submissions on whether it is highly likely that the outcome for the claimant would not have been substantially different if the conduct complained had not occurred. In such circumstances, the court must refuse permission unless there are reasons of exceptional public interest which make it appropriate for leave to be given. Rule 54.11A was inserted by the Civil Procedure (Amendment No.2) Rules 2015 (SI 2015/670) r.10 and came into effect on the day on which s.84(1) to (3) of the 2015 Act came into force, that is to say, on April 13, 2015 (see SI 2015/778 art.3). Section 84(1) to (3) and r.54.11A do not apply to an application for judicial review where the claim form was filed before that date (ibid art.4, Sch.2 para.6, and SI 2015/670 r.12(2)).

Effect of rule

Add at end, as a new paragraph:

Section 87(5) and (6) of the Criminal Justice and Courts Act 2015 (see Vol.2 **54.17.1** para.9A–1311) provide that a person may apply for costs from the intervener if it is satisfied that one of four conditions are satisfied and that costs have been incurred as a result. The conditions are that (a) the intervener has acted as the principal claimant or defendant; (b) the intervener's evidence and representations, taken as a whole, have not been of significant assistance to the court; (c) a significant part of the intervener's evidence and representations relate to matters that it was not necessary for the court to consider; or (d) the intervener has acted unreasonably. Rule 46.15 (Claim for judicial review: costs against interveners), which was inserted in Part 46 by the Civil Procedure (Amendment No.2) Rules 2015 (SI 2015/670) r.6, draws attention to s.87 of the 2015 Act. Section 87 and r.46.15 were brought into effect on April 13, 2105, but do not apply to an application for judicial review where the claim form was filed before that date (SI 2015/778 arts 3 & 4, and SI 2015/670 r.12(1)). See further commentary following r.46.15.

PART 55

POSSESSION CLAIMS

Pre–action Protocols for Possession claims

In the first paragraph, for "Pre–action Protocol for Possession claims based on Rent Arrears" substitute:

Pre–Action Protocol for Possession Claims by Social Landlords **55.2.1**

In the second paragraph, delete "In addition, the Pre–action Protocol for Possession Claims based on Residential Mortgage Arrears came into force on November 19, 2008." and substitute:

See too the Pre–Action Protocol for Possession Claims Based on Mortgage or Home Purchase Plan Arrears in Respect of Residential Property.

Delete paragraph 55.10.2 and substitute:

Mortgage Pre–Action Protocol

A new Pre–Action Protocol for Possession Claims Based on Mortgage or Home **55.10.2** Purchase Plan Arrears in Respect of Residential Property came into effect on 6 April 2015. See C12–001 and the annotations thereto.

PART 57

PROBATE, INHERITANCE AND PRESUMPTION OF DEATH

Editorial note

In the second sentence, for "57 PD" substitute:

57PDA **57.14.1**

Procedure

In the ninth paragraph, for "(para.2BPD.4)" substitute:

57.16.0   (para.2BPD.1.1C)

Compromise of claims under the Act

In the second paragraph, for "2BPD 5.1(a)" substitute:

57.16.1   2BPD.7B.1 (Master) and 7B.2 (District Judge)

The requirement to file a costs budget in claims under the Act

In the final paragraph, for "looks to recover" substitute:

57.16.5   intends to apply for an order for the payment of

PART 70

GENERAL RULES ABOUT ENFORCEMENT OF JUDGMENTS AND ORDERS

Delete paragraph 70.0.6 and substitute:

Money claims

70.0.6   With effect from March 19, 2012, Practice Direction 70 was substantially amended by TSO CPR Update 58 by which it was divided into two Sections with paras 8 to 11 added as Section II (see para.70PD.8 below). The provisions in Section 2 deal with the automatic transfer for enforcement of judgments in claims commenced in the County Court Money Claims Centre (formerly defined as "designated money claims"). Section II of Practice Direction 70 relates to a claim which (a) is started in the County Court under Pt 7, (b) is only a claim for either or both a specified amount of money or an unspecified amount of money, and (c) is not a claim for which special procedures are provided in the CPR (see 7APD.4A). Such claims are issued in the County Court Money Claims Centre ("CCMCC") situated at Salford. (A party commences such a claim by sending the appropriate practice form to the CCMCC; see para.7.2.2 above.) Provisions inserted in the CPR by the Civil Procedure (Amendment No.4) Rules 2011 (SI 2011/3103) and related amendments to practice directions made by TSO CPR Update 58 provide for the transfer of money claim cases from the CCMCC to County Court hearing centres for particular purposes before judgment (see rr.3.5A, 12.5A, 14.7A, 26.2A). Further provisions inserted in Pts 71 to 73 and CCR Ord.27 by the Civil Procedure (Amendment) Rules 2012 (SI 2012/505) deal with the transfer of money claims for enforcement purposes. The automatic transfer provisions in Section 2 of PD70 follow from those rule amendments and come into play where applications are made for orders to obtain information, for third party debt orders, charging orders and attachment of earnings orders. See, further, commentary in paras 71.2.3, 72.3.3, 73.3.3 and cc27.3.1 below.

PART 71

ORDERS TO OBTAIN INFORMATION FROM JUDGMENT DEBTORS

Venue

In the first paragraph, for "designated money claim" substitute:

71.2.3   money claim

In the first paragraph, for "courtas" substitute:
court as

Add new paragraph 71.2.9:

"produce at court documents in his control" (r.71.2(6))

71.2.9   The concept of "control" of documents for the purposes of the information–gathering exercise under Part 71 to enable enforcement of a judgment is different from control in the context of disclosure. Under Part 71, a person may have sufficient control to be required to produce a document if he is likely to have "a real say" as to whether or not to produce the document (*North Shore Ventures Ltd v Anstead Holdings Ltd* [2012] EWCA Civ 11, January 18, 2012, CA, unrep., per Toulson L.J. at [35]). If there are reasonable grounds to infer that the true nature of the relationship with a third party (such as a trustee) is that there is some understanding or arrangement by which the latter is to shelter assets or follow instructions, the judge may be entitled to infer that such assets and related documents are under the control of the person being examined (ibid at [38–40]). This is consistent with the approach of the court to provision of information in orders ancillary to freezing orders: the court can make an order under r.25.1(1)(g) for provision of information about relevant assets. Such orders provide to the claimant an opportunity of investigating the truth of the claim, for example, that assets are held on trust or by a third party for the defendant, in order to avoid sophisticated or wily operators from making themselves immune to the court's orders (see *JSC Mezhdunarodniy Promyshlenniy Bank v Pugachev* [2015] EWCA Civ 139, February 27, 2015, CA, unrep., at [58]).

PART 72

THIRD PARTY DEBT ORDERS

Venue

In the first paragraph, for "designated money claim" substitute:
money claim

72.3.3

PART 73

CHARGING ORDERS, STOP ORDERS AND STOP NOTICES

Venue

For "designated money claim" substitute:
money claim

73.3.3

PART 74

ENFORCEMENT OF JUDGMENTS IN DIFFERENT JURISDICTIONS

In the Table of Contents, before the entry for rule 74.36, add rule group heading "OUTGOING PROTECTION MEASURES" and, before the entry for rule 74.46, add rule group heading "INCOMING PROTECTION MEASURES".

Scope of this Part and interpretation

Rule 74.1(5)(d) as reproduced in the White Book 2015 Main Work contained some errors; please delete and substitute with the following version:

(d) "the Judgments Regulation" means Regulation (EU) No.1215/2012 of the European Parliament and of the Council of 12 December 2012 on jurisdiction and the recognition and enforcement of judgments in civil and commercial matters (recast), as amended from time to time and as applied pursuant to the Agreement made on 19 October 2005 between the European Community and the Kingdom of Denmark on jurisdiction and the recog-

74.1

nition and enforcement of judgments in civil and com-
mercial matters;
(For application of the recast Judgments Regulation to
Denmark, see also the Official Journal of the European
Union at OJ L79, 21.3.2013. p.4)

Delete the words in parentheses at the end of rule 74.1.

Procedure for enforcing judgments under the Judgments Regulation

Rule 74.4A as reproduced in the White Book 2015 Main Work contained some errors; please delete and substitute with the following version:

74.4A   **74.4A A person seeking the enforcement of a judgment which is
enforceable under the Judgments Regulation must, except in a case
falling within article 43(3) of the Regulation (protective measures),
provide the documents required by article 42 of the Regulation.**

Public policy

Add new paragraph at end:

74.7.3   In proceedings issued by a ship operating company on refund guarantees issued by
the defendant bank, *Spliethoff's Bevrachtingskantoor BV v Bank of China* [2015] EWHC
999 (Comm) the Commercial Court found that the claimant had voluntarily submitted
to the jurisdiction of the Chinese Court in proceedings brought by the Chinese
shipyard whose obligations were guaranteed by the bank. The Commercial Court went
on to hold that there was no valid public policy objection to the recognition of the
judgments of the Chinese court on grounds that the shipyard had obtained the judgments in breach of anti–suit injunctions issued in arbitration proceedings between the
claimant and the shipyard. This was despite a finding that there had bee "a flagrant
disregard of the anti–suit injunctions" which had been obtained in accordance with
English law, and where the parties had chosen English law and submitted to English
jurisdiction. The Court held that public policy grounds in s.32 of the 1982 Act are
clear. If a party submits for the purpose of s.32(1)(c), then it loses its shield against recognition under s.32 by reference to jurisdiction or arbitration clauses. It was noted
that anti–suit injunctions may be granted for many and varied reasons wholly unre-
lated to arbitration or jurisdiction clause, for example on grounds of oppression.

Refusal of recognition or enforcement under the Judgments Regulation

74.7A   *At the end of rule 74.7A(4)(a) delete "("the affected persons")".*

Relief against enforcement under the Judgments Regulation

Rule 74.7B as reproduced in the White Book 2015 Main Work contained some errors; please delete and substitute with the following version:

74.7B   **74.7B—(1) An application for relief under article 44 of the Judgments Regulation must be made—**

    (a) in accordance with Part 23; and

    **(b) to the court in which the judgment is being enforced or,
if the judgment debtor is not aware of any proceedings
relating to enforcement, the High Court.**

  **(2) The judgment debtor must, as soon as practicable, serve cop-
ies of any order made under article 44 on—**

    **(a) all other parties to the proceedings and any other person
affected by the order;**

(b) **any court in which proceedings relating to enforcement of the judgment are pending in England and Wales; and**

(c) **any enforcement agent or enforcement officer (as defined in rule 83.1(2)) instructed by the judgment creditor,**
and any such order will not have effect on any person until it has been served.

Appeals

In rule 74.8(3)(a) delete "or a Regulation State".   **74.8**

Appeals

Add new paragraph at end:

In *Christofi v National Bank of Greece (Cyprus) Ltd* [2015] EWHC 986 (QB) it was held **74.8.1** that he court had no general power to extend the mandatory two–month time limit for appealing in Regulation 44/2001 art.43(5) and CPR r.74.8(4)(a)(ii). It was obliged to enforce that time limit strictly, subject only to its residual power to extend it in the rare event that its application would impair the very essence of the right of appeal and strict adherence to it would infringe art.6 ECHR. The Regulation established an autonomous and complete system for the recognition and enforcement of judgments, and it excluded any separate challenge to an enforcement order under domestic law. Article 43(5) struck a balance between the need for expedition and a defendant's right to appeal. (See also the court's comments in relation to *Citibank NA v Rafidian Bank* above). This decision follows another recent High Court decision, *Taylor–Carr v Howkins and Harrison LLP* [2014] EWHC 3479 (QB), though the reasoning is fuller and applies more widely. It will have continuing relevance since, despite the new regime for enforcing judgments from EU countries which came into force on January 10, 2015, the old regime will still apply to judgments in proceedings instituted before that date.

Authentic instruments and court settlements

In rule 74.11, for "suspension of judgments" substitute:

suspension of any judgments   **74.11**

Adaptation of certain orders in foreign judgments subject to the Judgments Regulation

In rule 74.11A(4), after "article 54(2)" add:

of the Judgments Regulation   **74.11A**

IV. Enforcement in England and Wales of European Community Judgments

Interpretation

In rule 74.19(a)(iv), after "207/2009" add:

of 26 February 2009   **74.19**

Before rule 74.36 add rule group heading "OUTGOING PROTECTION MEASURES".
Before rule 74.46 add rule group heading "INCOMING PROTECTION MEASURES".

PART 81

APPLICATIONS AND PROCEEDINGS IN RELATION TO CONTEMPT OF COURT

Legal representation—legal aid

Add new paragraph at end:

81.1.5   In *Brown v Haringey LBC* [2015] EWCA Civ 483, May 14, 2015, CA, unrep., the Court of Appeal (1) endorsed the reasoning and the conclusion of the judge in the *King's Lynn and West Norfolk case* (above), (2) noted that under the relevant statutory provisions (a) the Crown Court, the High Court and the Court of Appeal (respectively) are authorised to make determinations under s.16 of the 2012 Act as to whether an individual qualifies for representation for the purposes of criminal proceedings before those courts, (b) however, there is no similar authorisation conferred upon the County Court, (c) accordingly, by virtue of s.18 it was for the Director of the LAA to make the determination in a case where committal proceedings are brought against an individual in the County Court. In allowing the appeal of an individual (D) committed for contempt in County Court proceedings, the Court held (1) that, in the circumstances, the judge ought to have made a full inquiry, adjourning the hearing if necessary, as to (a) whether D wanted legal representation, and (b) whether he had applied for the necessary funding and with what results, and (2) that the lack of legal representation for D before the judge (to which it seemed clear he was entitled) constituted a serious procedural flaw leading to a failure to hold a fair trial.

Disproportionate committal applications—abuse of process

In the first paragraph, for "(PJSC Vseukrainskyi Aktsionernyi Bank [2014] EWHC 3771 (Comm), November 17, 2014, unrep. (Hamblen J.))" substitute:

81.4.9   (*PJSC Vseukrainskyi Aktsionernyi Bank v Maksimov* [2014] EWHC 4370 (Comm), December 19, 2014, unrep. (Hamblen J.))

Effect of rule

Add new paragraph at end:

81.10.1   Generally, in an application to commit for breach of judgment or order as a practical matter the parties will be limited to the applicant and the respondent (the alleged contemnor). Nothing in the rules forbids the joinder of additional parties. In *Cambra v Jones* [2014] EWHC 913 (Fam); [2015] 1 F.L.R. 263, the joinder of a child was permitted in committal proceedings brought by her father against her mother following her failure to comply with a removal order made in family proceedings.

PART 82

CLOSED MATERIAL PROCEDURE

Consideration of closed material application or of objection to special advocate's communication

In rule 82.14(1)(b), after "special advocate" in the second instance, add:

82.14   **or to the form in which it is proposed to be made**

PART 83

WRITS AND WARRANTS—GENERAL PROVISIONS

Wrongful seizure by enforcement officer

83.0.13 *Delete the first paragraph starting "Where an enforcement officer, being misled..."*

Add new paragraph at end:
　Schedule 12 para.66 provides remedies for wrongful enforcement. The court may order the goods to be returned and order the enforcement agent or any related person (which includes the creditor) to pay damages for loss.

Staying execution of warrant of possession

In the third paragraph, for "9B" in the first instance, substitute:
　3A–39　　　　　　　　　　　　　　　　　　　　　　　　　　　　　　　**83.26.4**

In the third paragraph, for "9B" in the second instance, substitute:
　3A–58

PART 84

ENFORCEMENT BY TAKING CONTROL OF GOODS

The court's powers on the application

In the first paragraph, for "These are that the goods may be returned to the debtor or that the enforcement agent shall pay damages in respect of the loss suffered by the debtor as a result of the breach of Sch.12 or of anything done under a defective instrument." substitute:
　These are that the goods may be returned to the debtor and/or that the enforce- **84.13.4** ment agent or any related person (which includes the creditor) shall pay damages in respect of the loss suffered by the debtor as a result of the breach of Sch.12 or of anything done under a defective instrument.

SCHEDULE 1

RSC ORDER 115—CONFISCATION AND FORFEITURE IN CONNECTION WITH CRIMINAL PROCEEDINGS

"restraint order ... charging order"

1988 Act

For "R. v Ahmad (Shakeel) [2014] UKSC 36; [2014] 3 W.L.R. 23" substitute:
　R. v Ahmad (Shakeel) [2014] UKSC 36; [2015] A.C. 299; [2014] 3 W.L.R. 23　　**sc115.3.1**

In the fourth paragraph, for "CPS v Eastenders Group [2014] 2 W.L.R. 1269" substitute:
　Crown Prosecution Service v Eastenders Group [2014] UKSC 26; [2015] A.C. 1; [2014] 2 W.L.R. 1269

"where a receiver is appointed"

In the third paragraph, for "CPS v Eastenders Group [2014] 2 W.L.R. 1269" substitute:
　Crown Prosecution Service v Eastenders Group [2014] UKSC 26; [2015] A.C. 1; [2014] 2　**sc115.8.3** W.L.R. 1269

SCHEDULE 2

CCR ORDER 27—ATTACHMENT OF EARNINGS

Venue

In the first paragraph, for "designated money claim" substitute:
　money claim　　　　　　　　　　　　　　　　　　　　　　　　　　　**cc27.3.1**

SECTION B

MISCELLANEOUS PRACTICE DIRECTIONS AND PRACTICE STATEMENTS

PRACTICE DIRECTION—SOLICITOR'S NEGLIGENCE IN RIGHT TO BUY CASES (TRANSFER OF EXISTING AND NEW CLAIMS TO THE CHANCERY DIVISION AND APPOINTMENT OF DESIGNATED JUDGE)

Assignment to Mr Justice Sales

In paragraph 7.1, for "Mr Justice Sales" substitute:

B15–007 **7.1** a judge nominated by the Chancellor

In paragraph 7.2, for "Mr Justice Sales" substitute:

7.2 a judge nominated by the Chancellor

Substitution of Nominated Master and/or Judge

In paragraph 8, for "Mr Justice Sales" substitute:

B15–008 **8** a judge already so nominated

After paragraph B16–001 add new Practice Direction:

PRACTICE DIRECTION (COMMITTAL FOR CONTEMPT: OPEN COURT) [2015] 1 W.L.R. 2195, SEN CTS

Preamble

B17–001 **1.** This Practice Direction applies to all proceedings for committal for contempt of court, including contempt in the face of the court, whether arising under any statutory or inherent jurisdiction and, particularly, supplements the provisions relating to contempt of court in the Civil Procedure Rules 1998, the Family Procedure Rules 2010, the Court of Protection Rules 2007, and the Criminal Procedure Rules 2014 and any related Practice Directions supplementing those various provisions. It applies in all courts in England and Wales, including the Court of Protection, and supersedes the *Practice Guidance: Committal for Contempt* [2013] 1 WLR 1326, dated 3 May 2013; *Practice Guidance (Committal Proceedings: Open Court) (No. 2)* [2013] 1 WLR 1753, dated 4 June 2013; and *President's Circular: Committals* Family Court Practice 2024 at 2976, dated 2 August 2013.

2. Any reference in this Practice Direction to a judgment includes reference to written reasons provided in accordance with rule 27.2 of the Family Procedure Rules 2010.

Open Justice

B17–002 **3.** Open justice is a fundamental principle. The general rule is that hearings are carried out in, and judgments and orders are made in, public. This rule applies to all hearings, whether on application or otherwise, for committal for contempt irrespective of the court in which they are heard or of the proceedings in which they arise.

4. Derogations from the general principle can only be justified in exceptional circumstances, when they are strictly necessary as measures to secure the proper administration of justice. Derogations shall, where justified, be no more than strictly necessary to achieve their purpose.

Committal Hearings—in Public

5.(1) All committal hearings, whether on application or otherwise **B17–003** and whether for contempt in the face of the court or any other form of contempt, shall be listed and heard in public.

(2) They shall, except where paragraph 5(3) applies, be listed in the public court list as follows:

FOR HEARING IN OPEN COURT

Application by (*full name of applicant*) for

the Committal to prison of

(*full name of the person alleged to be in contempt*).

(3) In those cases where the person alleged to be in contempt is subject to arrest for an alleged breach of an order, including a location or collection order or an order made under the Family Law Act 1996, the hearing shall be listed in the public court list as follows:

FOR HEARING IN OPEN COURT [add, where there has been a remand in custody: in accordance with the order of (*name of judge*) dated (*date*)]

Proceedings for the Committal to prison of

(*full name of the person alleged to be in contempt*)

who was arrested on (*date*) in accordance with and for alleged breach of a [location/collection/ Family Law Act 1996/other] order made by (*name of judge*) on (*date*).

6. Where it is not possible to publish the details required by paragraph 5(3) in the public court list in the usual way the day before the hearing i.e., in such circumstances where the alleged contemnor is produced at court by the Tipstaff or a constable on the morning of the hearing, having been arrested over night, the following steps should be taken:

(1) Where, as in the Royal Courts of Justice, the public court list is prepared and accessible in electronic form, it should be updated with the appropriate entry as soon as the court becomes aware that the matter is coming before it;

(2) Notice of the hearing should at the same time be placed outside the door of the court in which the matter is being, or is to be heard, and at whatever central location in the building the various court lists are displayed;

(3) Notice should be given to the national print and broadcast media, via the Press Association's CopyDirect service, of the fact that the hearing is taking or is shortly due to take place.

If an alleged contemnor is produced at court, having been arrested overnight, the person shall immediately be produced before a judge who shall sit in public.

7. Where the committal hearing is brought by way of application notice, the court may authorise any person who is not a party to proceedings to obtain a copy of the application notice, upon request and subject to payment of any appropriate fee. Authorisation shall be granted in all but exceptional circumstances. Where authorisation is refused, the reasons for that refusal shall be set out in writing by the judge and supplied to the person who made the request.

Committal Hearings—in Private

B17–004   **8.** Where the court, either on application or otherwise, is considering derogating from the general rule and holding a committal hearing in private, or imposing any other such derogation from the principle of open justice:

> (1) it shall in all cases before the hearing takes place, notify the national print and broadcast media, via the Press Association's CopyDirect service, of the fact of the committal hearing (whether it is brought on application or otherwise) when and where it is listed for hearing, and the nature of the proposed derogation; and

> (2) at the outset of the committal hearing the court shall hear submissions from the parties and/or the media on the question whether to impose the proposed derogation.

9. In considering the question whether there are exceptional circumstances justifying a derogation from the general rule, and whether that derogation is no more than strictly necessary the fact that the committal hearing is made in the Court of Protection or in any proceedings relating to a child does not of itself justify the matter being heard in private. Moreover the fact that the hearing may involve the disclosure of material which ought not to be published does not of itself justify hearing the application in private if such publication can be restrained by an appropriate order.

10. Where the court decides to exercise its discretion to derogate from the general rule, and particularly where it decides to hold a committal hearing in private, it shall, before it continues to do so, sit in public in order to give a reasoned public judgment setting out why it is doing so.

11. Where, having decided to exercise its discretion to hold a committal hearing in private, the court further decides that the substantive committal application is to be adjourned to a future date, the adjourned hearing shall be listed in the public court list as follows:

> FOR HEARING IN PRIVATE
> In accordance with the order of (name of judge) dated (*date*)
> [On the application of (*full name of applicant*)]
> Proceedings for the Committal to prison of
> (*full name of the person alleged to be in contempt*).

12. Orders directing a committal hearing be heard in private or of other such derogations from the principle of open justice shall not be granted by consent of the parties: see *JIH v News Group Newspapers* [2011] EWCA Civ 42, [2011] WLR 1645 at [21].

Judgments

B17–005   **13.**(1) In all cases, irrespective of whether the court has conducted the hearing in public or in private, and the court finds that a person has committed a contempt of court, the court shall at the conclusion of that hearing sit in public and state:

(i) the name of that person;

(ii) in general terms the nature of the contempt of court in respect of which the committal order, which for this purpose includes a suspended committal order, is being made;

(iii) the punishment being imposed; and

(iv) provide the details required by (i) to (iii) to the national media, via the CopyDirect service, and to the Judicial Office, at judicialwebupdates@judiciary.gsi.gov.uk, for publication on the website of the Judiciary of England and Wales.

(2) There are no exceptions to these requirements. There are never any circumstances in which any one may be committed to custody or made subject to a suspended committal order without these matters being stated by the court sitting in public.

14. In addition to the requirements at paragraph 13, the court shall, in respect of all committal decisions, also either produce a written judgment setting out its reasons or ensure that any oral judgment is transcribed, such transcription to be ordered the same day as the judgment is given and prepared on an expedited basis. It shall do so irrespective of its practice prior to this Practice Direction coming into force and irrespective of whether or not anyone has requested this.

15. Copies of the written judgment or transcript of judgment shall then be provided to the parties and the national media via the Copy-Direct service. Copies shall also be supplied to BAILII and to the Judicial Office at judicialwebupdates@judiciary.gsi.gov.uk for publication on their websites as soon as reasonably practicable.

16. Advocates and the judge (except judges and justices of the peace in the Magistrates' courts) shall be robed for all committal hearings.

Lord Thomas L.C.J.

26 March 2015

After paragraph B17–005 add new Practice Note:

PRACTICE NOTE: FIXED–END TRIALS APRIL 24, 2015, UNREP

1. Following the success of last year's pilot scheme, all trials in the **B18–001** Chancery Division in London (including trials before Masters and Registrars) are in future to be conducted on a fixed–end basis. That means that each trial will, save in exceptional circumstances, be required to be completed within the period allocated to it.

2. The adoption of fixed–end trials makes it all the more important that parties should ensure that time estimates are accurate and, where appropriate, revise them. The parties need to consider carefully how long each element of the case is likely to take. Every time estimate should also take account of the length of time that the judge is likely to require for pre–reading. Where it is thought that it will be appropriate to have an interval between the close of evidence and final submissions, the time estimate should factor this in as well (taking into account both the preparation of the submissions and, where written submissions are to be supplied, the time that the judge will need to digest them). In practice, it is vital for the parties to agree a trial timetable at as early a stage as possible and to review it if circumstances change. In future, timetables (agreed, if possible) should always be filed at the same time as the skeleton arguments for the trial.

3. It is to be stressed that, as mentioned above (and also in the Chancery Guide), every time estimate must make a realistic allowance for pre–reading by the judge. The time within which a case must be concluded will thus run from the beginning of the judge's pre–reading. Should the period allowed for pre–reading prove inadequate, the time available in Court will be shortened correspondingly. The same principle will apply if too little time is allowed for the judge to read any written closing submissions.

4. A time estimate for the trial will typically have been provided at an early stage of the proceedings. Where, as will usually be appropriate, a case management conference has been held, this is likely to have fixed a time estimate. If an existing estimate now seems erroneous, it should be revised as soon as practicable, and in any event by the date of any pre–trial review. The Court will, if possible, seek to accommodate an increase (especially a modest one) if appropriate without changing the trial window.

5. Where one or more parties to a case propose that the time estimate for a trial should be changed but one or more other parties disagree, the matter must be referred to a Master, Registrar or Judge, as appropriate. Listing cannot change the time estimate given for a trial without either the parties' consent or a direction from a Master, Registrar or Judge.

6. A pre–trial review should be held about four weeks before the trial in any case estimated to last five days or more. Among other things, the judge hearing the pre–trial review will be concerned to check that the time estimate is realistic and that the parties have taken appropriate steps to agree a timetable for the trial. A trial will, however, be conducted on a fixed–end basis even where there has been no pre–trial review (as will typically be the case with trials lasting less than five days).

Sir Terence Etherton C.

24 April 2015

After Paragraph B18–001 add new Practice Direction:

PRACTICE DIRECTION (AUDIO RECORDING OF PROCEEDINGS: ACCESS) [2014] 1 W.L.R. 632 SEN CTS

B19–001   **1.** This Practice Direction is issued in order to clarify the practice and procedure governing access to CD or Digital Audio recordings of court proceedings. It applies to civil and family proceedings in all courts in England and Wales.

2. Where court proceedings, including judgments, are recorded by tape or other mechanical or digital means there is generally no right, either for a party or non–party, to listen to or receive a copy of such a recording. This is to minimise the risk of misuse of such recordings.

3. A person who has obtained a copy of the official transcript of proceedings or a judgment may apply, upon payment of the charges authorised by any scheme in force, for permission to listen to or receive a copy of an audio recording of the proceedings, the judgment, or a part thereof.

4. Applications should be made to the judge hearing the proceedings or, if the proceedings are taking place in theCourt of Appeal or a Divisional Court, to the presiding judge.

5. Subject to paragraph 6, permission will only be granted in exceptional circumstances, for example where there is cogent evidence that the official transcript may have been wrongly transcribed.

6. Permission will usually be granted to official law reporters, i.e., individuals who hold a Senior Courts qualification for the purposes of section 115 of the Courts and Legal Services Act 1990, if they require access to a recording in order to ensure that they can report a judgment with complete accuracy.

7. Permission may be granted subject to such conditions as the court considers necessary to protect recordings of confidential or legally privileged conversations between parties and their lawyers.

8. This Direction is made by the Lord Chief Justice, following consultation with the Master of the Rolls and President of the Family Division. It is issued in accordance with the procedure laid down in Part 1 of Schedule 2 to the Constitutional Reform Act 2005.

Lord Thomas of Cwmgiedd C.J.

14 February 2014

After paragraph B19–001 add Chancery Masters' Guidelines for the Transfer of Claims:

CHANCERY MASTERS' GUIDELINES FOR THE TRANSFER OF CLAIMS (MAY 20, 2015)

1. This document provides informal guidance for Chancery Masters and Deputies concerning the transfer of claims out of the Chancery Division in London. The guidance has been approved by The Chancellor.　　　　　　　　　　　　　　　　　　B20–001

2. Claims are transferred out where another court is more suitable for case management and trial of a claim. These guidelines relate to transfers to:

    (a) a Chancery District Registry outside London;

    (b) the County Court;

    (c) another Division of the High Court.

3. The objective of these guidelines is to ensure that only cases which may properly be regarded as being suitable for management and trial in the Chancery Division of the High Court in London are retained there. All other claims should be transferred out.

4. It is recognised that a decision to retain or transfer a case is an exercise of judicial discretion in accordance with the overriding objective and the other provisions of the CPR. This guidance is not intended to fetter the exercise of that discretion on a case by case basis.

5. Consideration should be given, where relevant, to:

    (a) PD29 2.1 to 2.6 (appendix 1) which provides guidance for case management within the High Court in London;

    (b) Part 30(3)(2) (appendix 2) which sets out criteria the court should take in to account when considering transfer. The criteria are not exclusive;

    (c) Part 49 and PD49A and PD49B—Specialist Proceedings;

(d) Part 57—Probate and Inheritance;

(e) Part 63—Intellectual Property.

6. Active consideration should be given at all stages of the management of a claim to the appropriate venue for the claim to be managed and tried. If a case is suitable for transfer, it is generally preferable for it to be transferred before detailed case management has taken place, leaving the receiving court to case manage the claim in accordance with its usual approach.

7. PD29 2.2 suggests that a claim with a value of less than £100,000 will generally be transferred to the County Court unless;

(a) it is required by an enactment to be tried in the High Court, or

(b) it falls within a specialist list, or

(c) it falls within one of the categories specified in the list at PD29 2.6.

8. The figure of £100,000 in PD29 2.2 accords with the current minimum value of money claims which may be issued in the High Court. The value of a claim is not a consideration which has greater weight than the other criteria set out in CPR 30(3)(2) but it is likely to be a factor with considerable influence in making a decision about transfer to the County Court or a specialist list. The figure of £100,000 mentioned in PD29 is not generally regarded as a relevant measure for money claims in the Chancery Division in London. Nor is £300,000 (the value figure beyond which court fees do not increase). Similarly, for probate and equity claims, the figures of £30,000 and £350,000 respectively are not determinative.

9. If the value of the claim is ascertainable, particular focus should be given to the possibility of transferring Part 7 claims with a value of less than £500,000. Factors which may point to retention of such claims in the High Court include:

(a) complex facts and/or

(b) complex or non–routine legal issues and/or

(c) complex relief and/or

(d) parties based outside the jurisdiction and/or

(e) public interest or importance and/or

(f) large numbers of parties and/or

(g) related claim and/or

(h) the saving of costs and/or

(i) efficiency in the use of judicial resources.

10. The availability of a judge with the specialist skills to deal with the claim is, however, always an important consideration when considering whether or not to transfer it. There are two circuit judges at Central London County Court who are specialised in Chancery work, and the waiting times at Central London are likely to be shorter than in the High Court for a trial before a judge. The delay in having a case heard should also be a consideration when deciding whether to transfer a case to the County Court or not and regard should be had to listing information provided by Central London CC, Chancery List.

11. When making an order for transfer of a claim to Central

London CC, Chancery List consideration should be given to including a direction in the order that the case is considered to be suitable for trial only by a specialist circuit judge. Such a direction is not binding on the County Court but should be taken into account.

12. PD 29 at 2.6(1), (3) and (7) indicates that professional negligence claims, fraud and undue influence claims and contentious probate claims are suitable for trial in the High Court, but it does not follow that claims within these categories should necessarily remain in the High Court. Less complex and/or lower value claims of these types are suitable for trial in Central London County Court, Chancery List. Serious cases of fraud, however, should generally remain in the High Court. Certain professional negligence claims may be better suited to the Queen's Bench Division.

13. Part 7 and Part 8 claims may sometimes be dealt with more efficiently by a Master rather than transferring the claim. Note the revised form of PD2B which came in to effect on 6 April 2015 and the Guidance Note relating to trials by Masters approved by the Chancellor.

14. Many claims under the Inheritance Act will be suitable for trial in the County Court and should generally be transferred to Central London County Court, Chancery List unless the Master is willing to try the claim and it is efficient to do so. Inheritance Act claims by a spouse will usually be suitable for transfer to the Family Division. Where there is a related Probate claim, or other Part 7 claim, the overall scope of the issues before the Court should be considered and generally all related claims should either be retained in the High Court or transferred out. The County Court limit for probate claims is £30,000, but claims well above that figure should be transferred to the County Court nonetheless.

15. Most claims under TOLATA will be suitable for transfer to the County Court.

16. Claims may only be transferred to the Commercial Court, the Mercantile Court or the TCC with the consent of the Chancellor and the senior judge in those venues (Part 30.5(4))

17. Whenever the parties and their witnesses are principally based within the area of a District Registry, the claim should normally be transferred. The place where the legal representatives are based is a relevant consideration, but no more than one factor to be taken into account.

Note

Please refer to PD29, 2.1 to 2.7, found at para.PD29.2 in Volume 1 of the White Book, and r.30.3(2), found at para.30.3 in Volume 1 of the White Book.

After paragraph B20–001 add Guidance for Masters concerning the grant of Injunctions and other interim relief:

GUIDANCE FOR MASTERS CONCERNING THE GRANT OF INJUNCTIONS AND OTHER INTERIM RELIEF

1. Freezing and search orders, including orders made under CPR **B21–001** 25.1(g), will only be made by a Judge or by an authorised Circuit Judge. Masters will not normally vary or discharge such orders, save where the parties consent.

2. The current arrangements for the grant of interim injunctions will continue to apply. Masters will not usually hear applications for interim injunctions where the American Cyanamid test must be applied. If such an application is made to a Master, unless there are good reasons for the Master to hear it, the application should be referred forthwith to a Judge.

3. Masters may hear interim applications which include an interim injunction if the injunction is secondary to the main relief which is sought.

4. Issues arising from the grant of an injunction may (as now) be referred by a Judge to a Master for determination.

5. Applications for interim relief, other than an injunction, may be heard by a Master.

6. All applications for interim relief which involve particular legal or factual complexity should normally be referred to a Judge.

7. Where there is doubt about the suitability of an application for an injunction or other interim application being dealt with by a Master, guidance may be obtained from one of the triage Judges.

8. Masters may grant final injunctions in connection with any application or trial (where the application or trial is suitable for disposal by a Master).

Approved by the Chancellor of the High Court
12th June 2015

After paragraph B21–001 add Guidance concerning the type of claims which are suitable for trial by a Master:

GUIDANCE CONCERNING THE TYPE OF CLAIMS WHICH ARE SUITABLE FOR TRIAL BY A MASTER

B22–001   **1.** This note provides broad guidance which will be developed in the light of experience.

2. The release of the restrictions preventing Masters trying Part 7 claims without the consent of the parties is intended to (a) facilitate the efficient use of judicial resources in the High Court and (b) further the requirements of the overriding objective. However, trials by Masters are likely to be the exception due to the pressure of other work currently undertaken by Masters.

3. Claims which are suitable for transfer to the County Court should not normally be tried by Masters unless it is more efficient to do so and in the interests of the parties.

4. Masters should not try claims involving issues of particular legal or factual complexity and not normally try cases where the trial is estimated to last more than 5 days.

5. Trials by Masters will normally be conducted in cases otherwise falling within listing category C or where the legal issues arising in the claim fall within the areas of expertise of the Master.

6. Preliminary issues may be suitable for trial by a Master such as where the speedy determination of issues may assist the parties to settle the overall claim.

7. Careful consideration should be given to objections by a party to trial by a Master. The wishes of the parties, however, are merely one factor to be taken into account.

8. If there is doubt about the suitability of a claim being tried by a Master, guidance may be obtained from one of the triage judges.
Approved by the Chancellor of the High Court
12th June 2015

SECTION C

PRE–ACTION CONDUCT AND PROTOCOLS

Delete "Practice Direction—Pre–Action Conduct" and substitute:

PRACTICE DIRECTION—PRE–ACTION CONDUCT AND PROTOCOLS

Introduction
1. Pre–action protocols explain the conduct and set out the steps C1–001 the court would normally expect parties to take before commencing proceedings for particular types of civil claims. They are approved by the Master of the Rolls and are annexed to the Civil Procedure Rules (CPR). (The current pre–action protocols are listed in paragraph 18.)
2. This Practice Direction applies to disputes where no pre–action protocol approved by the Master of the Rolls applies.

Objectives of Pre–Action Conduct and Protocols
3. Before commencing proceedings, the court will expect the par- C1–002 ties to have exchanged sufficient information to—
  (a) understand each other's position;
  (b) make decisions about how to proceed;
  (c) try to settle the issues without proceedings;
  (d) consider a form of Alternative Dispute Resolution (ADR) to assist with settlement;
  (e) support the efficient management of those proceedings; and
  (f) reduce the costs of resolving the dispute.

Proportionality
4. A pre–action protocol or this Practice Direction must not be C1–003 used by a party as a tactical device to secure an unfair advantage over another party. Only reasonable and proportionate steps should be taken by the parties to identify, narrow and resolve the legal, factual or expert issues.
5. The costs incurred in complying with a pre–action protocol or this Practice Direction should be proportionate (CPR 44.3(5)). Where parties incur disproportionate costs in complying with any pre–action protocol or this Practice Direction, those costs will not be recoverable as part of the costs of the proceedings.

Steps Before Issuing a Claim at Court
6. Where there is a relevant pre–action protocol, the parties should C1–004 comply with that protocol before commencing proceedings. Where there is no relevant pre–action protocol, the parties should exchange correspondence and information to comply with the objectives in paragraph 3, bearing in mind that compliance should be proportionate. The steps will usually include—

(a) the claimant writing to the defendant with concise details of the claim. The letter should include the basis on which the claim is made, a summary of the facts, what the claimant wants from the defendant, and if money, how the amount is calculated;

(b) the defendant responding within a reasonable time—14 days in a straight forward case and no more than 3 months in a very complex one. The reply should include confirmation as to whether the claim is accepted and, if it is not accepted, the reasons why, together with an explanation as to which facts and parts of the claim are disputed and whether the defendant is making a counterclaim as well as providing details of any counterclaim; and

(c) the parties disclosing key documents relevant to the issues in dispute.

Experts

C1–005   **7.** Parties should be aware that the court must give permission before expert evidence can be relied upon (see CPR 35.4(1)) and that the court may limit the fees recoverable. Many disputes can be resolved without expert advice or evidence. If it is necessary to obtain expert evidence, particularly in low value claims, the parties should consider using a single expert, jointly instructed by the parties, with the costs shared equally.

Settlement and ADR

C1–006   **8.** Litigation should be a last resort. As part of a relevant pre-action protocol or this Practice Direction, the parties should consider whether negotiation or some other form of ADR might enable them to settle their dispute without commencing proceedings.

9. Parties should continue to consider the possibility of reaching a settlement at all times, including after proceedings have been started. Part 36 offers may be made before proceedings are issued.

10. Parties may negotiate to settle a dispute or may use a form of ADR including—

(a) mediation, a third party facilitating a resolution;

(b) arbitration, a third party deciding the dispute;

(c) early neutral evaluation, a third party giving an informed opinion on the dispute; and

(d) Ombudsmen schemes.

(Information on mediation and other forms of ADR is available in the *Jackson ADR Handbook* (available from Oxford University Press) or at—

- http://www.civilmediation.justice.gov.uk/
- http://www.adviceguide.org.uk/england/law_e/law_legal system_e/law taking legal_action_e/alternatives_to_ court.htm)

11. If proceedings are issued, the parties may be required by the court to provide evidence that ADR has been considered. A party's silence in response to an invitation to participate or a refusal to participate in ADR might be considered unreasonable by the court and could lead to the court ordering that party to pay additional court costs.

Stocktake and List of Issues

12. Where a dispute has not been resolved after the parties have C1–007 followed a pre–action protocol or this Practice Direction, they should review their respective positions. They should consider the papers and the evidence to see if proceedings can be avoided and at least seek to narrow the issues in dispute before the claimant issues proceedings.

Compliance with this Practice Direction and the Protocols

13. If a dispute proceeds to litigation, the court will expect the par- C1–008 ties to have complied with a relevant pre–action protocol or this Practice Direction. The court will take into account non–compliance when giving directions for the management of proceedings (see CPR 3.1(4) to (6)) and when making orders for costs (see CPR 44.3(5)(a)). The court will consider whether all parties have complied in substance with the terms of the relevant pre–action protocol or this Practice Direction and is not likely to be concerned with minor or technical infringements, especially when the matter is urgent (for example an application for an injunction).

14. The court may decide that there has been a failure of compliance when a party has—

(a) not provided sufficient information to enable the objectives in paragraph 3 to be met;

(b) not acted within a time limit set out in a relevant protocol, or within a reasonable period; or

(c) unreasonably refused to use a form of ADR, or failed to respond at all to an invitation to do so.

15. Where there has been non–compliance with a pre–action protocol or this Practice Direction, the court may order that:

(a) the parties are relieved of the obligation to comply or further comply with the pre–action protocol or this Practice Direction;

(b) the proceedings are stayed while particular steps are taken to comply with the pre–action protocol or this Practice Direction;

(c) sanctions are to be applied.

16. The court will consider the effect of any non–compliance when deciding whether to impose any sanctions which may include—

(a) an order that the party at fault pays the costs of the proceedings, or part of the costs of the other party or parties;

(b) an order that the party at fault pay those costs on an indemnity basis;

(c) if the party at fault is a claimant who has been awarded a sum of money, an order depriving that party of interest on that sum for a specified period, and/or awarding interest at a lower rate than would otherwise have been awarded;

(d) if the party at fault is a defendant, and the claimant has been awarded a sum of money, an order awarding interest on that sum for a specified period at a higher rate, (not exceeding 10% above base rate), than the rate which would otherwise have been awarded.

Limitation

C1–009   17. This Practice Direction and the pre–action protocols do not alter the statutory time limits for starting court proceedings. If a claim is issued after the relevant limitation period has expired, the defendant will be entitled to use that as a defence to the claim. If proceedings are started to comply with the statutory time limit before the parties have followed the procedures in this Practice Direction or the relevant pre–action protocol, the parties should apply to the court for a stay of the proceedings while they so comply.

Protocols in Force

C1–010   18. The table sets out the protocols currently in force and from which date.

Protocol	Came into force
Personal Injury	6 April 2015
Resolution of Clinical Disputes	6 April 2015
Construction and Engineering	02 October 2000
Defamation	02 October 2000
Professional Negligence	16 July 2000
Judicial Review	6 April 2015
Disease and Illness	8 December 2003
Housing Disrepair	6 April 2015
Possession Claims by Social Landlords	6 April 2015
Possession Claims for Mortgage Arrears	6 April 2015
Dilapidation of Commercial Property	1 January 2012
Low Value Personal Injury Road Traffic Accident Claims	30 April 2010 extended from 31 July 2013
Low Value Personal Injury Employers' and Public Liability Claims	31 July 2013

Delete "Pre–Action Protocol for Personal Injury Claims" and substitute:

PRE–ACTION PROTOCOL FOR PERSONAL INJURY CLAIMS

1. Introduction

C2–001   **1.1**

1.1.1 This Protocol is primarily designed for personal injury claims which are likely to be allocated to the fast track and to the entirety of those claims: not only to the personal injury element of a claim which also includes, for instance, property damage. It is not intended to apply to claims which proceed under—

(a) the Pre–Action Protocol for Low Value Personal Injury Claims in Road Traffic Accidents from 31 July 2013;

(b) the Pre–Action Protocol for Low Value Personal Injury (Employers' Liability and Public Liability) Claims;

(c) the Pre–Action Protocol for the Resolution of Clinical Disputes; and

(d) the Pre–Action Protocol for Disease and Illness Claims.

1.1.2 If at any stage the claimant values the claim at more than the upper limit of the fast track, the claimant should notify the defendant as soon as possible. However, the "cards on the table" approach advocated by this Protocol is equally appropriate to higher value claims. The spirit, if not the letter of the Protocol, should still be followed for claims which could potentially be allocated multi–track.

1.2 Claims which exit either of the low value pre–action protocols listed at paragraph 1.1.1(a) and (b) ("the low value protocols") prior to Stage 2 will proceed under this Protocol from the point specified in those protocols, and as set out in paragraph 1.3.

1.3

1.3.1 Where a claim exits a low value protocol because the defendant considers that there is inadequate mandatory information in the Claim Notification Form ("CNF"), the claim will proceed under this Protocol from paragraph 5.1.

1.3.2 Where a defendant—

(a) alleges contributory negligence;

(b) does not complete and send the CNF Response; or

(c) does not admit liability,

the claim will proceed under this Protocol from paragraph 5.5.

1.4

1.4.1 This Protocol sets out conduct that the court would normally expect prospective parties to follow prior to the commencement of proceedings. It establishes a reasonable process and timetable for the exchange of information relevant to a dispute, sets standards for the content and quality of letters of claim, and in particular, the conduct of pre–action negotiations. In particular, the parts of this Protocol that are concerned with rehabilitation are likely to be of application in all claims.

1.4.2 The timetable and the arrangements for disclosing documents and obtaining expert evidence may need to be varied to suit the circumstances of the case. Where one or both parties consider the detail of the Protocol is not appropriate to the case, and proceedings are subsequently issued, the court will expect an explanation as to why the Protocol has not been followed, or has been varied.

1.5 Where either party fails to comply with this Protocol, the court may impose sanctions. When deciding whether to do so, the court will look at whether the parties have complied in substance with the relevant principles and requirements. It will also consider the effect any non–compliance has had on another party. It is not likely to be concerned with minor or technical shortcomings (see paragraphs 13 to 15 of the Practice Direction on Pre–Action Conduct and Protocols).

Early Issue

1.6 The Protocol recommends that a defendant be given three C2–002 months to investigate and respond to a claim before proceedings are issued. This may not always be possible, particularly where a claimant only consults a legal representative close to the end of any relevant limitation period. In these circumstances, the claimant's solicitor should give as much notice of the intention to issue proceedings as is practicable and the parties should consider whether the court might be invited to extend time for service of the claimant's supporting documents and for service of any defence, or alternatively, to stay the proceedings while the recommended steps in the Protocol are followed.

Litigants in Person

C2–003   **1.7** If a party to the claim does not have a legal representative they should still, in so far as reasonably possible, fully comply with this Protocol. Any reference to a claimant in this Protocol will also mean the claimant's legal representative.

2. Overview of Protocol—General Aim

C2–004   **2.1** The Protocol's objectives are to—
> (a) encourage the exchange of early and full information about the dispute;
> (b) encourage better and earlier pre–action investigation by all parties;
> (c) enable the parties to avoid litigation by agreeing a settlement of the dispute before proceedings are commenced;
> (d) support the just, proportionate and efficient management of proceedings where litigation cannot be avoided; and
> (e) promote the provision of medical or rehabilitation treatment (not just in high value cases) to address the needs of the Claimant at the earliest possible opportunity.

3. The Protocol

C2–005   An illustrative flow chart is attached at Annexe A which shows each of the steps that the parties are expected to take before the commencement of proceedings.

Letter of Notification

C2–006   **3.1** The claimant or his legal representative may wish to notify a defendant and/or the insurer as soon as they know a claim is likely to be made, but before they are able to send a detailed Letter of Claim, particularly, for instance, when the defendant has no or limited knowledge of the incident giving rise to the claim, or where the claimant is incurring significant expenditure as a result of the accident which he hopes the defendant might pay for, in whole or in part.

3.2 The Letter of Notification should advise the defendant and/or the insurer of any relevant information that is available to assist with determining issues of liability/suitability of the claim for an interim payment and/or early rehabilitation.

3.3 If the claimant or his legal representative gives notification before sending a Letter of Claim, it will not start the timetable for the Letter of Response. However the Letter of Notification should be acknowledged within 14 days of receipt.

4. Rehabilitation

4.1 The parties should consider as early as possible whether the **C2–007** claimant has reasonable needs that could be met by medical treatment or other rehabilitative measures. They should discuss how these needs might be addressed.

4.2 The Rehabilitation Code (which can be found at: http://www.iua.co.uk/IUA_Member/Publications) is likely to be helpful in considering how to identify the claimant's needs and how to address the cost of providing for those needs.

4.3 The time limit set out in paragraph 6.3 of this Protocol shall not be shortened, except by consent to allow these issues to be addressed.

4.4 Any immediate needs assessment report or documents associated with it that are obtained for the purposes of rehabilitation shall not be used in the litigation except by consent and shall in any event be exempt from the provisions of paragraphs 7.2 to 7.11 of this Protocol. Similarly, persons conducting the immediate needs assessment shall not be a compellable witness at court.

4.5 Consideration of rehabilitation options, by all parties, should be an on going process throughout the entire Protocol period.

5. Letter of Claim

5.1 Subject to paragraph 5.3 the claimant should send to the **C2–008** proposed defendant two copies of the Letter of Claim. One copy of the letter is for the defendant, the second for passing on to the insurers, as soon as possible, and, in any event, within 7 days of the day upon which the defendant received it.

5.2 The Letter of Claim should include the information described on the template at Annexe B1. The level of detail will need to be varied to suit the particular circumstances. In all cases there should be sufficient information for the defendant to assess liability and to enable the defendant to estimate the likely size and heads of the claim without necessarily addressing quantum in detail.

5.3 The letter should contain **a clear summary of the facts** on which the claim is based together with an indication of the **nature of any injuries** suffered, and the way in which these impact on the claimant's day to day functioning and prognosis. Any financial loss incurred by the claimant should be outlined with an indication of the heads of damage to be claimed and the amount of that loss, unless this is impracticable.

5.4 Details of the claimant's National Insurance number and date of birth should be supplied to the defendant's insurer once the defendant has responded to the Letter of Claim and confirmed the identity of the insurer. This information should not be supplied in the Letter of Claim.

5.5 Where a claim no longer continues under either low value protocol, the CNF completed by the claimant under those protocols can be used as the Letter of Claim under this Protocol unless the defendant has notified the claimant that there is inadequate information in the CNF.

5.6 Once the claimant has sent the Letter of Claim no further investigation on liability should normally be carried out within the Protocol period until a response is received from the defendant indicating whether liability is disputed.

Status of Letters of Claim and Response

C2–009 **5.7** Letters of Claim and Response are **not** intended to have the same formal status as a statement of case in proceedings. It would not be consistent with the spirit of the Protocol for a party to 'take a point' on this in the proceedings, provided that there was no obvious intention by the party who changed their position to mislead the other party.

6. The Response

C2–010 **6.1** Attached at Annexe B2 is a template for the suggested contents of the Letter of Response: the level of detail will need to be varied to suit the particular circumstances.

6.2 The **defendant must reply within 21 calendar days** of the date of posting of the letter identifying the insurer (if any). If the insurer is aware of any significant omissions from the letter of claim they should identify them specifically. Similarly, if they are aware that another defendant has also been identified whom they believe would not be a correct defendant in any proceedings, they should notify the claimant without delay, with reasons, and in any event by the end of the Response period. Where there has been no reply by the defendant or insurer within 21 days, the claimant will be entitled to issue proceedings. Compliance with this paragraph will be taken into account on the question of any assessment of the defendant's costs.

6.3 The **defendant** (insurer) will have a **maximum of three months** from the date of acknowledgment of the Letter of Claim (or of the CNF where the claim commenced in a portal) **to investigate**. No later than the end of that period, The defendant (insurer) should reply by no later than the end of that period, stating if liability is admitted by admitting that the accident occurred, that the accident was caused by the defendant's breach of duty, and the claimant suffered loss and there is no defence under the Limitation Act 1980.

6.4 Where the accident occurred outside England and Wales and/or where the defendant is outside the jurisdiction, the time periods of 21 days and three months should normally be extended up to 42 days and six months.

6.5 If a **defendant denies liability** and/or causation, their version of events should be supplied. The defendant should also enclose with the response, **documents** in their possession which are **material to the issues** between the parties, and which would be likely to be ordered to be disclosed by the court, either on an application for pre–action disclosure, or on disclosure during proceedings. No charge will be made for providing copy documents under the Protocol.

6.6 An admission made by any party under this Protocol may well be binding on that party in the litigation. Further information about admissions made under this Protocol is to be found in Civil Procedure Rules ("CPR") rule 14.1A.

6.7 Following receipt of the Letter of Response, if the claimant is aware that there may be a delay of six months or more before the claimant decides if, when and how to proceed, the claimant should keep the defendant generally informed.

7. Disclosure

Documents

7.1   C2–011

7.1.1 The aim of early disclosure of documents by the defendant is not to encourage 'fishing expeditions' by the claimant, but to promote an early exchange of relevant information to help in clarifying or resolving issues in dispute. The claimant's solicitor can assist by identifying in the Letter of Claim or in a subsequent letter the particular categories of documents which they consider are relevant and why, with a brief explanation of their purported relevance if necessary.

7.1.2 Attached at Annexe C are **specimen**, but non–exhaustive, **lists** of documents likely to be material in different types of claim.

7.1.3 Pre–action disclosure will generally be limited to the documents required to be enclosed with the Letter of Claim and the Response. In cases where liability is admitted in full, disclosure will be limited to the documents relevant to quantum, the parties can agree that further disclosure may be given. If either or both of the parties consider that further disclosure should be given but there is disagreement about some aspect of that process, they may be able to make an application to the court for pre–action disclosure under Part 31 of the CPR. Parties should assist each other and avoid the necessity for such an application.

7.1.4 The protocol should also contain a requirement that the defendant is under a duty to preserve the disclosure documents and other evidence (CCTV for example). If the documents are destroyed, this could be an abuse of the court process.

Experts

7.2 Save for cases likely to be allocated to the multi–track, the **C2–012** Protocol encourages joint selection of, and access to, quantum experts, and, on occasion liability experts e.g. engineers. The expert report produced is not a joint report for the purposes of CPR Part 35. The Protocol promotes the practice of the claimant obtaining a medical report, disclosing it to the defendant who then asks questions and/or agrees it and does not obtain their own report. The Protocol provides for nomination of the expert by the claimant in personal injury claims.

7.3 Before any party instructs an expert, they should give the other party a list of the **name**(s) of **one or more experts** in the relevant speciality whom they consider are suitable to instruct.

7.4 Some solicitors choose to obtain medical reports through medical agencies, rather than directly from a specific doctor or hospital.

The defendant's prior consent to this should be sought and, if the defendant so requests, the agency should be asked to provide in advance the names of the doctor(s) whom they are considering instructing.

7.5 Where a medical expert is to be instructed, the claimant's solicitor will organise access to relevant medical records – see specimen letter of instruction at Annexe D.

7.6 Within 14 days of providing a list of experts the other party may indicate **an objection** to one or more of the named experts. The first party should then instruct a mutually acceptable expert assuming there is one (this is not the same as a joint expert). It must be emphasised that when the claimant nominates an expert in the original Letter of Claim, the defendant has a further 14 days to object to one or more of the named experts after expiration of the 21 day period within which they have to reply to the Letter of Claim, as set out in paragraph 6.2.

7.7 If the defendant objects to all the listed experts, the parties may then instruct **experts of their own choice**. It will be for the court to decide, subsequently and if proceedings are issued, whether either party had acted unreasonably.

7.8 If the **defendant does not object to an expert nominated** by the claimant, they shall not be entitled to rely on their own expert evidence within that expert's area of expertise unless—

(a) the claimant agrees;

(b) the court so directs; or

(c) the claimant's expert report has been amended and the claimant is not prepared to disclose the original report.

7.9 Any party may send to an agreed expert written questions on the report, via the first party's solicitors. Such questions must be put within 28 days of service of the expert's report and must only be for the purpose of clarification of the report. The expert should send answers to the questions simultaneously to each party.

7.10 The cost of a report from an agreed expert will usually be paid by the instructing first party: the costs of the expert replying to questions will usually be borne by the party which asks the questions.

7.11 If necessary, after proceedings have commenced and with the permission of the court, the parties may obtain further expert reports. It would be for the court to decide whether the costs of more than one expert's report should be recoverable.

8. Negotiations following an admission

C2–013 **8.1**

8.1.1 Where a defendant admits liability which has caused some damage, before proceedings are issued, the claimant should send to that defendant—

(a) any medical reports obtained under this Protocol on which the claimant relies; and

(b) a schedule of any past and future expenses and losses which are claimed, even if the schedule is necessarily provisional. The schedule should contain as much detail as reasonably practicable and should identify those losses that are ongoing. If the schedule is likely to be updated before the case is concluded, it should say so.

8.1.2 The claimant should delay issuing proceedings for 21 days from disclosure of (a) and (b) above (unless such delay would cause his claim to become time–barred), to enable the parties to consider whether the claim is capable of settlement.

8.2 CPR Part 36 permits claimants and defendants to make offers to settle pre–proceedings. Parties should always consider if it is appropriate to make a Part 36 Offer before issuing. If such an offer is made, the party making the offer must always try to supply sufficient evidence and/or information to enable the offer to be properly considered.

The level of detail will depend on the value of the claim. Medical reports may not be necessary where there is no significant continuing injury and a detailed schedule may not be necessary in a low value case.

9. Alternative Dispute Resolution

9.1   C2–014

9.1.1 Litigation should be a last resort. As part of this Protocol, the parties should consider whether negotiation or some other form of Alternative Dispute Resolution ("ADR") might enable them to resolve their dispute without commencing proceedings.

9.1.2 Some of the options for resolving disputes without commencing proceedings are—
(a) discussions and negotiation (which may or may not include making Part 36 Offers or providing an explanation and/or apology);
(b) mediation, a third party facilitating a resolution;
(c) arbitration, a third party deciding the dispute; and
(d) early neutral evaluation, a third party giving an informed opinion on the dispute.

9.1.3 If proceedings are issued, the parties may be required by the court to provide evidence that ADR has been considered. It is expressly recognised that no party can or should be forced to mediate or enter into any form of ADR but unreasonable refusal to consider ADR will be taken into account by the court when deciding who bears the costs of the proceedings.

9.2 Information on mediation and other forms of ADR is available in the *Jackson ADR Handbook* (available from Oxford University Press) or at—

● http://www.civilmediation.justice.gov.uk/
● http://www.adviceguide.org.uk/england/law_e/law_legal_system_e/law_taking_legal_action_e/alternatives_to_court.htm

10. Quantification of Loss—Special damages

10.1 In all cases, if the defendant admits liability, the claimant will C2–015 send to the defendant as soon as reasonably practicable a schedule of any past and future expenses and losses which he claims, even if the schedule is necessarily provisional. The schedule should contain as much detail as reasonably practicable and should identify those losses that are ongoing. If the schedule is likely to be updated before the case is concluded, it should say so. The claimant should keep the defendant informed as to the rate at which his financial loss is progressing throughout the entire Protocol period.

11. Stocktake

C2–016 **11.1** Where the procedure set out in this Protocol has not resolved the dispute between the parties, each party should undertake a review of its own positions and the strengths and weaknesses of its case. The parties should then together consider the evidence and the arguments in order to see whether litigation can be avoided or, if that is not possible, for the issues between the parties to be narrowed before proceedings are issued. Where the defendant is insured and the pre–action steps have been taken by the insurer, the insurer would normally be expected to nominate solicitors to act in the proceedings and to accept service of the claim form and other documents on behalf of the defendant. The claimant or their solicitor is recommended to invite the insurer to nominate the insurer to nominate solicitors to act in the proceedings and do so 7 to 14 days before the intended issue date.

Annex A

Illustrative Flowchart of Likely Progression of the Claim Under this Protocol

C2–017

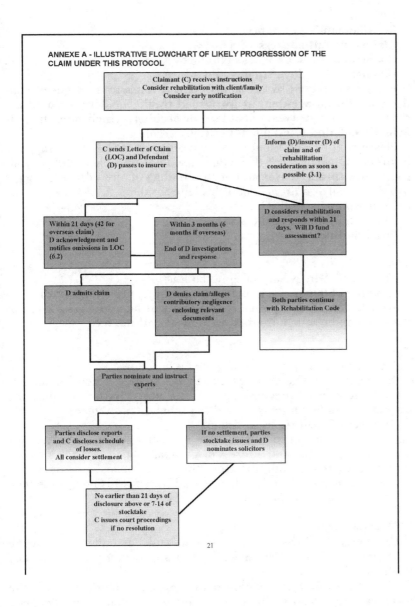

Annex B

Templates for Letters of Claim and Response

B1 Letter of Claim

C2–018   To

Defendant

Dear Sirs

Re: Claimant's full name

Claimant's full address

Claimant's Clock or Works Number

Claimant's Employer (name and address)

We are instructed by the above named to claim damages in connection with an **accident at work/road traffic accident/tripping accident** on...day of **(year)** at **(place of accident which must be sufficiently detailed to establish location)**

Please confirm the identity of your insurers. Please note that the insurers will need to see this letter as soon as possible and it may affect your insurance cover and/or the conduct of any subsequent legal proceedings if you do not send this letter to them.

Clear summary of the facts

The circumstances of the accident are:–

(brief outline)

Liability

The reason why we are alleging fault is:—

(simple explanation e.g. defective machine, broken ground)

We are obtaining a police report and will let you have a copy of the same upon your undertaking to meet half the fee.

Injuries

A description of our clients' injuries is as follows:—

(brief outline) The description should include a non–exhaustive list of the main functional effects on daily living, so that the defendant can begin to assess value / rehabilitation needs.

(In cases of road traffic accidents)

Our client (state hospital reference number) received treatment for the injuries at name and address of hospital).

Our client is still suffering from the effects of his/her injury. We invite you to participate with us in addressing his/her immediate needs by use of rehabilitation.

Loss of Earnings

He/She is employed as **(occupation)** and has had the following time off work **(dates of absence)**. His/Her approximate weekly income is (insert if known).

If you are our client's employers, please provide us with the usual earnings details which will enable us to calculate his financial loss.

Other Financial Losses

We are also aware of the following (likely) financial losses:—

Details of the insurer

We have also sent a letter of claim to **(name and address)** and a copy of that letter is attached. We understand their insurers are **(name, address and claims number if known)**.

At this stage of our enquiries we would expect the documents contained in parts **(insert appropriate parts of standard disclosure list)**to be relevant to this action.

A copy of this letter is attached for you to send to your insurers. Finally we expect an acknowledgment of this letter within 21 days by yourselves or your insurers.

Yours faithfully

B2 Letter of response

To Claimant's legal representative   C2–019
Dear Sirs

Letter of Response

[Claimant's name] v [Defendant's name]

Parties

We have been instructed to act on behalf of [defendant] in relation to your client's accident on [   ]. We note that you have also written to [defendant] in connection with this claim. We [do/do not] believe they are a relevant party because [   ]. [In addition we believe your claim should be directed against [defendant] for the following reasons:—

Liability

In respect of our client's liability for this accident we
admit the accident occurred and that our client is liable for loss and damage to the claimant the extent of which will require quantification.

Or

admit the accident occurred but deny that our client is responsible for any loss or damage alleged to have been caused for the following reasons:-

Or

do not admit the accident occurred either in the manner described in your letter of claim [or at all] because:—

Limitation

[We do not intend to raise any limitation defence]

Documents

We attach copies of the following documents in support of our client's position:—

You have requested copies of the following documents which we are not enclosing as we do not believe they are relevant for the following reasons:-

[It would assist our investigations if you could supply us with copies of the following documents]

Next Steps

In admitted cases
Please advise us which medical experts you are proposing to instruct.

Please also supply us with your client's schedule of past and future expenses [if any] which are claimed, even if this can only be supplied on a provisional basis at present to assist us with making an appropriate reserve.

If you have identified that the claimant has any immediate need for additional medical treatment or other early rehabilitation intervention so that we can take instructions pursuant to the Rehabilitation Code.

In non–admitted cases
Please confirm we may now close our file. Alternatively, if you intend to proceed please advise which experts you are proposing to instruct.

Alternative Dispute Resolution
Include details of any options that may be considered whether on a without prejudice basis or otherwise
Yours faithfully

Annex C

Pre-Action Personal Injury Protocol Standard Disclosure Lists

RTA Cases

Section A

C2–020 In all cases where liability is at issue—
   (i) documents identifying nature, extent and location of damage to defendant's vehicle where there is any dispute about point of impact;
   (ii) MOT certificate where relevant;
   (iii) maintenance records where vehicle defect is alleged or it is alleged by defendant that there was an unforeseen defect which caused or contributed to the accident.

Section B

Accident involving commercial vehicle as defendant—
   (i) tachograph charts or entry from individual control book;
   (ii) maintenance and repair records required for operators' licence where vehicle defect is alleged or it is alleged by defendant that there was an unforeseen defect which caused or contributed to the accident.

Section C

Cases against local authorities where highway design defect is alleged—

(i) documents produced to comply with Section 39 of the Road Traffic Act 1988 in respect of the duty designed to promote road safety to include studies into road accidents in the relevant area and documents relating to measures recommended to prevent accidents in the relevant area;

(ii) any Rule 43 reports produced at the request of a coroner pursuant to Schedule 5 of the Coroners & Justice Act 2009, for accidents occurring in the same locus as one covered by an earlier report.

Highway Tripping Claims

Documents from Highway Authority for a period of 12 months **C2–021** prior to the accident—

(i) records of inspection for the relevant stretch of highway;

(ii) maintenance records including records of independent contractors working in relevant area;

(iii) records of the minutes of Highway Authority meetings where maintenance or repair policy has been discussed or decided;

(iv) records of complaints about the state of highways;

(v) records of other accidents which have occurred on the relevant stretch of highway.

Workplace Claims

General Documents

(i) accident book entry; **C2–022**

(ii) other entries in the book or other accident books, relating to accidents or injuries similar to those suffered by our client (and if it is contended there are no such entries please confirm we may have facilities to inspect all accident books);

(iii) first aider report;

(iv) surgery record;

(v) foreman/supervisor accident report;

(vi) safety representative's accident report;

(vii) RIDDOR (Reporting of Injuries, Diseases and Dangerous Occurrences Regulations) reported to HSE or relevant investigatory agency;

(viii) back to work interview notes and report;

(ix) all personnel/occupational health records relating to our client;

(x) other communications between defendants and HSE or other relevant investigatory agency;

(xi) minutes of Health and Safety Committee meeting(s) where accident/matter considered;

(xii) copies of all relevant CCTV footage and any other relevant photographs, videos and/or DVDs;

(xiii) copies of all electronic communications/documentation relating to the accident;

(xiv) earnings information where defendant is employer;

(xv) reports to DWP;

(xvi) manufacturer's or dealers instructions or recommendations concerning use of the work equipment;

(xvii) service or maintenance records of the work equipment;

(xviii) all documents recording arrangements for detecting, removing or cleaning up any articles or substances on the floor of the premises likely to cause a trip or slip;

(xix) work sheets and all other documents completed by or on behalf of those responsible for implementing the cleaning policy and recording work done;

(xx) all invoices, receipts and other documents relating to the purchase of relevant safety equipment to prevent a repetition of the accident;

(xxi) all correspondence, memoranda or other documentation received or brought into being concerning the condition or repair of the work equipment/the premises;

(xxii) all correspondence, instructions, estimates, invoices and other documentation submitted or received concerning repairs, remedial works or other works to the work equipment/the premises since the date of that accident;

(xxiii) work sheets and all other documents recording work done completed by those responsible for maintaining the work equipment/premises;

(xxiv) all relevant risk assessments;

(xxv) all reports, conclusions or recommendations following any enquiry or investigation into the accident;

(xxvi) the record kept of complaints made by employees together with all other documents recording in any way such complaints or actions taken thereon;

(xxvii) all other correspondence sent, or received, relating to our client's injury prior to receipt of this letter of claim;

(xxviii) documents listed above relating to any previous/similar accident/matter identified by the claimant and relied upon as proof of negligence including accident book entries;

Workplace Claims—Disclosure where Specific Regulations Apply

Section A

Management of Health and Safety at Work Regulations 1999

C2-023   Documents including—

(i) Pre-accident Risk Assessment required by Regulation 3(1);

(ii) Post-accident Re-Assessment required by Regulation 3(2);

(iii) Accident Investigation Report prepared in implementing the requirements of Regulations 4, and 5;

(iv) Health Surveillance Records in appropriate cases required by Regulation 6;

(v) documents relating to the appointment of competent persons to assist required by Regulation 7;

(vi) documents relating to the employees health and safety training required by Regulation 8;

(vii) documents relating to necessary contacts with external services required by Regulation 9;

(viii) information provided to employees under Regulation 10.

Section B

Workplace (Health Safety and Welfare) Regulations 1992
Documents including—

(i) repair and maintenance records required by Regulation 5;

(ii) housekeeping records to comply with the requirements of Regulation 9;

(iii) hazard warning signs or notices to comply with Regulation 17 (Traffic Routes).

Section C

Provision and Use of Work Equipment Regulations 1998
Documents including—

(i) manufacturers' specifications and instructions in respect of relevant work equipment establishing its suitability to comply with Regulation 4;

(ii) maintenance log/maintenance records required to comply with Regulation 5;

(iii) documents providing information and instructions to employees to comply with Regulation 8;

(iv) documents provided to the employee in respect of training for use to comply with Regulation 9;

(v) risk assessments/documents required to comply with Regulation 12;

(vi) any notice, sign or document relied upon as a defence to alleged breaches of Regulations 14 to 18 dealing with controls and control systems;

(vii) instruction/training documents issued to comply with the requirements of Regulation 22 insofar as it deals with maintenance operations where the machinery is not shut down;

(viii) copies of markings required to comply with Regulation 23;

(ix) copies of warnings required to comply with Regulation 24.

Section D

Personal Protective Equipment at Work Regulations 1992
Documents including—

(i) documents relating to the assessment of the Personal Protective Equipment to comply with Regulation 6;

(ii) documents relating to the maintenance and replacement of Personal Protective Equipment to comply with Regulation 7;

(iii) record of maintenance procedures for Personal Protective Equipment to comply with Regulation 7;

(iv) records of tests and examinations of Personal Protective Equipment to comply with Regulation 7;

(v) documents providing information, instruction and training in relation to the Personal Protective Equipment to comply with Regulation 9;

(vi) instructions for use of Personal Protective Equipment to include the manufacturers' instructions to comply with Regulation 10.

Section E

Manual Handling Operations Regulations 1992
Documents including—

(i) Manual Handling Risk Assessment carried out to comply with the requirements of Regulation 4(1)(b)(i);

(ii) re–assessment carried out post–accident to comply with requirements of Regulation 4(1)(b)(i);

(iii) documents showing the information provided to the employee to give general indications related to the load and precise indications on the weight of the load and the heaviest side of the load if the centre of gravity was not positioned centrally to comply with Regulation 4(1)(b)(iii);

(iv) documents relating to training in respect of manual handling operations and training records.

Section F

Health and Safety (Display Screen Equipment) Regulations 1992
Documents including—

(i) analysis of work stations to assess and reduce risks carried out to comply with the requirements of Regulation 2;

(ii) re–assessment of analysis of work stations to assess and reduce risks following development of symptoms by the claimant;

(iii) documents detailing the provision of training including training records to comply with the requirements of Regulation 6;

(iv) documents providing information to employees to comply with the requirements of Regulation 7.

Section G

Control of Substances Hazardous to Health Regulations 2002
Documents including—

(i) risk assessment carried out to comply with the requirements of Regulation 6;

(ii) reviewed risk assessment carried out to comply with the requirements of Regulation 6;

(iii) documents recording any changes to the risk assessment required to comply with Regulation 6 and steps taken to meet the requirements of Regulation 7;

(iv) copy labels from containers used for storage handling and disposal of carcinogenics to comply with the requirements of Regulation 7(2A)(h);

(v) warning signs identifying designation of areas and installations which may be contaminated by carcinogenics to comply with the requirements of Regulation 7(2A)(h);

(vi) documents relating to the assessment of the Personal Protective Equipment to comply with Regulation 7(3A);

(vii) documents relating to the maintenance and replacement of Personal Protective Equipment to comply with Regulation 7(3A);

(viii) record of maintenance procedures for Personal Protective Equipment to comply with Regulation 7(3A);

(ix) records of tests and examinations of Personal Protective Equipment to comply with Regulation 7(3A);

(x) documents providing information, instruction and training in relation to the Personal Protective Equipment to comply with Regulation 7(3A);

(xi) instructions for use of Personal Protective Equipment to include the manufacturers' instructions to comply with Regulation 7(3A);

(xii) air monitoring records for substances assigned a maximum exposure limit or occupational exposure standard to comply with the requirements of Regulation 7;

(xiii) maintenance examination and test of control measures records to comply with Regulation 9;

(xiv) monitoring records to comply with the requirements of Regulation 10;

(xv) health surveillance records to comply with the requirements of Regulation 11;

(xvi) documents detailing information, instruction and training including training records for employees to comply with the requirements of Regulation 12;

(xvii) all documents relating to arrangements and procedures to deal with accidents, incidents and emergencies required to comply with Regulation 13;

(xvii) labels and Health and Safety data sheets supplied to the employers to comply with the CHIP Regulations.

Section H

Construction (Design and Management) Regulations 2007
Documents including—

(i) notification of a project form (HSE F10) to comply with the requirements of Regulation 7;

(ii) Health and Safety Plan to comply with requirements of Regulation 15;

(iii) Health and Safety file to comply with the requirements of Regulations 12 and 14;

(iv) information and training records provided to comply with the requirements of Regulation 17;

(v) records of advice from and views of persons at work to comply with the requirements of Regulation 18;

(vi) reports of inspections made in accordance with Regulation 33;

(vii) records of checks for the purposes of Regulation 34;

(viii) emergency procedures for the purposes of Regulation 39.

Section I

Construction (Health, Safety & Welfare) Regulations 1996
Documents including—

(i) documents produced to comply with requirements of the Regulations.

Section J

Work at Height Regulations 2005
Documents including—

(i) documents relating to planning, supervision and safety carried out for Regulation 4;

(ii) documents relating to training for the purposes of Regulation 5;

(iii) documents relating to the risk assessment carried out for Regulation 6;

(iv) documents relating to the selection of work equipment for the purposes of Regulation 7;

(v) notices or other means in writing warning of fragile surfaces for the purposes of Regulation 9;

(vi) documents relating to any inspection carried out for Regulation 12;

(vii) documents relating to any inspection carried out for Regulation 13;

(viii) reports made for the purposes of Regulation 14;

(ix) any certificate issued for the purposes of Regulation 15.

Section K

Pressure Systems and Transportable Gas Containers Regulations 1989
Documents including—

(i) information and specimen markings provided to comply with the requirements of Regulation 5;

(ii) written statements specifying the safe operating limits of a system to comply with the requirements of Regulation 7;

(iii) copy of the written scheme of examination required to comply with the requirements of Regulation 8;

(iv) examination records required to comply with the requirements of Regulation 9;

(v) instructions provided for the use of operator to comply with Regulation 11;

(vi) records kept to comply with the requirements of Regulation 13;

(vii) records kept to comply with the requirements of Regulation 22.

Section L

Lifting Operations and Lifting Equipment Regulations 1998
Documents including—
    (i) records kept to comply with the requirements of the Regulations including the records kept to comply with Regulation 6.

Section M

The Noise at Work Regulations 1989
Documents including—
    (i) any risk assessment records required to comply with the requirements of Regulations 4 and 5;
    (ii) manufacturers' literature in respect of all ear protection made available to claimant to comply with the requirements of Regulation 8;
    (iii) all documents provided to the employee for the provision of information to comply with Regulation 11.

Section N

Control of Noise at Work Regulations 1989
Documents including—
    (i) documents relating to the assessment of the level of noise to which employees are exposed to comply with Regulation 5;
    (ii) documents relating to health surveillance of employees to comply with Regulation 9;
    (ii) instruction and training records provided to employees to comply with Regulation 10.

Section O

Construction (Head Protection) Regulations 1989
Documents including—
    (i) pre–accident assessment of head protection required to comply with Regulation 3(4);
    (ii) post–accident re–assessment required to comply with Regulation 3(5).

Section P

The Construction (General Provisions) Regulations 1961
Documents including—
    (i) report prepared following inspections and examinations of excavations etc. to comply with the requirements of Regulation 9.

Section Q

Gas Containers Regulations 1989
Documents including—

    (i) information and specimen markings provided to comply with the requirements of Regulation 5;

    (ii) written statements specifying the safe operating limits of a system to comply with the requirements of Regulation 7;

    (iii) copy of the written scheme of examination required to comply with the requirements of Regulation 8;

    (iv) examination records required to comply with the requirements of Regulation 9;

    (v) instructions provided for the use of operator to comply with Regulation 11.

Section R

Control of Noise at Work Regulations 2005

Documents including—

    (i) risk assessment records required to comply with the requirements of Regulations 4 and 5;

    (ii) all documents relating to steps taken to comply with regulation 6;

    (iii) all documents relating to and/or arising out of actions taken to comply including providing consideration of alternative work that the claimant could have engaged to comply with Regulation 7.

Section S

Mine and Quarries Act 1954

Documents including—

    (i) documents produced to comply with requirements of the Act.

Section T

Control of Vibrations at Work Regulations 2005

Documents including—

    (i) risk assessments and documents produced to comply with requirements of Regulations 6 and 8;

    (ii) occupational health surveillance records produced to comply with Regulation 7.

Annex D

Letter of Instruction to Medical Expert

C2-024   Dear Sir,

Re: **(Name and Address)**

D.O.B.–

Telephone No.–

Date of Accident –

We are acting for the above named in connection with injuries received in an accident which occurred on the above date. A summary of the main facts of the accident circumstances is provided below.

The main injuries appear to have been (**describe main injuries and functional impact on day to day living as in Letter of Claim**).

In order to assist with the preparation of your report we have enclosed the following documents:

Enclosures

1. Hospital Records
2. GP records
3. Statement of Events

   We have not obtained [   ] records yet but will use our best endeavours to obtain these without delay if you request them.

   We should be obliged if you would examine our Client and let us have a full and detailed report dealing with any relevant pre–accident medical history, the injuries sustained, treatment received and present condition, dealing in particular with the capacity for work and giving a prognosis.

   It is central to our assessment of the extent of our Client's injuries to establish the extent and duration of any continuing disability. Accordingly, in the prognosis section we would ask you to specifically comment on any areas of continuing complaint or disability or impact on daily living. If there is such continuing disability you should comment upon the level of suffering or inconvenience caused and, if you are able, give your view as to when or if the complaint or disability is likely to resolve.

   If our client requires further treatment, please can you advise of the cost on a private patient basis.

   Please send our Client an appointment direct for this purpose. Should you be able to offer a cancellation appointment please contact our Client direct. We confirm we will be responsible for your reasonable fees.

   We are obtaining the notes and records from our Client's GP and Hospitals attended and will forward them to you when they are to hand/or please request the GP and Hospital records direct and advise that any invoice for the provision of these records should be forwarded to us.

   In order to comply with Court Rules we would be grateful if you would insert above your signature, the following statement: "I confirm that I have made clear which facts and matters referred to in this report are within my own knowledge and which are not. Those that are within my own knowledge I confirm to be true. The opinions I have expressed represent my true and complete professional opinions on the matters to which they refer".

   In order to avoid further correspondence we can confirm that on the evidence we have there is no reason to suspect we may be pursuing a claim against the hospital or its staff.

   We look forward to receiving your report within _____ weeks. If you will not be able to prepare your report within this period please telephone us upon receipt of these instructions.

When acknowledging these instructions it would assist if you could give an estimate as to the likely time scale for the provision of your report and also an indication as to your fee.

Yours faithfully,

Delete "Pre–Action Protocol for the Resolution of Clinical Disputes" and substitute:

PRE-ACTION PROTOCOL FOR THE RESOLUTION OF CLINICAL DISPUTES

1 Introduction

C3–001   **1.1** This Protocol is intended to apply to all claims against hospitals, GPs, dentists and other healthcare providers (both NHS and private) which involve an injury that is alleged to be the result of clinical negligence. It is not intended to apply to claims covered by—

(a) the Pre–Action Protocol for Disease and Illness Claims;

(b) the Pre–Action Protocol for Personal Injury Claims;

(c) the Pre–Action Protocol for Low Value Personal Injury Claims in Road Traffic Accidents;

(d) the Pre–Action Protocol for Low Value Personal Injury (Employers' Liability and Public Liability) Claims; or

(e) Practice Direction 3D—Mesothelioma Claims.

1.2 This Protocol is intended to be sufficiently broad–based and flexible to apply to all sectors of healthcare, both public and private. It also recognises that a claimant and a defendant, as patient and healthcare provider, may have an ongoing relationship.

1.3 It is important that each party to a clinical dispute has sufficient information and understanding of the other's perspective and case to be able to investigate a claim efficiently and, where appropriate, to resolve it. This Protocol encourages a cards–on–the–table approach when something has gone wrong with a claimant's treatment or the claimant is dissatisfied with that treatment and/or the outcome.

1.4 This Protocol is now regarded by the courts as setting the standard of normal reasonable pre–action conduct for the resolution of clinical disputes.

1.5

1.5.1 This Protocol sets out the conduct that prospective parties would normally be expected to follow prior to the commencement of any proceedings. It establishes a reasonable process and timetable for the exchange of information relevant to a dispute, sets out the standards for the content and quality of letters of claim and sets standards for the conduct of pre–action negotiations.

1.5.2 The timetable and the arrangements for disclosing documents and obtaining expert evidence may need to be varied to suit the circumstances of the case. Where one or more parties consider the detail of the Protocol is not appropriate to the case, and proceedings are subsequently issued, the court will expect an explanation as to why the Protocol has not been followed, or has been varied.

Early Issue

1.6   C3–002

1.6.1 The Protocol provides for a defendant to be given four
months to investigate and respond to a Letter of Claim before
proceedings are served. If this is not possible, the claimant's
solicitor should give as much notice of the intention to issue
proceedings as is practicable. This Protocol does not alter the
statutory time limits for starting court proceedings. If a claim
is issued after the relevant statutory limitation period has
expired, the defendant will be entitled to use that as a defence
to the claim. If proceedings are started to comply with the
statutory time limit before the parties have followed the
procedures in this Protocol, the parties should apply to the
court for a stay of the proceedings while they so comply.

1.6.2 The parties should also consider whether there is likely to be
a dispute as to limitation should a claim be pursued.

Enforcement of the Protocol and sanctions

1.7 Where either party fails to comply with this Protocol, the court   C3–003
may impose sanctions. When deciding whether to do so, the court
will look at whether the parties have complied in substance with the
Protocol's relevant principles and requirements. It will also consider
the effect any non–compliance has had on any other party. It is not
likely to be concerned with minor or technical shortcomings (see
paragraph 4.3 to 4.5 of the Practice Direction on Pre–Action Conduct
and Protocols).

Litigants in Person

1.8 If a party to a claim does not seek professional advice from a   C3–004
solicitor they should still, in so far as is reasonably possible, comply
with the terms of this Protocol. In this Protocol "solicitor" is intended
to encompass reference to any suitably legally qualified person.

If a party to a claim becomes aware that another party is a litigant
in person, they should send a copy of this Protocol to the litigant in
person at the earliest opportunity.

2 The Aims of the Protocol

2.1 The **general** aims of the Protocol are—   C3–005

    (a) to maintain and/or restore the patient/healthcare pro-
        vider relationship in an open and transparent way;

    (b) to reduce delay and ensure that costs are proportionate;
        and

    (c) to resolve as many disputes as possible without litigation.

2.2 The **specific** objectives are—

    (a) to encourage openness, transparency and early com-
        munication of the perceived problem between patients
        and healthcare providers;

    (b) to provide an opportunity for healthcare providers to
        identify whether notification of a notifiable safety incident
        has been, or should be, sent to the claimant in accor-
        dance with the duty of candour imposed by section 20 of
        the Health and Social Care Act 2008 (Regulated Activi-
        ties) Regulations 2014;

    (c) to ensure that sufficient medical and other information is disclosed promptly by both parties to enable each to understand the other's perspective and case, and to encourage early resolution or a narrowing of the issues in dispute;

    (d) to provide an early opportunity for healthcare providers to identify cases where an investigation is required and to carry out that investigation promptly;

    (e) to encourage healthcare providers to involve the *National Health Service Litigation Authority* (NHSLA) or their defence organisations or insurers at an early stage;

    (f) to enable the parties to avoid litigation by agreeing a resolution of the dispute;

    (g) to enable the parties to explore the use of mediation or to narrow the issues in dispute before proceedings are commenced;

    (h) to enable parties to identify any issues that may require a separate or preliminary hearing, such as a dispute as to limitation;

    (i) to support the efficient management of proceedings where litigation cannot be avoided;

    (j) to discourage the prolonged pursuit of unmeritorious claims and the prolonged defence of meritorious claims;

    (k) to promote the provision of medical or rehabilitation treatment to address the needs of the claimant at the earliest opportunity; and

    (l) to encourage the defendant to make an early apology to the claimant if appropriate.

2.3 This Protocol does not—

    (a) provide any detailed guidance to healthcare providers on clinical risk management or the adoption of risk management systems and procedures;

    (b) provide any detailed guidance on which adverse outcomes should trigger an investigation; or

    (c) recommend changes to the codes of conduct of professionals in healthcare.

3 The Protocol

C3–006   **3.1** An illustrative flowchart is attached at Annex A which shows each of the stages that the parties are expected to take before the commencement of proceedings.

Obtaining health records

C3–007   **3.2** Any request for records by the **claimant** should—

    (a) **provide sufficient information** to alert the defendant where an adverse outcome has been serious or has had serious consequences or may constitute a notifiable safety incident;

    (b) be as **specific as possible** about the records which are required for an initial investigation of the claim (including, for example, a continuous copy of the CTG trace in birth injury cases); and

(c) include a request for any relevant guidelines, analyses, protocols or policies and any documents created in relation to an adverse incident, notifiable safety incident or complaint.

3.3 Requests for copies of the claimant's clinical records should be made using the Law Society and Department of Health approved **standard forms** (enclosed at Annex B), adapted as necessary.

3.4

3.4.1 The copy records should be provided **within 40 days** of the request and for a cost not exceeding the charges permissible under the Access to Health Records Act 1990 and/or the Data Protection Act 1998. Payment may be required in advance by the healthcare provider.

3.4.2 The claimant may also make a request under the Freedom of Information Act 2000.

3.5 At the earliest opportunity, legible copies of the claimant's medical and other records should be placed in an indexed and paginated bundle by the claimant. This bundle should be kept up to date.

3.6 In the rare circumstances that the defendant is in difficulty in complying with the request within 40 days, the **problem should be explained** quickly and details given of what is being done to resolve it.

3.7 If the defendant fails to provide the health records or an explanation for any delay within 40 days, the claimant or their adviser can then apply to the court under rule 31.16 of the Civil Procedure Rules 1998 ('CPR') for an **order for pre–action disclosure**. The court has the power to impose costs sanctions for unreasonable delay in providing records.

3.8 If either the claimant or the defendant considers **additional health records are required from a third party**, in the first instance these should be requested by or through the claimant. Third party healthcare providers are expected to co–operate. Rule 31.17 of the CPR sets out the procedure for applying to the court for pre–action disclosure by third parties.

Rehabilitation

3.9 The claimant and the defendant shall both consider as early as C3–008 possible whether the claimant has reasonable needs that could be met by rehabilitation treatment or other measures. They should also discuss how these needs might be addressed. An immediate needs assessment report prepared for the purposes of rehabilitation should not be used in the litigation except by consent.

(A copy of the Rehabilitation Code can be found at: http:// www.iua.co.uk/IUA_Member/Publications)

Letter of Notification

3.10 Annex C1 to this Protocol provides a **template for the recom-** C3–009 **mended contents of a Letter of Notification**; the level of detail will need to be varied to suit the particular circumstances.

3.11

3.11.1 Following receipt and analysis of the records and, if appropriate, receipt of an initial supportive expert opinion, the claimant may wish to send a Letter of Notification to the defendant as soon as practicable.

3.11.2 The Letter of Notification should advise the defendant that this is a claim where a Letter of Claim is likely to be sent because a case as to breach of duty and/or causation has been identified. A copy of the Letter of Notification should also be sent to the NHSLA or, where known, other relevant medical defence organisation or indemnity provider.

3.12

3.12.1 On receipt of a Letter of Notification a defendant should—
    (a) acknowledge the letter within 14 days of receipt;
    (b) identify who will be dealing with the matter and to whom any Letter of Claim should be sent;
    (c) consider whether to commence investigations and/or to obtain factual and expert evidence;
    (d) consider whether any information could be passed to the claimant which might narrow the issues in dispute or lead to an early resolution of the claim; and
    (e) forward a copy of the Letter of Notification to the NHSLA or other relevant medical defence organisation/indemnity provider.

3.12.2 The court may question any requests by the defendant for extension of time limits if a Letter of Notification was sent but did not prompt an initial investigation.

Letter of Claim

C3–010   **3.13** Annex C2 to this Protocol provides **a template for the recommended contents of a Letter of Claim**: the level of detail will need to be varied to suit the particular circumstances.

3.14 If, following the receipt and analysis of the records, and the receipt of any further advice (including from experts if necessary – see Section 4), the claimant decides that there are grounds for a claim, a letter of claim should be sent to the defendant as soon as practicable. Any letter of claim sent to an NHS Trust should be copied to the National Health Service Litigation Authority.

3.16 This letter should contain—
    (a) a **clear summary of the facts** on which the claim is based, including the alleged adverse outcome, and the **main allegations of negligence;**
    (b) a description of the **claimant's injuries**, and present condition and prognosis;
    (c) an outline of the **financial loss** incurred by the claimant, with an indication of the heads of damage to be claimed and the scale of the loss, unless this is impracticable;
    (d) confirmation of the method of funding and whether any funding arrangement was entered into before or after April 2013; and
    (e) the discipline of any expert from whom evidence has already been obtained.

3.17 The Letter of Claim **should refer to any relevant documents**, including health records, and if possible enclose copies of any of those which will not already be in the potential defendant's possession, e.g. any relevant general practitioner records if the claimant's claim is against a hospital.

3.18 Sufficient information must be given to enable the defendant to **focus investigations** and to put an initial valuation on the claim.

3.19 Letters of Claim are **not** intended to have the same formal status as Particulars of Claim, nor should any sanctions necessarily apply if the Letter of Claim and any subsequent Particulars of Claim in the proceedings differ.

3.20 Proceedings should not be issued until after four months from the letter of claim.

In certain instances it may not be possible for the claimant to serve a Letter of Claim more than four months before the expiry of the limitation period. If, for any reason, proceedings are started before the parties have complied, they should seek to agree to apply to the court for an order to stay the proceedings whilst the parties take steps to comply.

3.21 The claimant may want to make an **offer to settle** the claim at this early stage by putting forward an offer in respect of liability and/or an amount of compensation in accordance with the legal and procedural requirements of CPR Part 36 (possibly including any costs incurred to date). If an offer to settle is made, generally this should be supported by a medical report which deals with the injuries, condition and prognosis, and by a schedule of loss and supporting documentation. The level of detail necessary will depend on the value of the claim. Medical reports may not be necessary where there is no significant continuing injury and a detailed schedule may not be necessary in a low value case.

Letter of Response

3.22 Attached at Annex C3 is a template for the suggested contents **C3–011** of the **Letter of Response**: the level of detail will need to be varied to suit the particular circumstances.

3.23 The defendant should **acknowledge** the Letter of Claim **within 14 days of receipt** and should identify who will be dealing with the matter.

3.24 The defendant should, **within four months** of the Letter of Claim, provide a **reasoned answer** in the form of a **Letter of Response** in which the defendant should—

- (a) if the **claim is admitted**, say so in clear terms;
- (b) if only **part of the claim is admitted**, make clear which issues of breach of duty and/or causation are admitted and which are denied and why;
- (c) state whether it is intended that any **admissions will be binding**;
- (d) if the **claim is denied**, include specific comments on the allegations of negligence and, if a synopsis or chronology of relevant events has been provided and is disputed, the defendant's version of those events;

    (e) if supportive expert evidence has been obtained, identify which disciplines of expert evidence have been relied upon and whether they relate to breach of duty and/or causation;

    (f) if known, state whether the defendant requires copies of any relevant medical records obtained by the claimant (to be supplied for a reasonable copying charge);

    (g) provide copies of any additional documents relied upon, e.g. an internal protocol;

    (h) if not indemnified by the NHS, supply details of the relevant indemnity insurer; and

    (i) inform the claimant of any other potential defendants to the claim.

3.25

3.25.1 If the defendant requires an extension of time for service of the Letter of Response, a request should be made as soon as the defendant becomes aware that it will be required and, in any event, within four months of the letter of claim.

3.25.2 The defendant should explain why any extension of time is necessary.

3.25.3 The claimant should adopt a reasonable approach to any request for an extension of time for provision of the reasoned answer.

3.26 If the claimant has made an offer to settle, the defendant should respond to that offer in the Letter of Response, preferably with reasons. The defendant may also make an offer to settle at this stage. Any offer made by the defendant should be made in accordance with the legal and procedural requirements of CPR Part 36 (possibly including any costs incurred to date). If an offer to settle is made, the defendant should provide sufficient medical or other evidence to allow the claimant to properly consider the offer. The level of detail necessary will depend on the value of the claim.

3.27 If the parties reach agreement on liability, or wish to explore the possibility of resolution with no admissions as to liability, but time is needed to resolve the value of the claim, they should aim to agree a reasonable period.

3.28 If the parties do not reach agreement on liability, they should discuss whether the claimant should start proceedings and whether the court might be invited to direct an early trial of a preliminary issue or of breach of duty and/or causation.

3.29 Following receipt of the Letter of Response, if the claimant is aware that there may be a delay of six months or more before the claimant decides if, when and how to proceed, the claimant should keep the defendant generally informed.

4 Experts

C3–012   **4.1** In clinical negligence disputes separate **expert opinions** may be needed—

- on breach of duty;
- on causation;
- on the patient's condition and prognosis;
- to assist in valuing aspects of the claim.

4.2 It is recognised that in clinical negligence disputes, the parties and their advisers will require flexibility in their approach to expert evidence. The parties should co–operate when making decisions on appropriate medical specialisms, whether experts might be instructed jointly and whether any reports obtained pre–action might be shared.

4.3 Obtaining expert evidence will often be an expensive step and may take time, especially in specialised areas of medicine where there are limited numbers of suitable experts.

4.4 When considering what expert evidence may be required during the Protocol period, parties should be aware that the use of any expert reports obtained pre–action will only be permitted in proceedings with the express permission of the court.

5 Alternative Dispute Resolution

5.1 Litigation should be a last resort. As part of this Protocol, the **C3–013** parties should consider whether negotiation or some other form of alternative dispute resolution ('ADR') might enable them to resolve their dispute without commencing proceedings.

5.2 Some of the options for resolving disputes without commencing proceedings are—

(a) discussion and negotiation (which may or may not include making Part 36 Offers or providing an explanation and/or apology);

(b) mediation, a third party facilitating a resolution;

(c) arbitration, a third party deciding the dispute;

(d) early neutral evaluation, a third party giving an informed opinion on the dispute; and

(e) Ombudsmen schemes.

5.3 Information on mediation and other forms of ADR is available in the *Jackson ADR Handbook* (available from Oxford University Press) or at—

● http://www.civilmediation.justice.gov.uk/

● http://www.adviceguide.org.uk/england/law_e/law_legal_system_e/law_taking_legal_action_e/alternatives_to_court.htm

5.4 If proceedings are issued, the parties may be required by the court to provide evidence that ADR has been considered. It is expressly recognised that no party can or should be forced to mediate or enter into any form of ADR, but a party's silence in response to an invitation to participate in ADR might be considered unreasonable by the court and could lead to the court ordering that party to pay additional court costs.

6 Stocktake

6.1 **C3–014**

6.1.1 Where a dispute has not been resolved after the parties have followed the procedure set out in this Protocol, the parties should review their positions before the claimant issues court proceedings.

6.1.2 If proceedings cannot be avoided, the parties should continue to co–operate and should seek to prepare a chronology of events which identifies the facts or issues that are agreed and those that remain in dispute. The parties should also seek to agree the necessary procedural directions for efficient case management during the proceedings.

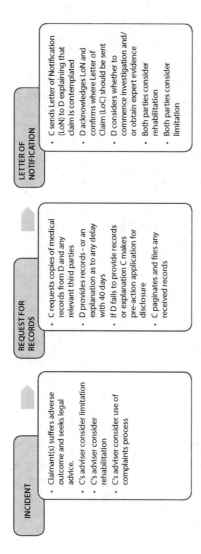

INCIDENT

- Claimant(s) suffers adverse outcome and seeks legal advice.
- C's adviser consider limitation
- C's adviser consider rehabilitation
- C's adviser consider use of complaints process

REQUEST FOR RECORDS

- C requests copies of medical records from D and any relevant third parties
- D provides records - or an explanation as to any delay with 40 days
- If D fails to provide records or explanation C makes pre-action application for disclosure
- C paginates and files any received records

LETTER OF NOTIFICATION

- C sends Letter of Notification (LoN) to D explaining that claim is contemplated
- D acknowledges LoN and confirms where Letter of Claim (LoC) should be sent
- D considers whether to commence investigation and/ or obtain expert evidence
- Both parties consider rehabilitation
- Both parties consider limitation

LETTER OF CLAIM

- C sends LoC to D and D's insurer detailing allegations as to breach of duty and causation
- C provides D with copies of relevant records and/or a list of all records obtained
- C sets out chronology of events
- C provides evidence as to condition, prognosis and alleged quantum losses
- Both parties consider rehabilitation

LETTER OF RESPONSE

- D provides C with detailed Letter of Response (LoR) within 4 months
- LoR will set out any admissions or denials as to breach of duty and/or causation
- D identifies relevant medical records not referred to in LoC
- D agree C's chronology or provides alternative chronology
- Both parties consider rehabilitation

ADR

- Parties consider whether matter can be resolved without further recourse to the court
- Parties consider non-financial resolution (eg. face-to-face explanation, further treatment and/or apology)
- Parties consider financial settlement (without without admission of liability)
- Parties consider rehabilitation

STOCKTAKE

- Parties seek to narrow issues to dispute
- Parties seek to agree chronology and key facts
- Parties seek to identify any matters that could be dealt with as preliminary issues (eg limitation)
- Parties consider rehabilitation
- Parties consider what further expert evidence will be issued
- Parties consider whether Protocol has been complied with

Annex B

Form for Obtaining Health Records

C3–016

Consent form
(Releasing health records under the Data Protection Act 1998)

About this form

In order to proceed with your claim, your solicitor may need to see your health records. Solicitors usually need to see all your records as they need to assess which parts are relevant to your case. (Past medical history is often relevant to a claim for compensation.) Also, if your claim goes ahead, the person you are making the claim against will ask for copies of important documents. Under court rules, they may see all your health records. So your solicitor needs to be familiar with all your records.

Part a – your, the health professionals' and your solicitor's or agent's details

Your full name:	
Your address:	
Date of birth:	
Date of incident:	
Solicitor's or agent's name and address:	
GP's name and address (and phone number if known):	
Name (and address if known) of the hospitals you went to in relation to this incident :	
If you have seen any other person or organisation about your injuries (for example, a physiotherapist) or have had any investigations (for example, x-rays) please provide details.	

Part b – your declaration and signature

Please see the 'Notes for the client' over the page before you sign this form.

To health professionals

I understand that filling in and signing this form gives you permission to give copies of all my GP records, and any hospital records relating to this incident, to my solicitor or agent whose details are given above.

Please give my solicitor or agent copies of my health records, in line with the Data Protection Act 1998, within 40 days.

Your signature: _____   Date: _____ / _____ / _____

Part c – your solicitor's or agent's declaration and signature

Please see the 'Notes for the solicitor or agent' over the page before you sign this form.

To health professionals

I have told my client the implications of giving me access to his or her health records. I confirm that I need the full records in this case. I enclose the authorised fee for getting access to records.

Solicitor's or agent's signature: _____   Date: _____ / _____ / _____

Notes for the client

Your health records contain information from almost all consultations you have had with health professionals. The information they contain usually includes:

- why you saw a health professional;
- details of clinical findings and diagnoses;
- any options for care and treatment the health professional discussed with you;
- the decisions made about your care and treatment, including evidence that you agreed; and
- details of action health professionals have taken and the outcomes.

By signing this form, you are agreeing to the health professional or hospital named on this form releasing copies of your health records to your solicitor or agent. During the process your records may be seen by people who are not health professionals, but they will keep the information confidential.

If you are making, or considering making, a legal claim against someone, your solicitor will need to see copies of all your GP records, and any hospital records made in connection with this incident, so he or she can see if there is anything in your records that may affect your claim. Once you start your claim, the court can order you to give copies of your health records to the solicitor of the person you are making a claim against so he or she can see if any of the information in your records can be used to defend his or her client.

If you decide to go ahead with your claim, your records may be passed to a number of people including:

- the expert who your solicitor or agent instructs to produce a medical report as evidence for the case;
- the person you are making a claim against and their solicitors;
- the insurance company for the person you are making a claim against;
- any insurance company or other organisation paying your legal costs; and
- any other person or company officially involved with the claim.

You do not have to give permission for your health records to be released but if you don't, the court may not let you go ahead with your claim and, in some circumstances, your solicitor may refuse to represent you.

If there is very sensitive information in the records, that is not connected to the claim, you should tell your solicitor. They will then consider whether this information needs to be revealed.

Notes for the solicitor or agent

Before you ask your client to fill in and sign this form you should explain that this will involve his or her full health records being released and how the information in them may be used. You should also tell your client to read the notes above.

If your client is not capable of giving his or her permission in this form, this form should be signed by:

- your client's litigation friend;
- someone who has enduring power of attorney to act for your client; or
- your client's receiver appointed by the Court of Protection.

When you send this form to the appropriate records controller please also enclose the authorised fees for getting access to records.

If you find out at any stage that the medical records contain information that the client does not know about (for example, being diagnosed with a serious illness), you should discuss this with the health professional who provided the records.

Unless your client agrees otherwise, you must use his or her health records only for the purpose for which the client signed this form (that is, making his or her claim). Under the Data Protection Act you have responsibilities relating to sensitive information. The entire health record should not be automatically revealed without the client's permission and you should not keep health records for any longer than you need them. You should return them to the client at the end of the claim if they want them. Otherwise, you are responsible for destroying them.

Notes for the medical records controller

This form shows your patient's permission for you to give copies of his or her full GP record, and any hospital records relating to this incident, to his or her solicitor or agent. You must give the solicitor or agent copies of these health records unless any of the exemptions set out in The Data Protection (Subject Access Modification) (Health) Order 2000 apply. The main exemptions are that you must not release information that:

- is likely to cause serious physical or mental harm to the patient or another person; or
- relates to someone who would normally need to give their permission (where that person is not a health professional who has cared for the patient).

Your patient's permission for you to release information is valid only if that patient understands the consequences of his or her records being released, and how the information will be used. The solicitor or agent named on this form must explain these issues to the patient. If you have any doubt about whether this has happened, contact the solicitor or agent, or your patient.

If your patient is not capable of giving his or her permission, this form should be signed by:

- a 'litigation friend' acting for your patient;
- someone with 'enduring power of attorney' to act for your patient; or
- a receiver appointed by the Court of Protection.

You may charge the usual fees authorised under the Data Protection Act for providing the records.

The BMA publishes detailed advice for doctors on giving access to health records, including the fees that you may charge. You can view that advice by visiting www.bma.org.uk/ap.nsf/Content/accesshealthrecords.

This form is published by the Law Society and British Medical Association. (2nd edition, October 2004)

The Law Society

Crystal Mark
Clarity
approved by
Plain English Campaign

Annex C

Templates for Letters of Notification, Claim and Response

C1 Letter of Notification

C3–017   **To**
Defendant
Dear Sirs
Letter of Notification

Re: [Claimant's Name, Address, DoB and NHS Number]
We have been instructed to act on behalf of [Claimant's name] in

relation to treatment carried out/care provided at [name of hospital or treatment centre] by [name of clinician(s) if known] on [insert date(s)].

The purpose of this letter is to notify you that, although we are not yet in a position to serve a formal Letter of Claim, our initial investigations indicate that a case as to breach of duty and/or causation has been identified. We therefore invite you to commence your own investigation and draw your attention to the fact that failure to do may be taken into account when considering the reasonableness of any subsequent application for an extension of time for the Letter of Response.

Defendant

We understand that you are the correct defendant in respect of treatment provided by [name of clinician] at [hospital/surgery/treatment centre] on [date(s)]. If you do not agree, please provide us with any information you have that may assist us to identify the correct defendant. Failure to do so may result in costs sanctions should proceedings be issued.

Summary of Facts and Alleged Adverse Outcome

[Outline what is alleged to have happened and provide a chronology of events with details of relevant known treatment/care.]

Medical Records

[Provide index of records obtained and request for further records/information if required.]

Allegations of Negligence

[Brief outline of any alleged breach of duty and causal link with any damage suffered.]

Expert Evidence

[State whether expert evidence has been obtained or is awaited and, if so, the relevant discipline.]

Damage

[Brief outline of any injuries attributed to the alleged negligence and their functional impact.]

Funding

[If known, state method of funding and whether arrangement was entered into before or after April 2013.]

Rehabilitation

As a result of the allegedly negligent treatment, our client has injuries/needs that could be met by rehabilitation. We invite you to consider how this could be achieved.

Limitation

For the purposes of limitation, we calculate that any proceedings will need to be issued on or before [date].

Please acknowledge this letter by [insert date 14 days after deemed receipt] and confirm to whom any Letter of Claim should be sent. We enclose a duplicate of the letter for your insurer.

Recoverable Benefits

The claimant's National Insurance Number will be sent to you in a separate envelope.

We look forward to hearing from you.

Yours faithfully,

C2 Letter of Claim

C3–018

To

Defendant

Dear Sirs

Letter of Claim

[Claimant's name] –v– [Defendant's Name]

We have been instructed to act on behalf of [Claimant's name] in relation to treatment carried out/care provided at [name of hospital or treatment centre] by [name of clinician(s) if known] on [insert date(s)]. Please let us know if you do not believe that you are the appropriate defendant or if you are aware of any other potential defendants.

Claimant's details

Full name, DoB, address, NHS Number.

Dates of allegedly negligent treatment

- include chronology based on medical records.

Events giving rise to the claim:

- an outline of what happened, including details of other relevant treatments to the client by other healthcare providers.

Allegation of negligence and causal link with injuries:

- an outline of the allegations or a more detailed list in a complex case;
- an outline of the causal link between allegations and the injuries complained of;
- a copy of any supportive expert evidence (optional).

The Client's injuries, condition and future prognosis

- A copy of any supportive expert report (optional);
- Suggestions for rehabilitation;
- The discipline of any expert evidence obtained or proposed.

Clinical records (if not previously provided)

We enclose an index of all the relevant records that we hold. We shall be happy to provide copies of these on payment of our photocopying charges.

We enclose a request for copies of the following records which we believe that you hold. We confirm that we shall be responsible for your reasonable copying charges. Failure to provide these records may result in costs sanctions if proceedings are issued.

The likely value of the claim

- an outline of the main heads of damage, or, in straightforward cases, the details of loss;
- Part 36 settlement offer (optional);
- suggestions for ADR.

Funding

[State method of funding and whether arrangement was entered into before or after April 2013.]

We enclose a further copy of this letter for you to pass to your insurer. We look forward to receiving an acknowledgment of this letter within 14 days and your Letter of Response within 4 months of the date on which this letter was received. We calculate the date for receipt of your Letter of Response to be [date].

Recoverable Benefits

The claimant's National Insurance Number will be sent to you in a separate envelope.

We look forward to hearing from you.

Yours faithfully

C3 Letter of Response

To   C3–019

Claimant

Dear Sirs

Letter of Response

[Claimant's name] –v– [Defendant's Name]

We have been instructed to act on behalf of [defendant] in relation to treatment carried out/care provided to [claimant] at [name of hospital or treatment centre] by [name of clinician(s) if known] on [insert date(s)].

The defendant [conveys sympathy for the adverse outcome/would like to offer an apology/denies that there was an adverse outcome].

Parties

It is accepted that [defendant] had a duty of care towards [claimant] in respect of [details if required] treatment/care provided to [claimant] at [location] on [date(s)].

However, [defendant] is not responsible for [details] care/treatment provided to [claimant] at [location] on [date(s)] by [name of clinician if known].

Records

We hold the following records...

We require copies of the following records...

Failure to provide these records may result in costs sanctions if proceedings are issued.

Comments on events and/or chronology:

We [agree the chronology enclosed with the Letter of Claim] [enclose a revised chronology of events].

We enclose copies of relevant [records/Protocols/internal investigations] in respect of the treatment/care that [claimant] received.

Liability

In respect of the specific allegations raised by the claimant, the defendant [has obtained an expert opinion and] responds as follows:–

[each allegation should be addressed separately. The defendant should explain which (if any) of the allegations of breach of duty and/or causation are admitted and why. The defendant should also make clear which allegations are denied and why].

Next Steps

The defendant suggests...

[e.g. no prospect of success for the claimant, resolution without admissions of liability, ADR, settlement offer, rehabilitation].

Yours faithfully,

Delete "Professional Negligence Pre–Action Protocol" and substitute:

PRE–ACTION PROTOCOL FOR PROFESSIONAL NEGLIGENCE

Introduction

1 Scope of the Protocol

C7–001 **1.1** This Protocol is designed to apply when a claimant wishes to claim against a professional (other than construction professionals and healthcare providers) as a result of that professional's alleged negligence or equivalent breach of contract or breach of fiduciary duty. Although these claims will be the usual situation in which the protocol will be used, there may be other claims for which the protocol could be appropriate.

1.2 "Professional" is deliberately left undefined in the protocol. If it becomes an issue as to whether a respondent to a claim is or is not a professional, parties are reminded of the overriding need to act reasonably (see paragraph 3.3 below). Rather than argue about the definition of "professional", therefore, the parties are invited to use this Protocol, adapting it where appropriate.

1.3 Allegations of professional negligence are sometimes made in response to an attempt by the professional to recover outstanding fees. Where possible these allegations should be raised before court proceedings have commenced, in which case the parties should comply with the protocol before either party commences court proceedings.

1.4 The protocol is not intended to apply to claims:

    (a) against architects, engineers and quantity surveyors— parties should use the Construction and Engineering Disputes (CED) protocol.

    (b) against healthcare providers—parties should use the pre-action protocol for the Resolution of Clinical Disputes.

    (c) concerning defamation—parties should use the pre–action protocol for defamation claims.

1.5 If at any time prior to the commencement of court proceedings the claimant decides not to proceed with the claim it should notify the professional as soon as reasonably practicable.

2 Aims of the Protocol

2.1 This Protocol sets out a code of good practice and contains the **C7–002** steps which parties should generally follow before commencing court proceedings in respect of a professional negligence claim.

2.2 The aims of the protocol are to enable parties to prospective claims to:

(a) understand and properly identify the issues in dispute in the proposed claim and share information and relevant documents;

(b) make informed decisions as to whether and how to proceed;

(c) try to settle the dispute without proceedings or reduce the issues in dispute;

(d) avoid unnecessary expense and keep down the costs of resolving the dispute; and

(e) support the efficient management of proceedings where court proceedings cannot be avoided.

2.3 This protocol is not intended to replace other forms of pre–action dispute resolution (such as those mentioned in paragraph 12 of this protocol). Where such procedures are available, parties are encouraged to consider whether they should be used. If, however, these other procedures are used and fail to resolve the dispute, the protocol should be used before court proceedings are started, adapting it where appropriate.

3 Compliance

3.1 The courts will treat the standards set out in this protocol as **C7–003** the normal reasonable approach for parties to a professional negligence claim. If court proceedings are started, it will be for the court to decide whether sanctions should be imposed as a result of substantial non–compliance with this protocol. Guidance on the courts' likely approach is given in the Practice Direction—Pre–Action Conduct and Protocols. The court is likely to disregard minor or technical departures from this protocol and so should the parties as between themselves.

3.2 Both in operating the timetable and in requesting and providing information during the protocol period, the parties are expected to act reasonably, in line with the court's expectations of them. Accordingly, in the event that the protocol does not specifically address a problem, the parties should comply with the spirit of the protocol by acting reasonably.

4 Limitation

4.1 The protocol does not alter the statutory time limits for com- **C7–004** mencing court proceedings. A claimant is required to start proceedings within those time limits. However, the claimant can request and the parties can agree a standstill agreement to extend the period in which a limitation defence will not be pursued. Alternatively, a claimant may commence court proceedings and invite the professional to agree to an immediate stay of the proceedings to enable the protocol procedures to be followed before the case is pursued.

The Protocol

5   Preliminary Notice
C7–005   **5.1** As soon as the claimant decides there is a reasonable chance that he will bring a claim against a professional, the claimant is encouraged to notify the professional in writing.

5.2 This letter (the "Preliminary Notice") should contain the following information:

(a) the identity of the claimant and any other parties;

(b) a brief outline of the claimant's grievance against the professional; and

(c) if possible, a general indication of the financial value of the potential claim.

5.3 The Preliminary Notice should be addressed to the professional and should ask the professional to inform his professional indemnity insurers, if any, immediately.

5.4 The Preliminary Notice should be acknowledged in writing within 21 days of receipt. Where the claimant is unrepresented the acknowledgment should enclose a copy of this protocol.

5.5 If, after 6 months from the date of the Preliminary Notice, the claimant has not sent any further correspondence to the professional regarding the claim, the claimant should notify the professional of its intentions with regard to the claim, i.e. whether the claimant is pursuing the claim, has decided not to pursue it or has yet to reach a decision and, if the latter, when the claimant envisages making a decision.

6   Letter of Claim
C7–006   **6.1** As soon as the claimant decides there are grounds for a claim against the professional, the claimant should write a detailed Letter of Claim to the professional.

6.2 The Letter of Claim will normally be an open letter (as opposed to being "without prejudice") and should include the following–

(a) The identity of any other parties involved in the dispute or a related dispute.

(b) A clear chronological summary (including key dates) of the facts on which the claim is based. Key documents should be identified, copied and enclosed.

(c) Any reasonable requests which the claimant needs to make for documents relevant to the dispute which are held by the professional.

(d) The allegations against the professional. What has been done wrong or not been done? What should the professional have done acting correctly?

(e) An explanation of how the alleged error has caused the loss claimed. This should include details of what happened as a result of the claimant relying upon what the professional did wrong or omitted to do, and what might have happened if the professional had acted correctly.

(f) An estimate of the financial loss suffered by the claimant and how it is calculated. Supporting documents should be identified, copied and enclosed. If details of the financial loss cannot be supplied, the claimant should explain why and should state when he will be in a position to provide the details. This information should be sent to the professional as soon as reasonably possible. If the claimant is seeking some form of non–financial redress, this should be made clear.

(g) Confirmation whether or not an expert has been appointed. If so, providing the identity and discipline of the expert, together with the date upon which the expert was appointed.

(h) A request that a copy of the Letter of Claim be forwarded immediately to the professional's insurers, if any.

6.3 The Letter of Claim is not intended to have the same formal status as a Statement of Case. If, however, the Letter of Claim differs materially from the Statement of Case in subsequent proceedings, the court may decide, in its discretion, to impose sanctions.

6.4 If the claimant has sent other Letters of Claim (or equivalent) to any other party in relation to the same dispute or a related dispute, those letters should be copied to the professional.

7 Letter of Acknowledgment

7.1 The Letter of Claim should be acknowledged in writing within **C7–007** 21 days of receipt.

7.2 Where the claimant is unrepresented, the Letter of Acknowledgment should enclose a copy of this protocol unless provided previously.

8 Investigations

8.1 If the professional considers that, for any reason, the Letter of **C7–008** Claim does not comply with section 6 above, the professional should as soon as reasonably practicable inform the claimant why and identify the further information which the professional reasonably requires.

8.2 The professional will have three months from the date of the Letter of Acknowledgment to investigate and respond to the Letter of Claim by the provision of a Letter of Response and/or a Letter of Settlement (as to which, see paragraph 9 below).

8.3 If the professional is in difficulty in complying with the three month time period, the problem should be explained to the claimant as soon as possible and, in any event, as long as possible before the end of the three month period. The professional should explain what is being done to resolve the problem and when the professional expects to be in a position to provide a Letter of Response and/or a Letter of Settlement. The claimant should agree to any reasonable requests for an extension of the three month period.

8.4 The parties should supply promptly, at this stage and throughout, whatever relevant information or documentation is reasonably requested.

8.5 If the professional intends to claim against someone who is not currently a party to the dispute, that third party should be identified to the claimant in writing as soon as possible.

9 Letter of Response and Letter of Settlement

C7–009   **9.1** As soon as the professional has completed his investigations (and in any event within 3 months of the Letter of Acknowledgment unless an extension has been agreed), the professional should send to the claimant:

    (a) a Letter of Response, or

    (b) a Letter of Settlement; or

    (c) both.

9.2 The Letter of Response

9.2.1 The Letter of Response should be an open letter (as opposed to being "without prejudice") and should be a reasoned answer to the claimant's allegations:

    (a) if the claim is admitted the professional should say so in clear terms.

    (b) if only part of the claim is admitted the professional should make clear which parts of the claim are admitted and which are denied.

    (c) if the claim is denied in whole or in part, the Letter of Response should include specific comments on the allegations against the professional and, if the claimant's version of events is disputed, the professional should provide his version of events.

    (d) if the professional is unable to admit or deny the claim, the professional should explain why and identify any further information which is required.

    (e) if the professional disputes the estimate of the claimant's financial loss, the Letter of Response should set out the professional's estimate. If an estimate cannot be provided, the professional should explain why and when he will be in a position to provide an estimate. The professional's estimate should be sent to the claimant as soon as reasonably possible.

    (f) to the extent not already exchanged in the protocol process, key documents should be identified, copied and enclosed.

9.2.2 The Letter of Response is not intended to have the same formal status as a Defence. If, however, the Letter of Response differs materially from the Defence in subsequent court proceedings, the court may decide, in its discretion, to impose sanctions.

9.3 The Letter of Settlement

9.3.1Any Letter of Settlement may be an open letter, a without prejudice letter, a without prejudice save as to costs letter or an offer made pursuant to Part 36 of the Civil Procedure Rules and should be sent if the professional intends to make proposals for settlement of all or part of the claim. It should:

(a) set out the professional's views on the claim identifying those issues which the professional believes are likely to remain in dispute and those which are not. (The Letter of Settlement does not need to include this information if it is already included in a Letter of Response.)

(b) make a settlement proposal or identify any further information which is required before the professional can formulate its proposal.

(c) where additional documents are relied upon, copies should be provided.

9.4 Effect of Letter of Response and/or Letter of Settlement

9.4.1 If the Letter of Response denies the claim in its entirety and there is no Letter of Settlement, it is open to the claimant to commence court proceedings.

9.4.2 In any other circumstance, the professional and the claimant should commence negotiations with the aim of resolving the claim within 6 months of the date of the Letter of Acknowledgment (NOT from the date of the Letter of Response).

9.4.3 If the claim cannot be resolved within this period:

(a) the parties should agree within 14 days of the end of the period whether the period should be extended and, if so, by how long.

(b) the parties should seek to identify those issues which are still in dispute and those which can be agreed.

(c) if an extension of time is not agreed it will then be open to the claimant to commence court proceedings.

10   Documents

10.1 This protocol is intended to encourage the early exchange of **C7–010** relevant information, so that issues in dispute can be clarified or resolved. The claimant should provide key documents with the Letter of Claim and (at any time) any other documents reasonably requested by the professional which are relevant to the issues in dispute. The professional should provide key documents with the Letter of Response, to the extent not provided by the claimant, and (at any time) any other documents reasonably requested by the claimant which are relevant to the issues in dispute.

10.2 Parties are encouraged to cooperate openly in the exchange of relevant information and documentation. However, the protocol should not be used to justify a 'fishing expedition' by either party. No party is obliged under the protocol to disclose any document which a court could not order them to disclose in the pre–action period under CPR 31.16.

10.3 This protocol does not alter the parties' duties to disclose documents under any professional regulation or under general law.

11   Experts

C7–011   **11.1** In professional negligence disputes, separate expert opinions may be needed on:

    (a) breach of duty;

    (b) causation; and/or

    (c) the quantification of the claimant's claim.

11.2 It is recognised that in professional negligence disputes the parties and their advisers will require flexibility in their approach to expert evidence. The parties should co–operate when making decisions on appropriate expert specialisms, whether experts might be instructed jointly and whether any reports obtained pre–action might be shared and should at all times have regard to the duty in CPR 35.1 to restrict expert evidence to that which is reasonably required to resolve the dispute.

11.3 When considering what expert evidence may be required during the protocol period, parties should be aware that any expert reports obtained pre–action will only be permitted in proceedings with the express permission of the court.

12   Alternative Dispute Resolution

C7–012   **12.1** Court proceedings should be a last resort. The parties should consider whether some form of alternative dispute resolution procedure might enable them to settle their dispute without commencing court proceedings, and if so, endeavour to agree which form to adopt.

12.2 Parties may negotiate to settle a dispute or may use a form of ADR including:

    (a) mediation—a third party facilitating a resolution;

    (b) arbitration—a third party deciding the dispute;

    (c) early neutral evaluation—a third party giving an informed opinion on the dispute;

    (d) adjudication—a process by which an independent adjudicator provides the parties with a decision that can resolve the dispute either permanently or on a temporary basis, pending subsequent court determination; and

    (e) Ombudsmen schemes.

(Information on mediation and other forms of ADR is available in the *Jackson ADR Handbook* (available from Oxford University Press) or at—

    ● http://www.civilmediation.justice.gov.uk/

    ● http://www.adviceguide.org.uk/england/law_e/law_legal_ system_e/law_taking_legal_action_e/alternatives_to_ court.htm)

12.3 If court proceedings are issued, the parties may be required by the court to provide evidence that ADR has been considered. A party's refusal to engage or silence in response to an invitation to participate in ADR might be considered unreasonable by the court and could lead to the court ordering that party to pay additional costs.

13   Stocktake

C7–013   **13.1** Where the procedure set out in this protocol has not resolved the dispute between the parties, they should undertake a further review of their respective positions. The parties should consider the state of the papers and the evidence in order to see if proceedings can be avoided and, at the least, narrow the issues between them.

14 Court proceedings

14.1 Unless it is necessary (for example, to obtain protection against the expiry of a relevant limitation period (see paragraph 4 above)) the claimant should not start court proceedings until: **C7–014**

(a) the Letter of Response denies the claim in its entirety and there is no Letter of Settlement (see paragraph 9.4.1 above); or

(b) the end of the negotiation period (see paragraphs 9.4.2 and 9.4.3 above).

14.2 If proceedings are for any reason started before the parties have followed the procedures in this protocol, the parties are encouraged to agree to apply to the court for a stay whilst the protocol is followed.

14.3 Where possible 14 days written notice should be given to the professional before proceedings are started, indicating the court within which the claimant is intending to commence court proceedings.

14.4 If proceedings are commenced they should be served in accordance with Part 6 of the Civil Procedure Rules.

Delete "Pre–Action Protocol for Judicial Review" and substitute:

PRE–ACTION PROTOCOL FOR JUDICIAL REVIEW

Introduction

1. This Protocol applies to proceedings within England and Wales only. It does not affect the time limit specified by Rule 54.5(1) of the Civil Procedure Rules (CPR), which requires that any claim form in an application for judicial review must be filed promptly and in any event not later than 3 months after the grounds to make the claim first arose. Nor does it affect the shorter time limits specified by Rules 54.5(5) and (6), which set out that a claim form for certain planning judicial reviews must be filed within 6 weeks and the claim form for certain procurement judicial reviews must be filed within 30 days. **C8–001**

2. This Protocol sets out a code of good practice and contains the steps which parties should generally follow before making a claim for judicial review.

3. The aims of the protocol are to enable parties to prospective claims to—

(a) understand and properly identify the issues in dispute in the proposed claim and share information and relevant documents;

(b) make informed decisions as to whether and how to proceed;

(c) try to settle the dispute without proceedings or reduce the issues in dispute;

(d) avoid unnecessary expense and keep down the costs of resolving the dispute; and

(e) support the efficient management of proceedings where litigation cannot be avoided.

4. Judicial review allows people with a sufficient interest in a decision or action by a public body to ask a judge to review the lawfulness of—

- an enactment; or
- a decision, action or failure to act in relation to the exercise of a public function.

5. Judicial review should only be used where no adequate alternative remedy, such as a right of appeal, is available. Even then, judicial review may not be appropriate in every instance. Claimants are strongly advised to seek appropriate legal advice as soon as possible when considering proceedings. Although the Legal Aid Agency will not normally grant full representation before a letter before claim has been sent and the proposed defendant given a reasonable time to respond, initial funding may be available, for eligible claimants, to cover the work necessary to write this. (See Annex C for more information.)

6. This protocol will not be appropriate in very urgent cases. In this sort of case, a claim should be made immediately. Examples are where directions have been set for the claimant's removal from the UK or where there is an urgent need for an interim order to compel a public body to act where it has unlawfully refused to do so, such as where a local housing authority fails to secure interim accommodation for a homeless claimant. A letter before claim, and a claim itself, will not stop the implementation of a disputed decision, though a proposed defendant may agree to take no action until its response letter has been provided. In other cases, the claimant may need to apply to the court for an urgent interim order. Even in very urgent cases, it is good practice to alert the defendant by telephone and to send by email (or fax) to the defendant the draft Claim Form which the claimant intends to issue. A claimant is also normally required to notify a defendant when an interim order is being sought.

7. All claimants will need to satisfy themselves whether they should follow the protocol, depending upon the circumstances of the case. Where the use of the protocol is appropriate, the court will normally expect all parties to have complied with it in good time before proceedings are issued and will take into account compliance or non–compliance when giving directions for case management of proceedings or when making orders for costs.

8. The Upper Tribunal Immigration and Asylum Chamber (UTIAC) has jurisdiction in respect of judicial review proceedings in relation to most immigration decisions. The President of UTIAC has issued a Practice Statement to the effect that, in judicial review proceedings in UTIAC, the parties will be expected to follow this protocol, where appropriate, as they would for proceedings in the High Court.

Alternative Dispute Resolution

C8–002   **9.** The courts take the view that litigation should be a last resort. The parties should consider whether some form of alternative dispute resolution ('ADR') or complaints procedure would be more suitable than litigation, and if so, endeavour to agree which to adopt. Both the claimant and defendant may be required by the court to provide evidence that alternative means of resolving their dispute were considered. Parties are warned that if the protocol is not followed (including this paragraph) then the court must have regard to such conduct when determining costs. However, parties should also note that a claim for judicial review should comply with the time limits set out in the Introduction above. Exploring ADR may not excuse failure to comply with the time limits. If it is appropriate to issue a claim to ensure compliance with a time limit, but the parties agree there should be a stay of proceedings to explore settlement or narrowing the issues in dispute, a joint application for appropriate directions can be made to the court.

10. It is not practicable in this protocol to address in detail how the parties might decide which method to adopt to resolve their particular dispute. However, summarised below are some of the options for resolving disputes without litigation which may be appropriate, depending on the circumstances—

- Discussion and negotiation.
- Using relevant public authority complaints or review procedures.
- Ombudsmen—the Parliamentary and Health Service and the Local Government Ombudsmen have discretion to deal with complaints relating to maladministration. The British and Irish Ombudsman Association provide information about Ombudsman schemes and other complaint handling bodies and this is available from their website at *www.bioa.org.uk*. Parties may wish to note that the Ombudsmen are not able to look into a complaint once court action has been commenced.
- Mediation—a form of facilitated negotiation assisted by an independent neutral party.

11. The Civil Justice Council and Judicial College have endorsed *The Jackson ADR Handbook* by Susan Blake, Julie Browne and Stuart Sime (2013, Oxford University Press). The Citizens Advice Bureaux website also provides information about ADR: http://www.adviceguide.org.uk/england/law_e/law_legal_system_e/law_taking_legal_action_e/alternatives_to_court.htm. Information is also available at: http://www.civilmediation.justice.gov.uk/.

12. If proceedings are issued, the parties may be required by the court to provide evidence that ADR has been considered. A party's silence in response to an invitation to participate in ADR or refusal to participate in ADR might be considered unreasonable by the court and could lead to the court ordering that party to pay additional court costs.

Requests for information and documents at the pre–action stage

13. Requests for information and documents made at the pre– C8–003 action stage should be proportionate and should be limited to what is properly necessary for the claimant to understand why the challenged decision has been taken and/or to present the claim in a manner that will properly identify the issues. The defendant should comply with any request which meets these requirements unless there is good reason for it not to do so. Where the court considers that a public body should have provided **relevant** documents and/or information, particularly where this failure is a breach of a statutory or common law requirement, it may impose costs sanctions.

The letter before claim

C8–004 **14.** In good time before making a claim, the claimant should send a letter to the defendant. The purpose of this letter is to identify the issues in dispute and establish whether they can be narrowed or litigation can be avoided.

15. Claimants should normally use the suggested **standard format** for the letter outlined at Annex A. For Immigration, Nationality and Asylum cases, the Home Office has a standardised form which can be used. It can be found online at: https://www.gov.uk/government/publications/chapter–27–judicial–review–guidance–part–1.

16. The letter should contain **the date and details of the decision, act or omission being challenged, a clear summary of the facts and the legal basis for the claim**. It should also contain the details of any information that the claimant is seeking and an explanation of why this is considered relevant. If the claim is considered to be an Aarhus Convention claim (see Rules 45.41 to 45.44 and Practice Direction 45), the letter should state this clearly and explain the reasons, since specific rules as to costs apply to such claims. If the claim is considered appropriate for allocation to the Planning Court and/or for classification as "significant" within that court, the letter should state this clearly and explain the reasons.

17. The letter should normally contain the **details of any person known to the claimant who is an Interested Party**. An Interested Party is any person directly affected by the claim. They should be sent a **copy** of the letter before claim **for information. Claimants are strongly advised to seek appropriate legal advice when considering proceedings which involve an Interested Party and, in particular, before sending the letter before claim to an Interested Party or making a claim**.

18. A claim should not normally be made until the proposed reply date given in the letter before the claim has passed, unless the circumstances of the case require more immediate action to be taken. The claimant should send the letter before claim in good time so as to enable a response which can then be taken into account before the time limit for issuing the claim expires, unless there are good reasons why this is not possible.

19. Any claimant intending to ask for a protective costs order (an order that the claimant will not be liable for the costs of the defendant or any other party or to limit such liability) should explain the reasons for making the request, including an explanation of the limit of the financial resources available to the claimant in making the claim.

The letter of response

C8–005 **20.** Defendants should normally respond within 14 days using the **standard format** at Annex B. Failure to do so will be taken into account by the court and sanctions may be imposed unless there are good reasons. Where the claimant is a litigant in person, the defendant should enclose a copy of this Protocol with its letter.

21. Where it is not possible to reply within the proposed time limit, the defendant should send an interim reply and propose a reasonable extension, giving a date by which the defendant expects to respond substantively. Where an extension is sought, reasons should be given and, where required, additional information requested. **This will not affect the time limit for making a claim for judicial review** nor will it bind the claimant where he or she considers this to be unreasonable. However, where the court considers that a subsequent claim is made prematurely it may impose sanctions.

22. If the **claim is being conceded in full**, the reply should say so in clear and unambiguous terms.

23. If the **claim is being conceded in part or not being conceded at all**, the reply should say so in clear and unambiguous terms, and—

(a) where appropriate, contain a new decision, clearly identifying what aspects of the claim are being conceded and what are not, or, give a clear timescale within which the new decision will be issued;

(b) provide a fuller explanation for the decision, if considered appropriate to do so;

(c) address any points of dispute, or explain why they cannot be addressed;

(d) enclose any **relevant** documentation requested by the claimant, or explain why the documents are not being enclosed;

(e) where documents cannot be provided within the time scales required, then give a clear timescale for provision. The claimant should avoid making any formal application for the provision of documentation/information during this period unless there are good grounds to show that the timescale proposed is unreasonable;

(f) where appropriate, confirm whether or not they will oppose any application for an interim remedy; and

(g) if the claimant has stated an intention to ask for a protective costs order, the defendant's response to this should be explained.

If the letter before claim has stated that the claim is an Aarhus Convention claim but the defendant does not accept this, the reply should state this clearly and explain the reasons. If the letter before claim has stated that the claim is suitable for the Planning Court and/or categorisation as "significant" within that court but the defendant does not accept this, the reply should state this clearly and explain the reasons.

24. The response should be sent to **all Interested Parties** identified by the claimant and contain details of any other persons who the defendant considers are Interested Parties.

Annex A

Letter before claim

Section 1.

Information required in a letter before claim

1 Proposed claim for judicial review
   To   C8–006

(Insert the name and address of the proposed defendant – see details in section 2.)

2 The claimant

(Insert the title, first and last name and the address of the claimant.)

3 The defendant's reference details

(When dealing with large organisations it is important to understand that the information relating to any particular individual's previous dealings with it may not be immediately available, therefore it is important to set out the relevant reference numbers for the matter in dispute and/or the identity of those within the public body who have been handling the particular matter in dispute—see details in section 3.)

4 The details of the claimants' legal advisers, if any, dealing with this claim

(Set out the name, address and reference details of any legal advisers dealing with the claim.)

5 The details of the matter being challenged

(Set out clearly the matter being challenged, particularly if there has been more than one decision.)

6 The details of any Interested Parties

(Set out the details of any Interested Parties and confirm that they have been sent a copy of this letter.)

7 The issue

(Set out a brief summary of the facts and relevant legal principles, the date and details of the decision, or act or omission being challenged, and why it is contended to be wrong.)

8 The details of the action that the defendant is expected to take

(Set out the details of the remedy sought, including whether a review or any interim remedy are being requested.)

9 ADR proposals

(Set out any proposals the claimant is making to resolve or narrow the dispute by ADR.)

10 The details of any information sought

(Set out the details of any information that is sought which is related to identifiable issues in dispute so as to enable the parties to resolve or reduce those issues. This may include a request for a fuller explanation of the reasons for the decision that is being challenged.)

11 The details of any documents that are considered relevant and necessary

(Set out the details of any documentation or policy in respect of which the disclosure is sought and explain why these are relevant.)

12 The address for reply and service of court documents

(Insert the address for the reply.)

13 Proposed reply date

(The precise time will depend upon the circumstances of the individual case. However, although a shorter or longer time may be appropriate in a particular case, 14 days is a reasonable time to allow in most circumstances.)

Section 2.

Address for sending the letter before claim

Public bodies have requested that, for certain types of cases, in order to ensure a prompt response, letters before claim should be sent to specific addresses.

- **Where the claim concerns a decision in an Immigration, Asylum or Nationality case (including in relation to an immigration decision taken abroad by an Entry Clearance Officer)—**

  The claim should be sent electronically to the following Home Office email address: **UKVIPAPhomeoffice.gsi.gov.uk**

  Alternatively the claim may be sent by post to the following Home Office postal address:

    Litigation Operations Allocation Hub
    Status Park 2
    4 Nobel Drive
    Harlington
    Hayes
    Middlesex UB3 5EY

  The Home Office has a standardised form which claimants may find helpful to use for communications with the Home Office in Immigration, Asylum or Nationality cases pursuant to this Protocol, to assist claimants to include all relevant information and to promote speedier review and response by the Home Office. The Home Office form may be filled out in electronic or hard copy format. It can be found online at: **https://www.gov.uk/government/publications/chapter–27–judicial–review–guidance–part–1**

- **Where the claim concerns a decision by the Legal Aid Agency—**

    The address on the decision letter/notification;
    Legal Director
    Corporate Legal Team
    Legal Aid Agency
    102 Petty France
    London SW1H 9AJ

- **Where the claim concerns a decision by a local authority—**

    The address on the decision letter/notification; and their legal department.

- **Where the claim concerns a decision by a department or body for whom Treasury Solicitor acts *and Treasury Solicitor has already been involved in the case* a copy should also be sent, quoting the Treasury Solicitor's reference, to—**

    The Treasury Solicitor,

One Kemble Street,
London WC2B 4TS.
In all other circumstances, the letter should be sent to the address on the letter notifying the decision.

Section 3.

Specific reference details required
Public bodies have requested that the following information should be provided, if at all possible, in order to ensure prompt response. **Where the claim concerns an Immigration, Asylum or Nationality case, dependent upon the nature of the case—**
- The Home Office reference number;
- The Port reference number;
- The Asylum and Immigration Tribunal reference number;
- The National Asylum Support Service reference number; or, if these are unavailable:
- The full name, nationality and date of birth of the claimant.
  Where the claim concerns a decision by the Legal Aid Agency—
- The certificate reference number.

Annex B

Response to a letter before claim

Information required in a response to a letter before claim

1 The claimant
C8–007 (*Insert the title, first and last names and the address to which any reply should be sent.*)

2 From
(*Insert the name and address of the defendant.*)

3 Reference details
(*Set out the relevant reference numbers for the matter in dispute and the identity of those within the public body who have been handling the issue.*)

4 The details of the matter being challenged
(*Set out details of the matter being challenged, providing a fuller explanation of the decision, where this is considered appropriate.*)

5 Response to the proposed claim
(*Set out whether the issue in question is conceded in part, or in full, or will be contested. Where an interim reply is being sent and there is a realistic prospect of settlement, details should be included. If the claimant is a litigant in person, a copy of the Pre–Action Protocol should be enclosed with the letter.*)

6 Details of any other Interested Parties
(*Identify any other parties who you consider have an interest who have not already been sent a letter by the claimant.*)

7 ADR proposals

(Set out the defendant's position on any ADR proposals made in the letter before claim and any ADR proposals by the defendant.)

8 Response to requests for information and documents

(Set out the defendant's answer to the requests made in the letter before claim including reasons why any requested information or documents are not being disclosed.)

9 Address for further correspondence and service of court documents

(Set out the address for any future correspondence on this matter)

Annex C

Notes on public funding for legal costs in judicial review

Public funding for legal costs in judicial review is available from **C8–008** legal professionals and advice agencies which have contracts with the Legal Aid Agency. Funding may be provided for—

- *Legal Help* to provide initial advice and assistance with any legal problem; or
- *Legal Representation* to allow you to be represented in court if you are taking or defending court proceedings. This is available in two forms—
  - *Investigative Help* is limited to funding to investigate the strength of the proposed claim. It includes the issue and conduct of proceedings only so far as is necessary to obtain disclosure of relevant information or to protect the client's position in relation to any urgent hearing or time limit for the issue of proceedings. This includes the work necessary to write a letter before claim to the body potentially under challenge, setting out the grounds of challenge, and giving that body a reasonable opportunity, typically 14 days, in which to respond.
  - *Full Representation* is provided to represent you in legal proceedings and includes litigation services, advocacy services, and all such help as is usually given by a person providing representation in proceedings, including steps preliminary or incidental to proceedings, and/or arriving at or giving effect to a compromise to avoid or bring to an end any proceedings. Except in emergency cases, a proper letter before claim must be sent and the other side must be given an opportunity to respond before Full Representation is granted.

Further information on the type(s) of help available and the criteria for receiving that help may be found in the Legal Aid Agency's pages on the Ministry of Justice website at: https://www.justice.gov.uk/legal–aid.

A list of contracted firms and Advice Agencies may be found at: http://find–legal–advice.justice.gov.uk

Delete "Pre–Action Protocol for Housing Disrepair Cases" and substitute:

PRE–ACTION PROTOCOL FOR HOUSING DISREPAIR CASES

1 Introduction

C10–001   **1.1** This Protocol applies to residential property situated in England and Wales. It relates to claims by tenants and others in respect of housing disrepair. Before using the Protocol tenants should ensure that their landlord is aware of the disrepair. The Protocol is intended for those cases where, despite the landlord's knowledge of the disrepair, the matter remains unresolved.

1.2 This Protocol describes the conduct the court will normally expect prospective parties in a housing disrepair claim to follow prior to the start of proceedings. It is intended to encourage the exchange of information between parties at an early stage and to provide a clear framework within which parties in a housing disrepair claim can attempt to achieve an early and appropriate resolution of the issues.

1.3 If a claim proceeds to litigation, the court will expect all parties to have complied with the Protocol as far as possible. The court has power to order parties who have unreasonably failed to comply with the Protocol to pay costs or to be subject to other sanctions.

2 Aims

C10–002   **2.1** The aims of this Protocol are to—
  (a) avoid unnecessary litigation;
  (b) promote the speedy and appropriate carrying out of any repairs which are the landlord's responsibility;
  (c) ensure that tenants receive any compensation to which they are entitled as speedily as possible;
  (d) promote good pre–litigation practice, including the early exchange of information and to give guidance about the instruction of experts; and
  (e) keep the costs of resolving disputes down.

3 The Scope of the Protocol

C10–003   **3.1** A disrepair claim is a civil claim arising from the condition of residential premises and may include a related personal injury claim (see 3.5 below). Although most claims are brought by a tenant against their landlord, this Protocol is not limited to such claims. It covers claims by any person with a disrepair claim including tenants, lessees and members of the tenant's family. The use of the word "tenant" in this Protocol is intended to cover all such people.

3.2 The types of claim which this Protocol is intended to cover include those brought under Section 11 of the Landlord and Tenant Act 1985, Section 4 of the Defective Premises Act 1972, common law nuisance and negligence, and those brought under the express terms of a tenancy agreement or lease. It does not cover claims brought under Section 82 of the Environmental Protection Act 1990 (which are heard in the Magistrates' Court).

3.3 This Protocol does not cover disrepair claims which originate as counterclaims or set–offs in other proceedings i.e. where the tenant is seeking to have the compensation due for disrepair set against money claimed by the landlord (typically in a possession claim for rent arrears). In such cases the landlord and tenant will still be expected to act reasonably in exchanging information and trying to settle the case at an early stage.

3.4 The Protocol should be followed in all cases, whatever the value of the damages claim.

3.5 Housing disrepair claims may contain a personal injury element. If the personal injury claim requires expert evidence other than a General Practitioner's letter, the Personal Injury Protocol should be followed for that element of the disrepair claim. If the personal injury claim is of a minor nature and will only be evidenced by a General Practitioner's letter, it is not necessary to follow the Personal Injury Protocol. If the disrepair claim is urgent, it would be reasonable to pursue separate disrepair and personal injury claims, which could then be case managed together or consolidated at a later date.

The Protocol

4 Alternative dispute resolution

4.1 The parties should consider whether some form of alternative C10–004 dispute resolution procedure would be more suitable than litigation and if so, try to agree which form to use. Both the landlord and the tenant may be required by the court to provide evidence that alternative means of resolving their dispute were considered. The courts take the view that litigation should be a last resort, and that claims should not be issued while a settlement is still actively being explored. Parties should be aware that the court will take into account the extent of the parties' compliance with this Protocol when making orders about who should pay costs.

4.2 Options for resolving a dispute include the following—

(a) mediation: information about mediation can be found at http://www.civilmediation.org/contact.php.

(b) for council tenants—

- Local authority repairs, complaints and/or arbitration procedures.
- The Right to Repair Scheme. The scheme is only suitable for small, urgent repairs of less than £250 in value. Information and leaflets about the scheme in England can be obtained from the Department for Communities and Local Government, Eland House, Bressenden Place, London SW1E 5DU. Tel: 0303 444 0000 (https://www.gov.uk/repair–council–property).
- Information about the scheme in Wales can be obtained from the National Assembly for Wales, Cardiff Bay, Cardiff, CF99 1NA. Tel. 0845 010 5500 http://www.assemblywales.org/index.htm
- In England, the Housing Ombudsman Service 81 Aldw-

ych London WC2B 4HN Tel 0300 111 3000 http://www.housing–ombudsman.org.uk/

- In Wales the Public Services Ombudsman for Wales. Tel. 0300 790 0203 http://www.ombudsman–wales.org.uk

(c) for housing association tenants and for tenants of qualifying private landlords—

- Any complaints procedure operated by the landlord.
- In England, the Housing Ombudsman Service, 81 Aldwych, London. WC2B 4HN Tel: 0300 111 3000 http://www.housing–ombudsman.org.uk/
- In Wales, the National Assembly for Wales, Cardiff Bay, Cardiff, CF99 1NA. Tel. 0845 010 5500 http://www.assemblywales.org/index.htm

Information about repair rights generally is available free of charge from the following web pages: http://england.shelter.org.uk/get__advice/repairs__and__bad__conditions and http://www.communitylegaladvice.org.uk/en/legalhelp/leaflet04__1.jsp.

The former Department for Transport, Local Government and the Regions issued Good Practice Guidance on Housing Disrepair Legal Obligations in January 2002. Copies of the Guidance (ISBN 185112523X) can be obtained from Communities and Local Government Publications, PO Box 236, Wetherby LS23 7NB. Tel: 0300 123 1124. Fax:0300 123 1125. Textphone: 0870 1207 405. E–mail: product@communities.gsi.gov.uk. (free to download from the Communities and Local Government website at http://www.communities.gov.uk/publications/housing/deliveringhousingadaptations2).

A summary, Housing Research Summary No. 154, is available free on the Communities and Local Government website at the following link http://www.communities.gov.uk/archived/publications/housing/housingdisrepair.

The Communities and Local Government website http://www.communities.gov.uk is a general source of information for landlords and tenants.

5 Tenant's Letter of Claim

C10–005   **5.1** It is recognised that disrepair cases can range from straightforward to highly complex, and that it is not always possible to obtain detailed information at an early stage. In order to avoid unnecessary delay and to ensure that notice of the claim is given to the landlord at the earliest possible opportunity, particularly where repairs are urgent, it may be appropriate for the tenant to send a letter notifying the landlord of the claim before a detailed Letter of Claim is sent.

5.2 The tenant should send to the landlord a Letter of Claim at the earliest reasonable opportunity. A specimen Letter of Claim is at Annex A. The letter may be suitably adapted as appropriate. The Letter of Claim should contain the following details—

(a) the tenant's name, the address of the property, the tenant's address if different, the tenant's telephone number and when access is available;

(b) details of the defects, including any defects outstanding, in the form of a schedule, if appropriate (See Annex C for a specimen schedule which can be used to inform the landlord of the disrepair);

(c) history of the defects, including any attempts to rectify them;

(d) details of any notification previously given to the landlord of the need for repair or information as to why the tenant believes that the landlord has knowledge of the need for repair;

(e) the effect of the defects on the tenant (including any personal injury claim by the tenant);

(f) the identities of all other persons who plan to make a personal injury claim and brief details of their personal injury claims;

(g) the details of any special damages (see the form at Annex D);

(h) the proposed expert (see paragraph 7);

(i) the proposed letter of instruction to the expert (See Annex B); and

(j) relevant documents disclosed by the tenant.

5.3 The Letter of Claim should also request disclosure from the landlord of all documents relevant to the disrepair including—

(a) a copy of the tenancy agreement including the tenancy conditions;

(b) the tenancy file;

(c) any documents relating to notice of disrepair given, including copies of any notes of meetings and oral discussions;

(d) any inspection reports or documents relating to works required to the property; and

(e) any computerised records.

5.4 Documents relating to rent arrears or other tenancy issues will not normally be relevant. Nothing in the Protocol restricts the right of the tenant to look personally at their file or to request a copy of the whole file. Neither is the landlord prevented from sending to the tenant a copy of the whole file, should the landlord wish.

5.5 A copy of the Protocol should be sent to the landlord if the tenant has reason to believe that the landlord will not have access to the Protocol e.g. because the landlord is an individual or small organisation. If in doubt, a copy should be sent.

6 Landlord's Response

6.1 Where a landlord is not an individual, a person should be C10–006 designated to act as a point of contact for the tenant (and their solicitor, if one is involved). The designated person's name and contact details should be sent to the tenant and their solicitor as soon as possible after the landlord receives the Letter of Claim from the tenant.

6.2 The landlord should normally reply to the Letter of Claim within 20 working days of receipt. Receipt is deemed to have taken place two days after the date of the letter. The landlord's response should include at least the following—

(a) copies of all relevant records or documents requested by the tenant; and

(b) a response to the tenant's proposals for instructing an expert including—

    i. whether or not the proposed single joint expert is agreed;

ii. whether the letter of instruction is agreed;

iii. if the single joint expert is agreed but with separate instructions, a copy of the letter of instruction; and

iv. if the appointment of a single joint expert is not agreed, whether the landlord agrees to a joint inspection.

6.3 The landlord must also provide a response dealing with the issues set out below, as appropriate. This can be provided either within the response to the Letter of Claim or within 20 working days of receipt of the report of the single joint expert or receipt of the experts' agreed schedule following a joint inspection—

(a) whether liability is admitted and, if so, in respect of which defects;

(b) if liability is disputed in respect of some or all of the defects, the reasons for this;

(c) any point which the landlord wishes to make regarding lack of notice of the disrepair or any difficulty in gaining access;

(d) a full schedule of intended works, including anticipated start and completion dates and a timetable for the works;

(e) any offer of compensation; and

(f) any offer in respect of costs.

6.4 Failure to respond within 20 working days of receipt of the Letter of Claim or at all, is a breach of the Protocol (see paragraph 1.3) and the tenant is then free to issue proceedings.

6.5 The Letter of Claim and the landlord's response are not intended to have the same status as a statement of case in court proceedings. Matters may come to light subsequently which mean that the case of one or both parties may be presented differently in court proceedings. Parties should not seek to take advantage of such discrepancies provided that there was no intention to mislead.

7 Experts

7.1 General

C10–007   (a) Parties are reminded that the Civil Procedure Rules provide that expert evidence should be restricted to that which is necessary and that the court's permission is required to use an expert's report. The court may limit the amount of experts' fees and expenses recoverable from another party.

(b) When instructing an expert, the parties must have regard to CPR Practice Direction 35 and the Guidance for the Instruction of Experts in Civil Claims 2014 at http:www.judiciary.gov.uk.

(c) In some cases it might not be necessary to instruct an expert to provide evidence of disrepair, for example, if the only issue relates to the level of any damages claimed. It may be advisable for tenants to take photographs or video footage of any defects before and after works.

(d) The expert should be instructed to report on all items of disrepair which the landlord ought reasonably to know about, or which the expert ought reasonably to report on. The expert should be asked to provide a schedule of works, an estimate of the costs of repair, and to list any urgent works.

7.2 Single Joint Expert

(a) If the landlord does not raise an objection to the proposed expert or letter of instruction within 20 working days of receipt of the Letter of Claim, the expert should be instructed as a single joint expert, using the tenant's proposed letter of instruction. (See Annex B for a specimen letter of instruction to an expert.)

(b) Alternatively, if the parties cannot agree joint instructions, the landlord and tenant should send their own separate instructions to the single joint expert. If sending separate instructions, the landlord should send the tenant a copy of the landlord's letter of instruction with their response to the Letter of Claim.

7.3 Joint Inspection

(a) If it is not possible to reach agreement to instruct a single joint expert, even with separate instructions, the parties should attempt to arrange a joint inspection, meaning an inspection by different experts instructed by each party to take place at the same time. If the landlord wishes their own expert to attend a joint inspection, they should inform both the tenant's expert and the tenant's solicitor.

(b) Should a case come before the court, it will be for the court to decide whether the parties have acted reasonably in instructing separate experts and whether the costs of more than one expert should be recoverable.

7.4 Time Limits

(a) Whether a single joint expert or a joint inspection is used, the property should be inspected within 20 working days of the date that the landlord responds to the tenant's Letter of Claim.

(b) If a single joint expert is instructed, a copy of the expert's report should be sent to both the landlord and the tenant within 10 working days of the inspection. Either party can ask relevant questions of the expert who should send the answers to both parties.

(c) If there is a joint inspection, the experts should produce an agreed schedule of works detailing—

    i the defects and required works which are agreed and a timetable for the agreed works;

    ii the areas of disagreement and the reasons for disagreement.

(d) The agreed schedule should be sent to both the landlord and the tenant within 10 working days of the joint inspection.

7.5 Urgent Cases

The Protocol does not prevent a tenant from instructing an expert at an earlier stage if this is considered necessary for reasons of urgency. Appropriate cases may include—

(a) where the tenant reasonably considers that there is a significant risk to health and safety;

(b) where the tenant is seeking an interim injunction;

(c) where it is necessary to preserve evidence.

7.6 Access

Tenants must allow the landlord reasonable access for inspection and repair in accordance with the tenancy agreement. The landlord should give reasonable notice of the need for access, except in the case of an emergency. The landlord must give access to common parts as appropriate, for example, for the inspection of a shared heating system. If the tenant is no longer in occupation of the premises the landlord should take all reasonable steps to give access to the tenant for the purpose of an inspection.

7.7 Expert's fees

(a) Experts' terms of appointment should be agreed at the outset, including the basis of charging and time for delivery of the report.

(b) If a single joint expert is instructed, each party will pay one half of the cost of the report. If a joint inspection is carried out, each party will pay the full cost of the report from their own expert.

7.8 Information about independent experts can be obtained from—

(a) The Chartered Institute of Environmental Health, Chadwick Court, 15 Hatfields, London. SE1 8DJ Tel: 020 7928 6006 http://www.cieh.org/about_us.html. Ask for a copy of the Consultants and Trainers Directory;

(b) The Expert Witness Directory http://www.sweetandmaxwell.co.uk/our-businesses/directories.aspx

(c) The Royal Institution of Chartered Surveyors, 12 Great George Street, Parliament Square, London. SW1P 3AD, Tel: 024 7686 8555 http://www.ricsfirms.com/ Ask for a copy of the relevant regional directory.

Taking stock

C10–008   8 Where the procedure set out in this Protocol has not resolved the dispute between the landlord and the tenant, they should undertake a review of their respective positions to see if proceedings can be avoided and, at the least, to narrow the issues between them.

Time limits

C10–009   9 (a) The time scales given in the Protocol are long stops and every attempt should be made to comply with the Protocol as soon as possible. If parties are able to comply earlier than the time scales provided, they should do so.

(b) Time limits in the Protocol may be changed by agreement. However, it should always be borne in mind that the court will expect an explanation as to why the Protocol has not been followed or has been varied and breaches of the Protocol may lead to costs or other orders being made by the court.

Limitation period

C10–010   10 (a) There are statutory time limits for starting proceedings ('the limitation period'). If a tenant starts a claim after the limitation period applicable to that type of claim has expired, the landlord will be entitled to use that as a defence to the claim. In cases where the limitation period is about to expire, the tenant should ask the landlord to agree not to rely on a limitation defence, so that the parties can comply with the Protocol.

(b) If proceedings have to be started before the parties have complied with the Protocol, they should apply to the court for an order to stay (i.e. suspend) the proceedings until the steps under the Protocol have been completed.

Costs

11 If the tenant's claim is settled without litigation on terms which justify bringing it, the landlord will pay the tenant's reasonable costs. The Statement of Costs Form N260 available on the HMCTS website can be used to inform the landlord of the costs of the claim. **C10–011**

Annexes

1212 The following documents are annexed to this pre–action protocol— **C10–012**

Annex A
Letter of Claim
(a) for use by a solicitor; and
(b) for use by the tenant.

Annex B
Letter of Instruction to Expert
(a) for use by a solicitor, and
(b) for use by the tenant.

Annex C
Schedule of Disrepair

Annex D
Special Damages Form

Annex A

Letter of Claim

(a) Letter from solicitor
To Landlord   C10–013
Dear Sirs,
RE: TENANT'S NAME AND ADDRESS OF PROPERTY
We are instructed by your above named tenant. (*Where the tenant is legally aided or a party to a conditional fee agreement entered into before 1 April 2013 insert a sentence stating how their case is being funded.*) We are using the Housing Disrepair Protocol. *We enclose a copy of the Protocol for your information.*

Repairs
Your tenant complains of the following defects at the property (*set out nature of defects*).

We enclose a schedule which sets out the disrepair in each room.

The history of the disrepair is as follows: (*set out history of defects*).

You received notice of the defects as follows: (*list details of notice relied on*).

The defects at the property are causing (*set out the effects of the disrepair on the client and their family, including any personal injury element. Specify if there will be any additional claimants*).

Please arrange to inspect the property as soon as possible. Access will be available on the following dates and times: (*list dates and times as appropriate*).

Please confirm whether you intend to carry out repairs at this stage or whether you wish to wait until the property has been inspected by the expert(s) as set out below. If you intend to carry out repairs at this stage, please set out a full schedule of intended works including anticipated start and completion dates and a timetable for the works.

Disclosure

Please also provide within 20 working days of this letter the following:

All relevant records or documents including:

(i) a copy of the tenancy agreement including the tenancy conditions;

(ii) the tenancy file;

(iii) documents relating to notice of disrepair given, including copies of any notes of meetings and oral discussions;

(iv) inspection reports or documents relating to works required to the property;

(iv) computerised records.

We enclose a signed authority from our client for you to release this information to us.

We also enclose copies of the following relevant documents from our client:

Expert

If agreement is not reached about the carrying out of repairs within 20 working days of this letter, we propose that the parties agree to jointly instruct a single joint expert (*insert expert's name and address*) to carry out an inspection of the property and provide a report. We enclose a copy of their CV, plus a draft letter of instruction. Please let us know if you agree to his/her appointment. If you object, please let us know your reasons within 20 working days.

If you do not object to the expert being instructed as a single joint expert, but wish to provide your own instructions, you should send those directly to (*insert expert's name*) within 20 working days of this letter. Please send us a copy of your letter of instruction. If you do not agree to a single joint expert, we will instruct (*insert expert's name*) to inspect the property in any event. In those circumstances, if you wish to instruct your expert to attend at the same time, please let us and (*insert expert's name*) know within 20 working days.

Claim

We take the view that you are in breach of your repairing

138

obligations. Please provide us with your proposals for compensation. *(Alternatively, set out suggestions for general damages i.e. £x for x years). Our client also requires compensation for special damages, and we attach a schedule of the special damages claimed.*
Yours faithfully,

Annex A

Letter of Claim

(b)   Letter from tenant
To Landlord   C10–014
Dear Sirs,
RE: YOUR NAME AND ADDRESS OF PROPERTY
I write regarding disrepair at the above address. I am using the Housing Disrepair Protocol. *I enclose a copy of the Protocol for your information.*

Repairs
The following defects exist at the property *(set out nature of defects).*
I enclose a schedule which sets out the disrepair in each room.
The history of the disrepair is as follows: *(set out history of defects).*
You received notice of the defects as follows: *(list details of notice relied on).*
The defects at the property are causing *(set out the effects of the disrepair on you and your family, including any personal injury element. Specify if there will be any additional claimants).*
Please arrange to inspect the property as soon as possible. Access will be available on the following dates and times: *(list dates and times as appropriate).*
Please confirm whether you intend to carry out repairs at this stage or whether you wish to wait until the property has been inspected by the expert(s) as set out below. If you intend to carry out repairs at this stage, please set out a full schedule of intended works including anticipated start and completion dates and a timetable for the works.

Disclosure
Please also provide within 20 working days of this letter the following:
All relevant records or documents including:
   (i) a copy of the tenancy agreement including the tenancy conditions;
   (ii) the tenancy file;
   (iii) documents relating to notice of disrepair given, including copies of any notes of meetings and oral discussions;
   (iv) inspection reports or documents relating to works required to the property;
   (iv) computerised records.
I enclose copies of the following relevant documents:

Expert
If agreement is not reached about the carrying out of repairs within 20 working days of this letter, I propose that we jointly instruct a

single joint expert (*insert expert's name and address*) to carry out an inspection of the property and provide a report. I enclose a copy of their CV, plus a draft letter of instruction. Please let me know if you agree to his/her appointment. If you object, please let me know your reasons within 20 working days.

If you do not object to the expert being instructed as a single joint expert, but wish to provide your own instructions, you should send those directly to (*insert expert's name*) within 20 working days of this letter. Please send me a copy of your letter of instruction. If you do not agree to a single joint expert, I will instruct (*insert expert's name*) to inspect the property in any event. In those circumstances, if you wish to instruct your expert to attend at the same time, please let me and (*insert expert's name*) know within 20 working days.

Claim
I take the view that you are in breach of your repairing obligations. Please provide me with your proposals for compensation. (*Alternatively, set out suggestions for general damages i.e. £x for x years). I also require compensation for special damages, and I attach a schedule of the special damages claimed.*

Yours faithfully,

Annex B

Letter of Instruction to Expert

(a) Letter from solicitor
C10–015 Dear
RE: TENANT'S NAME AND ADDRESS OF PROPERTY
We act for the above named in connection with a housing disrepair claim at the above property. We are using the Housing Disrepair Protocol. *We enclose a copy of the Protocol for your information.*

Please carry out an inspection of the above property by (date) [The date to be inserted should be 20 working days from the date of the letter] and provide a report covering the following points:

  (a) whether you agree that the defects are as claimed;
  (b) whether any of the defects is structural;
  (c) the cause of the defect(s);
  (d) the age, character and prospective life of the property;
  (e) a schedule of works;
  (f) an estimate of the costs of repair.

Access will be available on the following dates and times: (*list dates and times as appropriate*).

You are instructed as a single joint expert / The landlord is (landlord's name and details) / The landlord will be providing you with their own instructions direct / The landlord will contact you to confirm that their expert will attend at the same time as you to carry out a joint inspection.

Please provide the report within 14 days of the inspection. Please contact us immediately if there are any works which require an interim injunction.

If the case proceeds to court, the report may be used in evidence.

Please ensure that the report complies with Civil Procedure Rules Practice Direction 35.3 and the Guidance for the Instruction of Experts in Civil Claims 2014 at http:www.judiciary.gov.uk. If you do not have a copy please let us know.

Insert details as to cost and payment

Yours sincerely,

Annex B

Letter of Instruction to Expert

(b)   Letter from tenant

Dear   C10–016

RE: YOUR NAME AND ADDRESS OF PROPERTY

I am currently in dispute with my landlord about disrepair at the above property. I am using the Housing Disrepair Protocol. *I enclose a copy of the Protocol for your information.*

Please carry out an inspection of the above property by (date) [The date to be inserted should be 20 working days from the date of the letter] and provide a report covering the following points:

(a) whether you agree that the defects are as claimed;

(b) whether any of the defects is structural;

(c) the cause of the defect(s);

(d) the age, character and prospective life of the property;

(e) a schedule of works;

(f) an estimate of the costs of repair.

Access will be available on the following dates and times: (*list dates and times as appropriate*)

You are instructed as a single joint expert / The landlord is (landlord's name and details) / The landlord will be providing you with their own instructions direct / The landlord will contact you to confirm that their expert will attend at the same time as you to carry out a joint inspection.

Please provide the report within 14 days of the inspection. Please contact me immediately if there are any works which require an interim injunction.

If the case proceeds to court, the report may be used in evidence. Please ensure that the report complies with Civil Procedure Rules Practice Direction 35.3 and the Guidance for the Instruction of Experts in Civil Claims 2014 at http:www.judiciary.gov.uk. If you do not have a copy please let me know.

Insert details as to cost and payment

Yours sincerely,

Annex C

Schedule of Disrepair

C10–017

Schedule
Disrepair Protocol
TENANT

	Item Number	Room (tick where appropriate)	Disrepair (identify briefly)	Notice given (How was the landlord made aware of the problem)	Inconvenience suffered (How has the disrepair affected you)
Exterior of premises, roof and access Comment:					
Entrance, hall and storage Comment:					
Living room (s) Comment:					
Kitchen Comment:					
Bathroom Comment:					
Bedroom 1 Comment:					
Bedroom 2 Comment:					
Bedroom 3 Comment:					
Other Comment:					

Annex D

Special Damages Form

C10–018

SPECIAL DAMAGES FORM

	ITEM	DATE PURCHASED	WHERE PURCHASED	PRICE	RECEIPTS – YES/NO	HOW DAMAGED
1						
2						
3						
4						
5						
6						
7						
8						
9						
10						

Delete "Pre–Action Protocol for Possession Claims Based on Rent Arrears" and substitute:

PRE–ACTION PROTOCOL FOR POSSESSION CLAIMS BY SOCIAL LANDLORDS

Part 1

Aims and Scope of the Protocol

C11–001 **1.1** This Protocol applies to residential possession claims by social landlords (such as local authorities, Registered Social Landlords and Housing Action Trusts) and private registered providers of social housing. Part 2 relates to claims which are based solely on claims for rent arrears. Part 3 relates to claims where the Court's discretion to postpone possession is limited by s.89(1) Housing Act 1980. The protocol does not apply to claims in respect of long leases or to claims for possession where there is no security of tenure.

1.2 Part 3 of the protocol does not apply to cases brought by social landlords solely on grounds where if the case is proved, there is a restriction on the Court's discretion on making an order for possession and/or to which s.89 Housing Act 1980 applies.

1.3 Part 2 of the protocol reflects the guidance on good practice given to social landlords and private registered providers in the collection of rent arrears. It recognises that it is in the interests of both landlords and tenants to ensure that rent is paid promptly and to ensure that difficulties are resolved wherever possible without court proceedings.

1.4 Part 3 seeks to ensure that in cases where Article 8 of the European Convention on Human Rights is raised the necessary information is before the Court at the first hearing so that issues of proportionality may be dealt with summarily, if appropriate, or that appropriate directions for trial may be given.

1.5 The aims of the protocol are:

(a) to encourage more pre–action contact and exchange of information between landlords and tenants;

(b) to enable the parties to avoid litigation by settling the matter if possible; and

(c) to enable court time to be used more effectively if proceedings are necessary.

1.6 Courts should take into account whether this protocol has been followed when considering what orders to make. Social Landlords and private registered providers of social housing should also comply with guidance issued from time to time by the Homes and Communities Agency, the Department for Communities and Local Government and the Welsh Ministers.

(a) If the landlord is aware that the tenant has difficulty in reading or understanding information given, the landlord should take reasonable steps to ensure that the tenant understands any information given. The landlord should be able to demonstrate that reasonable steps have been taken to ensure that the information has been appropriately communicated in ways that the tenant can understand.

(b) If the landlord is aware that the tenant is under 18 or is particularly vulnerable, the landlord should consider at an early stage—

144

(i) whether or not the tenant has the mental capacity to defend possession proceedings and, if not, make an application for the appointment of a litigation friend in accordance with CPR 21;

(ii) whether or not any issues arise under Equality Act 2010; and

(iii) in the case of a local authority landlord, whether or not there is a need for a community care assessment in accordance with National Health Service and Community Care Act 1990.

Part 2

Possession Claims Based upon Rent Arrears

Initial contact

2.1 The landlord should contact the tenant as soon as reasonably **C11–002** possible if the tenant falls into arrears to discuss the cause of the arrears, the tenant's financial circumstances, the tenant's entitlement to benefits and repayment of the arrears. Where contact is by letter, the landlord should write separately to each named tenant.

2.2 The landlord and tenant should try to agree affordable sums for the tenant to pay towards arrears, based upon the tenant's income and expenditure (where such information has been supplied in response to the landlord's enquiries). The landlord should clearly set out in pre–action correspondence any time limits with which the tenant should comply.

2.3 The landlord should provide, on a quarterly basis, rent statements in a comprehensible format showing rent due and sums received for the past 13 weeks. The landlord should, upon request, provide the tenant with copies of rent statements in a comprehensible format from the date when arrears first arose showing all amounts of rent due, the dates and amounts of all payments made, whether through housing benefit, discretionary housing payments or by the tenant, and a running total of the arrears.

2.4 If the tenant meets the appropriate criteria, the landlord should arrange for arrears to be paid by the Department for Work and Pensions from the tenant's benefit.

2.5 The landlord should offer to assist the tenant in any claim the tenant may have for housing benefit, discretionary housing benefit or universal credit (housing element).

2.6 Possession proceedings for rent arrears should not be started against a tenant who can demonstrate that—

(a) the local authority or Department for Work and Pensions have been provided with all the evidence required to process a housing benefit or universal credit (housing element) claim;

(b) a reasonable expectation of eligibility for housing benefit or universal credit (housing element); and

(c) paid other sums due not covered by housing benefit or universal credit (housing element).

The landlord should make every effort to establish effective ongoing liaison with housing benefit departments and DWP and, with the tenant's consent, make direct contact with the relevant housing benefit department or DWP office before taking enforcement action.

The landlord and tenant should work together to resolve any housing benefit or universal credit (housing element) problems.

2.7 Bearing in mind that rent arrears may be part of a general debt problem, the landlord should advise the tenant to seek assistance from CAB, debt advice agencies or other appropriate agencies as soon as possible. Information on debt advice is available on the Money Advice Service website https://www.moneyadviceservice.org.uk/en/articles/whereto–go–to–get–free–advice–debt–advice.

After service of statutory notices

C11–003   **2.8** After service of a statutory notice but before the issue of proceedings, the landlord should make reasonable attempts to contact the tenant, to discuss the amount of the arrears, the cause of the arrears, repayment of the arrears and the housing benefit or universal credit (housing element) position and send a copy of this protocol.

2.9 If the tenant complies with an agreement to pay the current rent and a reasonable amount towards arrears, the landlord should agree to postpone issuing court proceedings so long as the tenant keeps to such agreement. If the tenant ceases to comply with such agreement, the landlord should warn the tenant of the intention to bring proceedings and give the tenant clear time limits within which to comply.

Alternative dispute resolution

C11–004   **2.10** The parties should consider whether it is possible to resolve the issues between them by discussion and negotiation without recourse to litigation. The parties may be required by the court to provide evidence that alternative means of resolving the dispute were considered. Courts take the view that litigation should be a last resort, and that claims should not be issued prematurely when a settlement is still actively being explored.

2.11 The Civil Justice Council and Judicial College have endorsed *The Jackson ADR Handbook* by Susan Blake, Julie Browne and Stuart Sime (2013, Oxford University Press). The Citizens Advice Bureaux website also provides information about ADR: http://www.adviceguide.org.uk/england/law_e/law_legal_system_e/law_taking_legal_action_e/alternatives_to_court.htm. Information is also available at: http://www.civilmediation.justice.gov.uk/.

Court proceedings

C11–005   **2.11** Not later than ten days before the date set for the hearing, the landlord should—

(a) provide the tenant with up to date rent statements; and

(b) disclose what knowledge it possesses of the tenant's housing benefit or universal credit (housing element) position to the tenant.

2.12 (a) The landlord should inform the tenant of the date and time of any court hearing and provide an up to date rent statement and the order applied for. The landlord should advise the tenant to attend the hearing as the tenant's home is at risk. Records of such advice should be kept.

(b) If the tenant complies with an agreement made after the issue of proceedings to pay the current rent and a reasonable amount towards arrears, the landlord should agree to postpone court proceedings so long as the tenant keeps to such agreement.

(c) If the tenant ceases to comply with such agreement, the landlord should warn the tenant of the intention to restore the proceedings and give the tenant clear time limits within which to comply.

2.13 If the landlord unreasonably fails to comply with the terms of the protocol, the court may impose one or more of the following sanctions—

(a) an order for costs; and

(b) in cases other than those brought solely on mandatory grounds, adjourn, strike out or dismiss claims.

2.14 If the tenant unreasonably fails to comply with the terms of the protocol, the court may take such failure into account when considering whether it is reasonable to make possession orders.

Part 3

Mandatory Grounds for Possession

3.1 This part applies in cases where if a social landlord proves its **C11–006** case, there is a restriction on the Court's discretion on making an order for possession and/or to which s.89 Housing Act 1980 applies (e.g. non–secure tenancies, unlawful occupiers, succession claims, and severing of joint tenancies).

3.2 In cases where the court must grant possession if the landlord proves its case then before issuing any possession claim social landlords—

(a) should write to occupants explaining why they currently intend to seek possession and requiring the occupants within a specified time to notify the landlord in writing of any personal circumstances or other matters which they wish to take into account. In many cases such a letter could accompany any notice to quit and so would not necessarily delay the issue of proceedings; and

(b) should consider any representations received, and if they decide to proceed with a claim for possession give brief written reasons for doing so.

3.3 In these cases the social landlord should include in its particulars of claim, or in any witness statement filed under CPR 55.8(3), a schedule giving a summary—

(a) of whether it has (by statutory review procedure or otherwise) invited the defendant to make representations of any personal circumstances or other matters which they wish to be taken into account before the social landlord issues proceedings;

147

(b) if representations were made, that they were considered;

(c) of brief reasons for bringing proceedings; and

(d) copies of any relevant documents which the social landlord wishes the Court to consider in relation to the proportionality of the landlord's decision to bring proceedings.

Delete "Pre–Action Protocol for Possession Claims Based on Mortgage or Home Purchase Plan Arrears in Respect of Residential Property" and substitute:

PRE–ACTION PROTOCOL FOR POSSESSION CLAIMS BASED ON MORTGAGE OR HOME PURCHASE PLAN ARREARS IN RESPECT OF RESIDENTIAL PROPERTY

I Introduction

Definitions

C12–001   **1.1** In this Protocol—

(a) 'possession claim' means a claim for the recovery of possession of property under Part 55 of the Civil Procedure Rules 1998;

(b) 'home purchase plan' means a method of purchasing a property by way of a sale and lease arrangement that does not require the payment of interest;

(c) 'bank holiday' means a bank holiday under the Banking and Financial Dealings Act 1971;

(d) 'business day' means any day except Saturday, Sunday, a bank holiday, Good Friday or Christmas day; and

(e) 'authorised tenant' means a tenant whose tenancy is authorised as between the borrower and the lender.

Preamble

C12–002   **2.1** This Protocol describes the behaviour the court will normally expect of the parties prior to the start of a possession claim within the scope of paragraph 3.1 below.

2.2 This Protocol does not alter the parties' rights and obligations.

2.3 It is in the interests of the parties that mortgage payments or payments under home purchase plans are made promptly and that difficulties are resolved wherever possible without court proceedings. However in some cases an order for possession may be in the interest of both the lender and the borrower.

Aims

C12–003   **3.1** The aims of this Protocol are to—

(a) ensure that a lender or home purchase plan provider (in this Protocol collectively referred to as 'the lender') and a borrower or home purchase plan customer (in this Protocol collectively referred to as 'the borrower') act fairly and reasonably with each other in resolving any matter concerning mortgage or home purchase plan arrears;

(b) encourage greater pre–action contact between the lender and the borrower in order to seek agreement between the parties, and where agreement cannot be reached, to enable efficient use of the court's time and resources; and

148

(c) encourage lenders to check who is in occupation of the property before issuing proceedings.

3.2 Where either party is required to communicate and provide information to the other, reasonable steps should be taken to do so in a way that is clear, fair and not misleading. If the lender is aware that the borrower may have difficulties in reading or understanding the information provided, the lender should take reasonable steps to ensure that information is communicated in a way that the borrower can understand.

Scope

4.1 This Protocol applies to arrears on—   C12–004

(a) first charge residential mortgages and home purchase plans regulated by the Financial Conduct Authority under the Financial Services and Markets Act 2000 (as amended by the Financial Services Act, 2012);

(b) second charge mortgages over residential property and other secured loans regulated under the Consumer Credit Act 1974 on residential property; and

(c) unregulated residential mortgages.

4.2 Where a potential claim includes a money claim and a possession claim, this protocol applies to both.

4.3 The protocol does not apply to Buy To Let mortgages.

II Actions Prior to the Start of a Possession Claim

Initial contact and provision of information

5.1 Where a borrower falls into arrears, the lender must provide C12–005
the borrower with—

(a) where appropriate, the required regulatory information sheet or the National Homelessness Advice Service/Shelter/Cymru booklet on mortgage arrears;

(b) information on the current monthly instalments and the amounts paid for the last 2 years; and

(c) information on the amount of arrears, which should include—
   (i) the total amount of the arrears;
   (ii) the total outstanding of the mortgage or the home purchase plan; and
   (iii) whether interest or charges have been or will be added, and, where appropriate, details or an estimate of the interest or charges that may be payable.

5.2 The lender should also seek information about whether the property is occupied by an authorised tenant.

5.3 The lender must advise the borrower to make early contact with the housing department of the borrower's Local Authority and, should, where relevant refer the borrower to appropriate sources of independent debt advice.

5.4 The parties, or their representatives, must take all reasonable steps to discuss with each other the reasons for the arrears, the borrower's financial circumstances and proposals for repayment of the arrears (see paragraph 7.1). For example, parties should consider whether the reasons for the arrears are temporary or long–term, and whether the borrower may be able to pay the arrears in a reasonable time.

5.5 The lender must consider a reasonable request from the borrower to change the date of regular payment (within the same payment period) or the method by which payment is made. The lender must either agree to such a request or, where it refuses such a request, it must, within a reasonable period of time, give the borrower a written explanation of its reasons for the refusal.

5.6 The lender must respond promptly to any proposal for payment made by the borrower. If the lender does not agree to such a proposal it should give reasons in writing to the borrower within 10 business days of the proposal.

5.7 If the lender submits a proposal for payment, the borrower must be given a reasonable period of time in which to consider such proposals. The lender must set out the proposal in sufficient detail to enable the borrower to understand the implications of the proposal.

5.8 If the borrower fails to comply with an agreement, the lender should warn the borrower, by giving the borrower 15 business days notice in writing, of its intention to start a possession claim unless the borrower remedies the breach in the agreement.

Postponing the start of a possession claim

C12–006 **6.1** A lender must not consider starting a possession claim for mortgage arrears where the borrower can demonstrate to the lender that the borrower has—

    (a) submitted a claim to—

        (i) the Department for Works and Pensions ('DWP') for Support for Mortgage Interest (SMI) or if appropriate Universal Credit; or

        (ii) an insurer under a mortgage payment protection policy; or

        (iii) a participating local authority for support under a Mortgage Rescue Scheme, or other means of homelessness prevention support provided by the local authority,

        (iv) and has provided all the evidence required to process a claim;

    (b) a reasonable expectation of eligibility for payment from the DWP or from an insurer or support from the local authority or welfare or charitable organisation such as the Veterans Welfare Scheme or Royal British Legion;

    (c) an ability to pay a mortgage instalment not covered by a claim to the DWP or the insurer in relation to a claim under paragraph 6.1(1)(a) or (b);

    (d) difficulty in respect of affordability or another specific personal or financial difficulty, and requires time to seek free independent debt advice, or has a confirmed appointment with a debt adviser, and

    (e) a reasonable expectation, providing evidence where possible, of an improvement in their financial circumstances in the foreseeable future (for example a new job or increased income from a lodger).

6.2 If a borrower can demonstrate that reasonable steps have been or will be taken to market the property at an appropriate price in accordance with reasonable professional advice, the lender must consider postponing starting a possession claim to allow the borrower a realistic period of time to sell the property. The borrower must continue to take all reasonable steps actively to market the property where the lender has agreed to postpone starting a possession claim.

6.3 Where, notwithstanding paragraphs 6.1 an 6.2, the lender has agreed to postpone starting a possession claim, the borrower should provide the lender with a copy of the particulars of sale, the Energy Performance Certificate ('EPC') or proof that an EPC has been commissioned and (where relevant) details of purchase offers received within a reasonable period of time specified by the lender. The borrower should give the lender details of the estate agent and the conveyancer instructed to deal with the sale. The borrower should also authorise the estate agent and the conveyancer to communicate with the lender about the progress of the sale and the borrower's conduct during the process.

6.4 Where the lender decides not to postpone the start of a possession claim, it must inform the borrower of the reasons for this decision at least 5 business days before starting proceedings.

Further matters to consider before starting a possession claim

7.1 Starting a possession claim should be a last resort and must not normally be started unless all other reasonable attempts to resolve the situation have failed.. The parties should consider whether, given the individual circumstances of the borrower and the form of the agreement, it is reasonable and appropriate to do one or more of the following— C12–007

(a) extend the term of the mortgage;

(b) change the type of mortgage;

(c) defer payment of interest due under the mortgage;

(d) capitalise the arrears; or

(e) make use of any Government forbearance initiatives in which the lender chooses to participate.

7.2 Where there is an authorised tenant in occupation of the property, at the possession hearing the court will consider whether—

(a) further directions are required;

(b) to adjourn the possession claim until possession has been recovered against the tenant; or

(c) to make an order conditional upon the tenant's right of occupation.

Complaints to the Financial Services Ombudsman

8.1 The lender must consider whether to postpone the start of a possession claim where the borrower has made a genuine complaint to the Financial Ombudsman Service ('FOS') about the potential possession claim. C12–008

8.2 Where a lender does not intend to await the decision of the FOS, it must give notice to the borrower, with reasons, that it intends to start a possession claim.

PRE–ACTION PROTOCOL FOR LOW VALUE PERSONAL INJURY CLAIMS IN ROAD TRAFFIC ACCIDENTS FROM 31 JULY 2013

Scope

In paragraph 4.7(2) and the table below it, for "www.ask.CUEPI.com" substitute:

C13–005   http://www.askCUE.co.uk

Section II — General Provisions

Claimants without a legal representative

In paragraph 5.10(3), for "www.ask.CUEPI.com" substitute:

C13–006   http://www.askCUE.co.uk

Section III — The Stages of the Process
Stage 1

Completion of the Claim Notification Form

In paragraph 6.3A(1), for "www.ask.CUEPI.com" substitute:

C13–007   http://www.askCUE.co.uk

PRE–ACTION PROTOCOL FOR LOW VALUE PERSONAL INJURY (EMPLOYERS' LIABILITY AND PUBLIC LIABILITY) CLAIMS

Stage 2

Non–settlement payment by the defendant at the end of Stage 2

In paragraph 7.58, for "7.54 or 7.56" substitute:

C15–013   7.55 or 7.57

VOLUME 2

CIVIL PROCEDURE RULES

SECTION A1

PROCEDURAL GUIDES

15. INSOLVENCY

15.2. Proceedings under s.6 of the Company Directors Disqualification Act 1986 (CDDA 1986)

In Guide 15.2, add new entry at the beginning:

Prospective changes

A1.15–002

Small Business, Enterprise and Employment Act 2015 (SBEEA 2015)	Part 9 of SBEEA 2015 makes provision for a number of substantial changes to CDDA 1986. These will come into force on a day to be appointed. When they come into force, consequential changes to this procedural guide will be required. No day for them to come into force has yet been appointed.

SECTION 2

SPECIALIST PROCEEDINGS

2A COMMERCIAL COURT

PART 58—COMMERCIAL COURT

Related sources

After "http://www.justice.gov.uk/courts/rcj–rolls–building/admiralty–commercial–mercantile–courts." add:

- Commercial Court Updates and Guidance at *http://www.combar.com.*   **2A–3**

Delete "Heavy and Complex Cases—Checklist (see para.2A–18.1)."

Electronic working

Add at end:

See also *Southern Rock Insurance Co Ltd v Brightside Group Ltd* [2015] EWHC 757 **2A–9.1** (Comm) where Leggatt J., refusing to transfer an insurance matter from the Chancery List in Bristol, emphasised the crossover between the expertise available in the Chancery Division and the Commercial Court.

Add new paragraph 2A–39.0:

Note

2014 and 2015 have seen a succession of guidance notes and cases in which the **2A–39.0** importance of compliance with the Admiralty and Commercial Courts Guide has been strongly emphasised by judges. See, for example the four pieces of guidance issued since October 2014 at *http://www.combar.com, Tchenguiz v Grant Thornton UK LLP* [2015] EWHC 405 (Comm), (Leggatt J. – pleadings of excessive length), *Richardson v Glencore*

Energy [2014] EWHC 3990 (Comm) (Paul Walker J., failure to observe conditions for holding CMCs by consent).

Admiralty and Commercial Courts Guide

F5 Ordinary applications

At the end of paragraph F5.4, add as a footnote:

2A–89 F5.4[1]

[1] By a Note of April 2015 from the Judge in charge of the Commercial List, the following wording has been added to this paragraph: "Skeletons should not without good reason be more than 15 pages in length".

F6 Heavy applications

At the end of paragraph F6.5, add as a footnote:

2A–90 F6.5[2]

[2] By a Note of April 2015 from the Judge in charge of the Commercial List, the following wording has been added to this paragraph: "Skeletons should not be more than 25 pages in length. The court will give permission for a longer skeleton where a party shows good reason for doing so. Any application to serve a longer skeleton should be made on paper to the court briefly stating the reasons for exceeding the 25 page limit. Such application should be made sufficiently in advance of the deadline for service to enable the court to rule upon it before then".

2B MERCANTILE COURTS

Mercantile Court Guide

APPENDIX A

COURT ADDRESSES AND OTHER INFORMATION

1.

LONDON AND SOUTH EAST

Delete the entry for "Judge" and substitute:

Judge

2B–35   His Honour Judge Waksman QC
    Clerk—Adham Harker
    Email: Adham.Harker@hmcts.gsi.gov.uk
    Tel: 020 7947 6265

3.

NORTH EAST (LEEDS)

Judges

Delete "Listing Officer—Richard Sutherland" and substitute:
2B–37   Listing Officer – Richard Marsland

Delete "email: richard.sutherland@hmcts.gsi.gov.uk" and substitute:
    email: richard.marsland@hmcts.gsi.gov.uk

4.

NORTH EAST (NEWCASTLE UPON TYNE)

Judges

Add after "His Honour Judge Raeside QC":
2B–38   His Honour Judge Behrens

Delete "Clerk—Phil Lloyd" and substitute:
Clerk—Richard Marsland

Delete "email: phil.lloyd@hmcts.gsi.gov.uk" and substitute:
Email: richard.marsland@hmcts.gsi.gov.uk

5.

NORTH WEST (LIVERPOOL)

Judges

Delete "His Honour Judge Waksman QC".   **2B–39**

Delete the entry for "Listing and Enquiries" and substitute:

Listing and Enquiries

Mercantile Manager: Elizabeth Taylor (elizabeth.taylor@hmcts.gsi.gov.uk)
Email (for filing and enquiries): e–filingliverpool@countycourt.gsi.gov.uk
Tel: 0151 296 2445
Fax (Goldfax): 01264 785321 (not a dedicated fax so clearly mark "Mercantile Court")

6.

NORTH WEST (MANCHESTER)

Delete the entry for "Judges and Listing" and substitute:

Judges and Listing

His Honour Judge Bird   **2B–40**
Manager of Mercantile Listing—Lesley Armstrong
Clerk to Mercantile Judges: 0161 240 5305
Email: manchester.mercantile@hmcts.gsi.gov.uk
Fax (Goldfax): 01264 785034

7.

SOUTH WEST (BRISTOL)

Judge and Listing

Delete "Special Listing Officers—Dawn Slade and Amy Smallcombe" and substitute:
Specialist Listing Officers—Debbie Thal–Jantzen and Amy Smallcombe   **2B–41**

8.

WALES (CARDIFF)

Delete the entry for "Wales (Cardiff)" and substitute:

Address

Cardiff Civil Justice Centre   **2B–42**
2 Park Street
Cardiff CF10 1ET
DX 99500 Cardiff 6

Judge

His Honour Judge Keyser QC
Clerk—Amanda Barrago
Email: amanda.barrago@hmcts.gsi.gov.uk
Tel: 02920 376411
Fax: 02920 376475
Listing Clerk—Amanda Thomas

Email: amanda.thomas@hmcts.gsi.gov.uk
Tel: 029 20376412
Fax: 029 20376475

Video–conferencing
Contact: Circuit Judges Listing
Tel: 029 20376412
E–mail hearings@cardiff.countycourt.gsi.gov.uk

PSU
Tel: 02920 343 685
E–mail: cardiff@thepsu.org.uk

9.

WALES (MOLD)

Delete the entry for "Wales (Mold)" and substitute:

Address
2B–43   Law Courts
Civic Centre
Mold Flintshire
CH7 1AE
DX 702521 Mold 2

Postal Address
Wrexham Law Courts
Bodhyfryd
Wrexham
LL12 7BP
DX 745320 Wrexham 9

Judge and Listing
His Honour Judge Keyser QC
Listing: Clerk—Tracy Paterson
Tel: 01978 317406
Fax: 01978 358213
Email: northwalescivillisting@wrexham.countycourt.gsi.gov.uk

Video–conferencing
Contact: Civil listing at Wrexham,

2E   ARBITRATION PROCEEDINGS

Arbitration Act 1996

THE ARBITRATION AGREEMENT

Agreement to submit to arbitration

In the fifth paragraph, for "Christian Kruppa v Alessandro Benedetti and Bertrand de Pallieres [2014] EWHC 1887 (Comm); [2014] 2 All E.R. (Comm) 617" substitute:
2E–99   *Kruppa v Benedetti* [2014] EWHC 1887 (Comm); [2014] 2 All E.R. (Comm) 617; [2014] 2 Lloyd's Rep. 421

STAY OF LEGAL PROCEEDINGS

Onus of showing that claim should proceed

At the end of the second paragraph, add:
2E–112   However, in *Salford Estates (No.2) Ltd v Altomart Ltd* [2014] EWCA Civ 1575; [2015]

B.C.C. 306, the Court of Appeal held that where a number of disputes concerning liability for the payment of service charges and insurance rent were referred to arbitration under the provisions of a lease, the Arbitration Act 1996 s.9 did not apply to a winding–up petition presented by the lessor based on the lessee company's inability to pay its debts, because the substance of the dispute was the existence of a particular debt mentioned in the petition.

THE ARBITRAL TRIBUNAL

Change title from "Consolidation by court" to:

Exercise of court's powers

Delete from ", but the court in such a case" to "presumably for separate arbitrations".

Add at end: **2E–137**

In *Shagang South–Asia (Hong Kong) Trading Co Ltd v Daewoo Logistics* [2015] EWHC 194 (Comm); [2015] 1 All E.R. (Comm) 545; [2015] 1 Lloyd's Rep. 504 Hamblen J. held that where an arbitrator had been appointed without any attempt to follow the procedures set out in section 16(3) and without recourse to the court under this section, the appointment made was invalid.

Note

Add at end:

The exercise of this power is rare. An example of a case where it was exercised is **2E–147** *Sierra Fishing Co v Farran* [2015] EWHC 140 (Comm); [2015] 1 All E.R. (Comm) 560; [2015] 1 Lloyd's Rep. 514 (Popplewell J.) where an arbitrator failed to disclose to the parties at the outset of the case that he had a financial interest in his father's law firm, the firm and his father acted for one of the parties and derived significant financial benefit from that continuing commercial relationship; circumstances within the "non–waivable red list" of situations regarded as giving rise to justifiable doubts about an arbitrator's impartiality in the International Bar Association Guidelines on Conflicts of Interest in International Arbitration.

POWERS OF THE COURT IN RELATION TO AWARD

Application

Add at end:

In *Y v S* [2015] EWHC 612 (Comm) Eder J. expressed the tentative view that the **2E–250** court had no power to order the provision of security on an application under the Arbitration Act 1996 s.66 for leave to enforce an arbitration award.

Note

In the first paragraph, for "Central Trading & Exports Ltd v Fioralba Shipping Co ("The Kalisti") [2014] EWHC 2397 (Comm)" substitute:

Central Trading & Exports Ltd v Fioralba Shipping Co [2014] EWHC 2397 (Comm); **2E–256** [2015] 1 All E.R. (Comm) 580; [2014] 2 Lloyd's Rep. 449

Add at end:

In *Emirates Trading Agency LLC v Sociedade de Fomento Industrial Private Ltd* [2015] EWHC 1452 (Comm) Popplewell J. held that an application under this section to set aside a final merits award for lack of jurisdiction should be refused where the tribunal had already made a partial award on jurisdiction which was binding and had not been challenged.

"On the ground of serious irregularity"

In the seventh paragraph, for "Transition Feeds LLP v Itochu Europe PLC [2013] EWHC 3629 (Comm) Field J.." substitute:

2E–262   *Transition Feeds LLP (formerly Advanced Liquid Feeds LLP) v Itochu Europe Plc* [2013] EWHC 3629 (Comm); [2013] 2 C.L.C. 920 Field J. The test for whether such an irregularity caused, or would cause, a substantial injustice was whether the irregularity caused the arbitrator to reach a conclusion which, but for the irregularity, he might not have reached, as long as the alternative was reasonably arguable: *Maass v Musion Events Ltd* [2015] EWHC 1346 (Comm) (Andrew Smith J.).

Change title from "Jurisdiction of arbitrator on remission" to:

Remission and setting aside

For "(Interbulk Ltd v Aiden Shipping Co Ltd; The Vimiera (No.3) [1986] 2 Lloyd's Rep. 75). Setting aside in whole or in part (s.68(3))." substitute:

2E–263   *(Interbulk Ltd v Aiden Shipping Co (The Vimeira)* [1986] 2 Lloyd's Rep. 75 (s.68(3)). In *Secretary of State for the Home Department v Raytheon Systems Ltd* [2015] EWHC 311 (TCC); [2015] 1 Lloyd's Rep. 493 Akenhead J. held that where the court had found that there was a serious irregularity in an arbitral process pursuant to the Arbitration Act 1996 s.68(2)(d), causing substantial injustice, the arbitral award should be set aside and the matter remitted to a new tribunal because the grounds were towards the more serious end of the spectrum, much of the factual and expert evidence would be redeployed before the new tribunal, and it would be invidious for the tribunal to be required to re–determine the same issues.

Time for appeal/Exhaustion of Specified Remedies s.70(2)

In the first paragraph, for "A Ltd v B Ltd [2014] EWHC 1870 (Comm)" substitute:

2E–271   *A Ltd v B Ltd* [2014] EWHC 1870 (Comm); [2014] 2 Lloyd's Rep. 393; [2014] 1 C.L.C. 958

Section 70(7)

In the first paragraph, for "Konkola Copper Mines v U&M Mining Zambia [2014] EWHC 2146 (Comm)" substitute:

2E–274   *Konkola Copper Mines Plc v U&M Mining Zambia Ltd* [2014] EWHC 2146 (Comm); [2014] 2 Lloyd's Rep. 507

Grounds of refusal

At the end of the second paragraph, add:

2E–360   In *Malicorp Ltd v Egypt* [2015] EWHC 361 (Comm); [2015] 1 Lloyd's Rep. 423 Walker J. held that where the award had been set aside by a competent authority it would generally be right to respect that decision unless it offended basic principles of honesty, natural justice and domestic concepts of public policy.

Subsection (5)

For "Dowans Holdings SA v Tanzania Electric Supply" substitute:

2E–361   *Dowans Holding SA v Tanzania Electric Supply Co Ltd* [2011] EWHC 1957 (Comm); [2012] 1 All E.R. (Comm) 820; [2011] 2 Lloyd's Rep. 475

2F   INTELLECTUAL PROPERTY PROCEEDINGS

Part 63 — Intellectual Property Claims

Delete paragraph 2F–17.6 and substitute:

Appeals to the Appointed Person: Registered Designs

2F–17.6   Section 10(2) of the Intellectual Property Act 2014 inserted into the Registered Designs Act 1949 ("RDA") ss. 27A and 27B. It took effect on April 6, 2015. New section 27A of the RDA provides as follows:

27A Appeals from decisions of registrar

(1) An appeal against a decision of the registrar under this Act may be made to—

    (a) a person appointed by the Lord Chancellor (an "appointed person"), or

    (b) the court.

(2) On an appeal under this section to an appointed person, the appointed person may refer the appeal to the court if—

    (a) it appears to the appointed person that a point of general legal importance is involved,

    (b) the registrar requests that the appeal be so referred, or

    (c) such a request is made by any party to the proceedings before the registrar in which the decision appealed against was made.

(3) Before referring an appeal to the court under subsection (2), the appointed person must give the appellant and any other party to the appeal an opportunity to make representations as to whether it should be so referred.

(4) Where, on an appeal under this section to an appointed person, the appointed person does not refer the appeal to the court—

    (a) the appointed person must hear and determine the appeal, and

    (b) the appointed person's decision is final.

(5) Sections 30 and 31 (costs, evidence) apply to proceedings before an appointed person as they apply to proceedings before the registrar.

(6) In the application of this section to England and Wales, "the court" means the High Court.

Section 27B provides the eligibility requirements for Appointed Persons. The effect of new s.27A is to introduce a new, alternative route for appeals from registration decisions regarding registered designs. It means that—as with the practice with appealing decisions of the Registrar in relation to Trade Marks (s.76 Trade Marks Act 1994)—an appellant will have the choice of an appeal to the High Court or to an appointed person.

Section 28 of the RDA, which provided for a Registered Designs Appeal Tribunal, is repealed by s.10(4) of the Intellectual Property Act 2014.

Delete "Guide to the Patents County Court Small Claims Track" and substitute:

Guide to the Intellectual Property Enterprise Court Small Claims Track

1. Introduction

This Guide applies to the small claims track within the Intellectual Property **2F–183** Enterprise Court ("IPEC"). It aims to help users and potential users of the IPEC small claims track by giving practical tips and explaining:

- how to decide if the IPEC small claims track is suitable for a claim
- how claims proceed in the IPEC small claims track
- what procedures apply in the IPEC small claims track
- how to contact the IPEC small claims track.

A number of legal terms used in this Guide are explained in the section of Commonly Used Terms in Annex B.

The Civil Procedure Rules ("CPR") govern proceedings in civil courts in England and Wales. They can be found at www.justice.gov.uk/courts/procedure–rules/civil/rules.

Part 63—Intellectual Property Claims ("CPR 63") and *Practice Direction 63—Intellectual Property Claims* ("PD 63") set out additional rules that apply only to intellectual property claims. The rules which apply specifically to the IPEC small claims are:

- CPR 63.27 and CPR 63.28
- PD63 para.32.2
- all other rules and paragraphs referred to in CPR 63.27, CPR 63.28 and PD63 para.32.2

- CPR 27 (which deals with the small claims track in general)

Where there is any conflict or confusion between the provisions of this Guide and the CPR, you must follow the rules and practices as set out in the CPR.

Further useful information can be found in the *Guide to the Intellectual Property Enterprise Court*, the *Patents Court Guide* and the *Chancery Guide* which can be found at www.justice.gov.uk.

2. Courts that Deal with Intellectual Property Claims

2F–184   Intellectual property claims are heard in the Chancery Division of the High Court, either by the Patents Court or the IPEC. The IPEC provides a streamlined and more cost–effective forum to hear lower value and less complex intellectual property claims than the Patents Court. IPEC cases are allocated either to the multi track or the small claims track.

The IPEC small claims track provides a forum with simpler procedures by which the most straightforward intellectual property claims with a low financial value can be decided:

- without the need for parties to be legally represented
- without substantial pre–hearing preparation
- without the formalities of a traditional trial and
- without the parties putting themselves at risk of anything but very limited costs.

IPEC small claims track cases are heard by three District Judges (District Judge Melissa Clarke, District Judge Lambert or District Judge Hart) or by deputy District Judges. IPEC multi–track cases are heard by enterprise judges, usually circuit judge HHJ Hacon. Patents Court cases are heard by High Court Judges and their deputies.

On 1 October 2013, the IPEC took over all claims issued in the Patents County Court, and the Patents County Court was abolished.

3. Location of the IPEC small claims track

2F–185   The main home of IPEC is in the Rolls Building in Fetter Lane, London. However, much of the work of the IPEC small claims track (including all hearings) takes place in the Thomas More Building which is part of the main Royal Courts of Justice complex on the Strand, London.

Annex A to this guide contains a table setting out which steps in an IPEC small claim need to be done in which building. It also contains postal addresses and useful contact details.

4. Is a Claim Suitable for the IPEC small claims track?

2F–186   Whether a claim is suitable for the IPEC small claims track depends mainly on:

- the *type of intellectual property rights* it relates to; and
- its *value*; and
- the *remedies* sought

4.1 Type of Intellectual Property Rights

2F–187   The IPEC small claims track is only suitable for claims which relate to the following intellectual property rights:

- copyright
- UK and Community registered trade marks
- passing off
- UK and Community unregistered design rights

The IPEC small claims track cannot be used for claims relating to certain other intellectual property rights, including:

- patents
- registered designs (including UK and Community registered designs)
- plant varieties

For full information about what types of claims can and cannot be brought on the IPEC small claims track, see CPR 63.2(1) and PD63 para.16.1.

If a claim is not suitable for the IPEC small claims track because of the type of intellectual property right it relates to, you may wish to consider whether it is suitable for the IPEC multi track or the Patents Court instead. The General IPEC Guide and the Patents Court Guide may assist you in reaching this decision.

162

A claim relating to a type of intellectual property right which is suitable for the IPEC small claims track, must also fit within the value limits of the small claims track.

4.2 Value

The IPEC small claims track is only suitable for claims where the amount in dispute **2F–188** (not including costs) is £10,000 or less. If the claim has a value of more than £10,000, it is unlikely to be suitable for hearing in the small claims track, unless the court orders otherwise.

The IPEC multi track is suitable for claims with a value above £10,000 but not exceeding £500,000. Higher value claims are usually suitable for the Patents Court.

Before bringing a claim in the IPEC small claims track, the claimant should also make certain that each of the remedies it seeks is available.

4.3 Remedies

The IPEC small claims track is suitable for claims where the remedies being sought **2F–189** are damages for infringement, an account of profits, delivery up or destruction of infringing items and/or a final injunction to prevent infringement in the future.

Interim remedies (which are remedies ordered before the final hearing of the claim) such as interim injunctions, asset freezing orders and search and seizure orders are not available on the IPEC small claims track. A claim seeking these remedies, which would otherwise be suitable for the IPEC small claims track, should be made on the IPEC multi track instead.

5. Who Decides Whether a Claim Starts and/or Stays on the IPEC small claims track?

The Claimant must state clearly in the Particulars of Claim if it wishes the claim to **2F–190** be allocated to the IPEC small claims track. It is also helpful to the court if the Claimant writes "Small Claims Track" on the front of the Claim Form. If the Claimant does so, the claim will be allocated to the IPEC small claims track unless a Defendant objects in its Defence or the court considers the IPEC multi–track or Patents Court to be more appropriate.

If the Claimant does not opt for the small claims track but the Defendant does, or the Claimant opts for the small claims track but the Defendant objects, the court will send the parties a directions questionnaire. The parties must send the completed questionnaire to the court within the time stated in the questionnaire and serve a copy on all the other parties within 14 days. The court will then allocate the claim to either the small claims track or multi track as it thinks appropriate.

In deciding on allocation, the court will take into account the value of the claim, the type of intellectual property rights it relates to, the likely complexity and the number of witnesses that may be needed to give oral evidence. Cases concerned with the validity of trade marks (rather than the infringement of a trade mark), for example, are unlikely to be suitable for the IPEC small claims track.

Where cases are transferred from one track to another, the costs rules applicable to the original track will apply up to the date of re–allocation and the costs rules on the new track will apply from the date of re–allocation onwards.

6. Do Parties need Legal Representation in the IPEC Small Claims Track?

The IPEC small claims track is designed to be used by parties who do not have a **2F–191** legal representative acting for them. Accordingly it has more simplified procedures than a standard civil claim, hearings are more informal in nature and evidence is not usually taken on oath. Additionally, if all the parties agree, the court may deal with the claim without a hearing at all, by considering the documents in the case and the written arguments of the parties instead (CPR 27.10). It should be noted, however, that the court will still apply the law and will decide the case on the evidence the parties have made available.

The choice whether to be legally represented or not in the IPEC small claims track is one for each party to make for themselves.

Many parties who are not legally represented choose to bring a friend or family member to hearings. That person may speak for the party or provide moral and practical support if the judge agrees. Corporate parties may be represented by any officer or employee authorised by the company.

If a party chooses to be legally represented in the IPEC small claims track, the costs of doing so are not recoverable from the other party except in exceptional circumstances (see "*Costs Recovery*" below).

There are various sources of free (or "pro bono") legal advice available to parties. A good place to start is a Citizen's Advice Bureau or Law Centre. There is a Citizen's Advice Bureau office on the Ground Floor of the Thomas More Building which operates every day the courts are open on a first–come first–served basis and which offers advice and assistance on the procedural aspects of bringing or defending a claim.

Further information about free legal advice can be obtained from the National Pro Bono Centre which houses national clearing houses for legal pro bono work in England and Wales, for example:

- the Bar Pro Bono Unit
- Law Works (the Solicitors' Pro Bono Group)
- ILEX Pro Bono Forum

The National Pro Bono Centre website is at www.nationalprobonocentre.org.uk.

7. Procedure in the Small Claims Track

7.1 Before issuing proceedings

2F–192   Claimants in the IPEC small claims track should be aware of the Practice Direction (Pre Action Conduct), which can be found on the Ministry of Justice website at www.justice.gov.uk. This encourages disputing parties to communicate with each other with a view to avoiding litigation or, at least, narrowing the areas of dispute between them. Compliance with it is not a requirement, but it does affect the timing for the service of any defence once a claim has been issued (see "*Time Limits for Serving Documents*" below).

Claimants must state in the Particulars of Claim whether or not they have complied with paragraph 7.1 (1) and Annex A (paragraph 2) of the Practice Direction (Pre Action Conduct) (CPR 63.20 (2)).

As unjustified threats to bring legal proceedings in respect of many intellectual property rights can themselves be subject to litigation, each Claimant will need to make their own decision as to whether it is appropriate to contact a prospective defendant to see if matters can be resolved before any proceedings are issued.

If a Claimant chooses not to comply with the Practice Direction (Pre Action Conduct) this may be taken into account against him when the court considers the issue of costs recovery.

7.2 Issuing Claims

2F–193   All claims should be issued at the public counter for IPEC in the Rolls Building. The Claim Form should be marked "*Intellectual Property Enterprise Court*" in the top right hand corner and it would be helpful to the court if it was also marked "*Small Claims Track*".

The proceedings start with the issue of the Claim Form, which the court will "seal" with a court stamp. However, the time for a Defendant to file a Defence does not run until the Claimant serves both a sealed copy of the Claim Form and the Particulars of Claim on that Defendant. The Particulars of Claim may be contained in the Claim Form or served separately. See "*Time limits for Serving Documents*" below.

7.3 Service of Documents

2F–194   CPR 6 sets out the rules that apply to the service of documents, including the service of the Claim Form and the Particulars of Claim. The deadline for a party to take a step in the proceedings is often within a specific number of days after service of a document, e.g. "within 14 days after service of the Particulars of Claim". In order to know when a deadline expires, you therefore need to know the date of service of the document.

Please note that the date of service of a document is not necessarily the date the document is actually received. The time limit will run from a "deemed date of service" which is a date determined in accordance with CPR 6. Parties must therefore check CPR 6 to be certain of the time limits that apply to them.

7.4 Service of the claim

2F–195   It is the Claimant's responsibility to serve each Defendant with the Claim Form together with a response pack and the Particulars of Claim (at the same time or later) in IPEC small claims track cases. The court will not do it. The Claimant should therefore make sure that the Defendant's copy of the Claim Form (sealed by the court) is obtained at the time of issue. Details of how to obtain the response pack will be given to the Claimant by the court on issue of the claim.

The Claimant must file a certificate of service of the Claim Form within 21 days of service of the Particulars of Claim, unless all the Defendants have served Acknowledgments of Service within that time (CPR 6.17). A Claimant may not obtain judgment in default under CPR 12 unless a certificate of service has been filed at court.

7.5 Time Limits for Filing and Serving Documents

The Claimant must serve the Claim Form on a Defendant within 4 months after the **2F–196** date of issue of the Claim Form unless it is to be served outside the jurisdiction when it must be served within 6 months of issue. These are strict time limits.

The Claimant must serve the Particulars of Claim on a Defendant either at the same time as the Claim Form or within 14 days after deemed service of the Claim Form.

If the Defendant does not respond to the Particulars of Claim, default judgment may be entered against him.

There are two ways for the Defendant to respond. If he is ready to do so, he can simply file and serve his Defence, with or without a Counterclaim, within 14 days after deemed service of the Particulars of Claim (unless the Particulars of Claim have been served out of the jurisdiction when a longer period may apply).

If he needs some more time to produce his Defence, or if he wants to contest the court's jurisdiction, he must file and serve an Acknowledgment of Service within 14 days of deemed service of the Particulars of Claim. He must then file and serve his Defence and any Counterclaim in accordance with the following time limits:

- within 42 days of deemed service of the Particulars of Claim, if it contains the Claimant's statement of compliance with the Practice Direction (Pre–Action Conduct) (see "*Before Issuing Proceedings*" above);
- within 70 days of deemed service of the Particulars of Claim if it does not contain the Claimant's statement of compliance with the Practice Direction (Pre–Action Conduct).

For further time limits, e.g. for filing Defences to Counterclaims and Replies, see CPR 63.22.

The parties are not permitted to extend the time limits set out in the CPR without the prior order of the court. Applications for extensions of time must therefore be made before the time expires or as soon as possible afterwards, and must set out clearly why they are required.

7.6 Contents of Particulars of Claim, Defence and Reply to Defence

The Claimant's Particulars of Claim, the Defendant's Defence and Counterclaim (if **2F–197** any) and any Replies of the parties are known as the "statements of case".

The parties must make sure that their statements of case set out their position in full, but they should not be unnecessarily long. They should set out briefly and accurately all the facts and arguments that the party wants to rely upon, so that the court and all the other parties understand what issues the court is being asked to decide.

A party may attach relevant documents to the statement of case, such as documents establishing any copyright or trade marks or screenshots evidencing the internet publication of a work where breach of copyright is claimed.

All statements of case should be signed with a statement of truth in the following words: "[I believe] *or* [The [*party*] believes] that the facts stated in this [*name of document being verified*] are true".

7.7 Default Judgment

If the Defendant fails to respond to the claim within the time limits referred to **2F–198** above, the Claimant may apply to the court to enter default judgment against the Defendant, by filling in and returning the "Request for Judgment" form at the bottom of the Notice of Issue that was given to them when they issued the claim.

If the court is satisfied that the Claim Form and Particulars of Claim have been properly served on the Defendant and the time for service of an Acknowledgment of Service or Defence has expired, it will usually give judgment for the Claimant against the Defendant and give directions for damages to be assessed by the court and for other remedies to be considered by the court. This may be done at a hearing, in which case notice of the hearing date will be sent to the parties, or it may be done without a hearing, in which case the court may ask the parties for written submissions or arguments and a written judgment will subsequently be produced by the judge.

The Court will not enter default judgment unless the Claimant has filed with the Court a certificate of service of the Claim Form and Particulars of Claim.

7.8 Progress of the Case Once a Defence has been Filed

2F–199   Shortly after a Defence has been filed at court, the court will send out an order containing directions for the management and progress of the case leading up to the trial. These directions will usually be issued without a hearing and will be based on the court's consideration of the Claim, Particulars of Claim and Defence. Exceptionally, it may set a preliminary hearing for the parties to attend at which an order for directions will be made.

All orders for directions must be complied with by the parties by the dates specified.

The order for directions will set a timetable for each party to disclose relevant documents to the other parties, and for the evidence of any witnesses to be filed and served. It will include a date for the final hearing of the claim, unless all the parties have agreed that the claim can be decided by the judge without a hearing. In such a case, the order will give a date by which a written judgment will be made available. The court may make other directions as it considers appropriate.

7.9 Experts

2F–200   No expert may give evidence at the final hearing of an IPEC small claims track claim, whether written or oral, without the permission of the court. If experts are necessary, the claim is likely to be re–allocated to the IPEC multi track or, rarely, the Patents Court.

7.10 Hearings

2F–201   All IPEC small claims track hearings take place on the Fourth Floor of the Thomas More Building. They are heard in a courtroom and are open to the public, unless the court orders otherwise in exceptional circumstances. All hearings are tape recorded by the court. A party may obtain a transcript of an oral judgment given in a hearing on payment of a fee.

Any party may give the court and the other parties no less than 7 days notice that he does not intend to attend the final hearing and to request the court decide the claim taking into account his statement of case and other documents. CPR 27.9 sets out the effect of giving the required notice and the potential effects of non–attendance without such notice, which may include striking out that party's case.

At an IPEC small claims track final hearing, the judge may adopt any method of proceeding she considers to be fair. This may include the judge asking questions of witnesses herself or limiting cross–examination of witnesses by others.

7.11 Court Fees

2F–202   Fees are payable to the court by the Claimant when issuing a claim in the IPEC small claims track and when the final hearing is fixed, and by a party who issues an application. There may be exemptions available depending on the payer's financial circumstances. *Guidance on Fees* is available on the website of the Ministry of Justice at www.justice.gov.uk.

7.12 Small Claims Mediation and other Alternative Dispute Resolution

2F–203   Like all civil courts, the IPEC small claims track encourages parties to consider the use of Alternative Dispute Resolution (ADR), as an alternative means of resolving disputes or particular issues within disputes.

Parties to IPEC small claims track cases may use the **Small Claims Mediation Service** which is a FREE service provided by HM Courts & Tribunals Service. It may only be accessed after a claim has been issued. Mediation appointments are conducted by telephone and so the parties are not required to attend at court or at the mediators' offices. Parties can also mediate through the small claims mediator without speaking to one another.

The mediation appointment is:

- limited to one hour
- confidential
- can be done any time up to 10 working days before the final hearing of the IPEC small claims case

If mediation is unsuccessful then the parties will continue to a final hearing of their IPEC small claim as usual.

If you would like to arrange a mediation appointment with the Small Claims Mediation Service, contact HM Courts & Tribunals Service by telephone on 01604 795511 or by email on scmreferrals@hmcts.gsi.gov.uk, providing a return telephone number and your case number.

Further information on mediation can be obtained online at www.gov.uk. Further information about alternative forms of ADR can be found in the General IPEC Guide.

7.13 Settlement/Discontinuance of the Claim

The parties may settle the case by agreement between them at any time before judg- **2F–204** ment is given in the final hearing. A case in the IPEC small claims track can be brought to an end before a final judgment either by the parties' agreement or the discontinuance of the proceedings by the Claimant.

If the parties reach a settlement agreement, it is important that they both notify the court as soon as possible. If the court is notified in writing at least 7 days before the final hearing date that the case has settled, the Claimant (who is responsible for paying the hearing fee) may obtain a full refund of that fee.

Please note that the court will not remove the hearing from the court list (known as "vacating a hearing") on the basis of a letter from one party only. In addition, the court will usually not vacate the hearing unless it is satisfied that the parties have agreed what should happen in relation to the costs of the proceedings.

If the parties would like the terms of their agreement to be recorded in a court order, they will need to request the court to make a "consent order". The benefit of a consent order is that in the event of one party breaching the agreement, the other party can enforce it in the same way as they can enforce any other order of the court.

The court should be notified by both parties of the following:

- that the case has settled;
- that the hearing on [date] is no longer required;
- if damages is to be paid, stating that [party] shall pay [party] the sum of [amount] [inclusive/exclusive of VAT, if applicable] by [payment date] (or by [x] monthly instalments of [amount], first instalment date being [date]) in full and final settlement of the claim;
- stating what has been agreed about the costs of the parties. This may be an order for one party to pay agreed costs of [amount] to the other by [payment date] OR it may be "no order for costs" (ie that each party is responsible for their own costs);
- any other terms that the parties have agreed (e.g. for the return or destruction of infringing goods).

This notification may be made by sending the court a draft consent order or a letter containing the information, in each case signed by **both** parties, or by each party sending the court a signed letter containing the same terms of agreement.

A case may also be brought to an end by the Claimant discontinuing the claim. Please see CPR 38 for the procedure to be followed in that case. CPR 38.6 should be particularly noted because filing a notice of discontinuance has a number of consequences in relation to the costs of the proceedings.

8. Costs Recovery

The general principle that an unsuccessful party will pay the legal costs of a success- **2F–205** ful party does not apply to IPEC small claims track claims.

In the IPEC small claims track there are only very limited circumstances in which the court will order one party to contribute to the costs of another (CPR 27.14). These include:

- fixed sums in relation to issuing the claim;
- court fees (including the hearing fee);
- expenses which a party or witness has reasonably incurred travelling to or

from a hearing or staying away from home for the purpose of attending the hearing;

- loss of earnings or loss of leave evidenced by a party or witness caused by attending a court hearing, limited to £90 per day for each person (PD27 para.7.3);
- in proceedings which include a claim for an injunction, a sum for legal advice and assistance relating to that claim, not exceeding £260 (PD27 para.7.2);
- such further costs as the court may decide at the conclusion of the hearing should be paid by a party who has behaved unreasonably. A party's rejection of an offer of settlement will not of itself constitute unreasonable behaviour but the court may take it into consideration (CPR 27.14 (3)).

9. Paying Damages and Costs

2F–206   All court–ordered or agreed payments for damages and costs should be paid directly to the receiving party and not the court. The paying party should ask the receiving party for details of where electronic payments and/or cheques should be sent.

10. Appeals

2F–207   An appeal from a decision made by a district judge of the IPEC small claims track should be made to an enterprise judge of the IPEC (CPR 63.19(3)).

An appeal can only be made with permission. A party should ask for permission to appeal from the district judge who made the decision, at end of the hearing in which the decision was made. If that district judge refuses permission, or if a party did not ask for permission at the hearing but wants to do so later, he should apply for permission to appeal to an enterprise judge within 21 days of the date of the decision he wishes to appeal.

Annex A—Contact details and addresses for the IPEC small claims track

To issue a claim form, make an application, seek permission to appeal or pay all court fees:

2F–208   The Rolls Building,
7 Rolls Building,
Fetter Lane, London, EC4A 1NL
DX160040 STRAND 4

Claims, general applications and applications for permission to appeal may be issued at the public counter for IPEC, which is on the ground floor of the Rolls Building. The counter is open Monday to Friday (except public holidays) from 10am–4.30pm.

For general correspondence and filing documents:

Fourth Floor Reception for Courts 88, 89 and 90,
Thomas More Building, Royal Courts of Justice,
Strand, London WC2A 2LL
DX 44450 STRAND

The public counter for IPEC small claims track matters is on the first floor of the Thomas More Building. The counter is open Monday to Friday (except public holidays) from 10am–4.30pm.

Documents which are filed in advance of a preliminary or small claims hearing should be handed in at this counter or sent by post to this address.

Clerks to the enterprise judges and the District Judges of the IPEC small claims track:

Enquiries relating to the IPEC in general may be addressed to the Clerk to the enterprise judges, Christy Irvine:

Christy.Irvine@hmcts.gsi.gov.uk

Enquiries relating to an IPEC small claims track claim may be made to the Clerks to the District Judges of the IPEC small claims track:

Tel 020 7947 7387/6187
Fax 0870 761 7695
Email: IPECsmallclaimstrack@hmcts.gsi.gov.uk

Please note that court staff cannot give legal advice or enter into prolonged correspondence.

Table of what to do where in the IPEC small claims track

Where should I...	
...issue a claim form?	Rolls Building
...pay any court fee?	Rolls Building
...issue an application?	Rolls Building
...send correspondence about an allocated IPEC small claim?	Thomas More Building
...file documents for any hearing to be heard by a district judge?	Thomas More Building
...attend any hearing before a district judge?	Thomas More Building
...apply for permission to appeal the decision of a district judge?	Rolls Building

Other Resources

Copies of this Guide, the General IPEC Guide and other materials you may find useful are available on the website of the Ministry of Justice at www.justice.gov.uk.

Annex B—Tips for the Litigant in Person

This section is primarily aimed at those litigants using the IPEC small claims track who have no **2F–209** previous experience of civil proceedings. It is in two parts: an explanation of commonly used terms and what to expect in your dealings with the court.

Commonly used terms

Notice of Discontinuance	A notice by a claimant that they are not intending to pursue their claim.
Consent Order	An order of the court that is agreed by the parties and approved by a judge.
Directions	An order of the court that sets out what the parties are required to do and by when.
File	A party ordered by the court to file a document or witness statement should send or deliver this to the court within the time stated in the order.
Injunction	A court order prohibiting a person from doing something or requiring a person to do something.
Issue	A claim form or application must be issued before being served on the other party/ies. A fee is paid (unless fee exemption applies) and the claim form or application is sealed with a court stamp.
Privilege	The right of a party to refuse to disclose a document or to produce a document or to refuse to answer questions in certain circumstances.
Sealed	Stamped with the court's stamp.
Service	Formally sending a document to someone other than the court (usually the other party). The rules of service in CPR Part 6 apply, including dates of deemed service. If you are required to serve a document, please check whether you need to serve a sealed copy.

Set aside	An order cancelling a judgment or order.
Stay	A stay imposes a halt on a particular order or on the proceedings. This may be for a defined period or indefinite until revived by a court order.
Statement of case	The Claim Form, Particulars of Claim, Defence, any Counterclaim and any Replies. In order to rely on the contents of a statement of case as evidence, it should be signed with a statement of truth.
Statement of truth	A confirmation that the content of a document is true. A statement of case and a witness statement should conclude with a signed and dated statement of truth, e.g.: "The facts stated in this [witness statement] [defence] are true".
Strike out	An order of the court deleting all or part of a statement of case, so that it may no longer be relied on.
Without prejudice	Negotiations and documents expressed to be without prejudice mean that their content may only be revealed to the court in very limited circumstances.
Without prejudice except as to costs	Negotiations and documents expressed to be without prejudice except as to costs mean that their content can be produced to a judge who is deciding whether one party should pay the other's costs.

What to expect in your dealings with the court

The Impartiality of the Court

It is a fundamental principle of justice in this country that the court must remain impartial as between the parties to a case. For this reason, neither the court staff nor the judges are able to give any party legal advice. If you raise a query that the court declines to answer, this is often why. Section 7 of this document sets out some ways that you can obtain free legal advice and assistance.

For the same reason, you should copy all email, documents and correspondence you send to the court to the other parties to your case. This is so that the court does not have any information which one or more of the parties do not also have.

If you send information to the court without copying it to the other side, the court will either ignore it or send it to the other parties, even if you indicate that you would prefer it to be kept confidential. For example, if you send confidential medical information to the court in support of an application to adjourn, you should be aware that it is likely to be sent to all other parties to your case.

Without prejudice correspondence and other privileged material

You should be particularly careful about sending the court material which is "without prejudice" or otherwise privileged. In the absence of legal advice about your particular circumstances, you should be cautious about disclosing such material to the court or (if it is not known to them) the other party/ies.

As a general principle, it is usually **not** appropriate to send the court details of settlement offers that have passed between the parties but which have not resulted in an agreement to settle. It is often preferable to bring letters containing such offers to the hearing (rather than filing them in advance). The district judge dealing with the hearing will then be able to explore with the parties whether it can be relied upon without seeing it inadvertently.

Correspondence with the court

Please help the court to administer proceedings efficiently by:
- taking care to address your correspondence correctly;
- including the correct case number on everything you send to court;
- not sending duplicate copies of documents to the court, for example by fax and email and post. This contributes to delay;

- seeking orders and directions by the court by making an application, copied to the other parties, rather than in correspondence;
- seeking legal advice from legal advisors and sources of free legal advice and support rather than from the court;
- looking for the answers to your questions about procedure and practice in the CPR, this guide and the General IPEC guide rather than asking the court.

Distinguishing between correspondence and applications

The court staff and judges will not usually enter into correspondence with a party. There are, of course, times when you will have a purely administrative query for the court, but correspondence should generally be restricted to these matters. The district judges will not comment on decisions or revise orders as a result of correspondence, except in very limited circumstances (for example, if the correspondence points out a typographical error in an order).

If you wish the court to make or vary an order, you will usually need to issue a formal application (form N244) and to pay the appropriate fee. Common examples where correspondence is insufficient are:

- requests for the adjournment of a forthcoming hearing;
- a request that the other party/ies be required to take a step in the proceedings (e.g. to comply with the court's timetable of directions);
- if you wish to challenge a decision that has been made;

Most applications are "on notice". This means that once you have issued your application with the court, you will have to serve a copy of the application notice and any supporting evidence on the other party/ies. You should file a certificate of service with the court to confirm how and when you served it.

If you are served with an application by another party, you should write to the court within 5 days of the date of service with your response. You should also send this to the other party/ies. If possible, the court will then determine the application without a hearing.

It is also not appropriate to "explain your case" to the court in correspondence. This should be done formally by particulars of claim or defence (as appropriate) and witness statement(s).

Follow the court's orders and timetable

This is one of the best ways to put your case before the court effectively. You should not assume that you will be able to rely on documents that are filed late.

If the court directs you to file a document, you will usually also be required to send a copy to the other party/ies. It is important that you do this without delay.

If you are unable to comply with the court's directions, you should make a formal application to the court for a variation in the timetable. The court is more likely to grant an extension of a deadline if you issue your application before the original deadline expires.

2G COMPANIES ACT PROCEEDINGS

PRACTICE DIRECTION 49A—APPLICATIONS UNDER THE COMPANIES ACT AND RELATED LEGISLATION

Companies Court

After the first paragraph, add as new paragraphs:

2G-39 As a result of the County Court at Central London acquiring both Companies Act jurisdiction (as aforesaid) and limited insolvency jurisdiction (as a result of a change to r.7.11 of the Insolvency Rules 1986 effected by the Insolvency (Amendment) Rules 2015 (SI 2015/443)), after consultation with the registrars, the County Court and users, the following note has been agreed by the Chancellor as to the basis on which work previously done in the High Court may be transferred to the County Court at Central London:

Note on listing and criteria for the transfer of work from the registrars to The County Court sitting in Central London

The Insolvency (Amendment) Rules 2015 (SI 2015/443) have amended, with effect from April 6, 2015, r.7.11 Insolvency Rules 1986 so as to allow the High Court in London to transfer certain cases to the County Court sitting at Central London. Following consultation with users and others, the Chancellor has agreed the following criteria which the registrars will apply when considering whether to retain a case in the High Court or transfer it to Central London.

(1) All winding up petitions must be issued and listed for initial hearing in the Royal Courts of Justice sitting in the Rolls Building.

(2) All bankruptcy petitions must be listed and allocated in accordance with rule 6.9A Insolvency Rules 1986.

(3) Save as provided above, all High Court proceedings which are to be listed before a registrar in accordance with the Practice Direction—Insolvency Proceedings will continue to be issued and listed in the Royal Courts of Justice sitting in the Rolls Building. In each case consideration will be given by a registrar at an appropriate stage to whether the proceedings should remain in the High Court or be transferred to the County Court sitting in Central London.

(4) When deciding whether proceedings which have been issued in the High Court should be transferred to the County Court sitting in Central London, the registrar should have regard to the following factors:

   (a) the complexity of the proceedings;

   (b) whether the proceedings raise new or controversial points of law;

   (c) the likely date and length of the hearing;

   (d) public interest in the proceedings;

   (e) (where it is ascertainable) the amount in issue in the proceedings.

(5) As a general rule, and subject to 4 (a)–(d) above, where the amount in issue in the proceedings is £100,000 or less, the proceedings should be transferred to the County Court sitting in Central London.

(6) Subject to paragraph 4 (a)–(e), the following will be transferred to be heard in the County Court sitting in Central London:

   (a) private examinations ordered to take place under ss.236 or 366 Insolvency Act 1986 (but not necessarily the application for the private examination);

   (b) applications to extend the term of office of an administrator (para.76 Sch.B1 Insolvency Act 1986);

   (c) applications for permission to distribute the prescribed part (para.65(3) Sch.B1 Insolvency Act 1986);

   (d) applications to disqualify a director and applications for a bankruptcy restrictions order where it appears likely that an order will be made for a period not exceeding five years.

(7) With effect from 6 April 2015 the following proceedings will be issued and heard in the County Court sitting in Central London:

   (a) applications for the restoration of a company to the register (s.1029ff. Companies Act 2006);

   (b) applications to extend the period allowed for the delivery of particulars relating to a charge (s.859F Companies Act 2006);

   (c) applications to rectify the register by reason of omission or mis–statement in any statement or notice delivered to the registrar of companies (s.859M Companies Act 2006) or to replace an instrument or debenture delivered to the registrar of companies (s.859N Companies Act 2006).

Issuing proceedings

After "or district judge in a District Registry" add:

2G–41   or the County Court

Applications to extend time for registering a charge or to rectify an omission or mis–statement

Add new paragraph at beginning:

2G–45   Note that with effect from 6 April 2015 the High Court in London no longer deals with these applications which should be issued and heard in the County Court in

Central London (see the Note on listing and criteria for the transfer of work from the registrars to the County Court sitting in Central London (para.2G–39)).

Unfair Prejudice Applications (2006 Act Pt 30)

Add new paragraphs at end:

Following consultation with the Chancery Modernisation Review Implementation **2G–46.1** Committee and users, with effect from 1 May 2015 until further notice, in respect of any unfair prejudice petition issued in the High Court (Rolls Building) for initial hearing before a registrar, the court will give automatic directions in the form attached.

The rationale for doing so is as follows:

(a) in a significant number of cases the directions given on the first return date of the petition are in standard form and are often agreed; automatic directions may therefore save costs as well as court time;

(b) there can be no meaningful costs management until the issues between the parties have been defined, which requires, at least, an exchange of pleadings;

(c) the court cannot engage in meaningful costs management without having some regard to what the parties believe the value in issue in the proceedings might be; for that reason the directions require the parties to provide a non–binding estimate of the value of the shares in issue.

The effectiveness of automatic directions will be reviewed from time to time, and any decision to continue to give automatic directions or revert to the previous practice of giving an initial return date before the court will be taken in the light of experience and any representations made by parties to unfair prejudice petitions or their advisers. Any comments or suggestions (whether positive or negative) should be sent to the chief registrar at *rcjcompanies.orders@hmcts.gsi.gov.uk*.

IN THE HIGH COURT OF JUSTICE
CHANCERY DIVISION
COMPANIES COURT

IN THE MATTER OF [NAME OF COMPANY]
AND IN THE MATTER OF THE COMPANIES ACT 2006

BETWEEN

[   ]

                                          Petitioner(s)

                    -and-

[   ]

                                          Respondents

UPON THE PETITION of the above named Petitioner(s) presented to the court on [insert date of presentation]

OF ITS OWN MOTION THE COURT ORDERS:

1.   The Petitioner(s) serve the petition by 4.00 pm [insert date 14 days after date of issue];

2.   the petition stand as points of claim;

3.   the Respondent(s) (save for the company) file and serve points of defence by 4.00 pm [insert date 28 days after date in 1. above];

4.   the Petitioner(s) file and serve points of reply (if so advised) by 4.00 pm [insert date 14 days after date in 3. above];

5.   the petition be adjourned to [insert date 28 days after date in 4. above – 1 hour appointment] for case management and (where appropriate) costs management[1];

6.   where there is to be costs management:

    (a) the parties file and exchange costs budgets by 4.00 pm [21 days before hearing fixed by para 5 above];

---

[1] The parties should presume that the court will engage in costs budgeting unless one of the exceptions provided for by the CPR applies. They should notify the court as soon as possible if the 1 hour time estimate is too long or too short.

(b) the parties consider each other's costs budget(s) and by 4.00 pm [insert date 14 days before date in 5 above] identify to each other which phases in the other party's/parties' budget(s) are agreed and which are not agreed, in the latter case giving brief reasons and suggested alternative figures;

(c) by 4.00 pm [7 days before hearing fixed by para 5 above] the Petitioner's solicitors file and serve:

    (i)   confirmation that all phases in the budgets are agreed; or
    (ii)   a one page summary in tabular form setting out the figures for the phases in the budgets indicating which phases have been agreed and which have not been agreed together with a summary of the reasons for disagreement and suggested alternative figures;

(d) the parties file and serve in the form below a non-binding indication of what they believe to be the approximate value of the shares in issue in the petition by 4.00 pm [insert date 7 days before the date in 5];

7.   the parties be permitted to vary the above orders by consent so as to extend any period provided for by no more than 28 days (the court to be notified so that the hearing fixed by paragraph 5 can be vacated and re-fixed) or to apply to the court to vary the foregoing;

8.   costs be in the petition.

Estimate of value

For the purpose of the hearing mentioned in paragraph 6 of the order dated [   ]
I/ we put the following non-binding estimate on the value of the shares in issue in this petition on [insert date(s)   ]: £

Petitioner/petitioner's solicitors/Respondent/respondent's solicitors

PRACTICE DIRECTION 49B—ORDER UNDER SECTION 127 INSOLVENCY ACT 1986

Companies Court—Practice Note

Editorial note

Add new paragraph at end:
Note that with effect from 6 April 2015 the High Court in London no longer deals **2G–55** with these applications which should be issued and heard in the County Court in Central London (see the Note on listing and criteria for the transfer of work from the registrars to the County Court sitting in Central London (para.2G–39)).

SECTION 3

OTHER PROCEEDINGS

3A HOUSING

Administration of Justice Act 1970

Mortgage Pre–Action Protocol

For "A pre–action protocol for possession claims based on residential mortgage arrears came into force on November 19, 2008." substitute:

3A–41.1 A new Pre–Action Protocol for Possession Claims Based on Mortgage or Home Purchase Plan Arrears in Respect of Residential Property came into effect on 6 April 2015.

Housing Act 1985

Note

For "That amendment is not yet in force." substitute:

3A–350 The amendment was brought into force on March 23, 2015 by the Anti–social Behaviour, Crime and Policing Act 2014 (Commencement No.8, Saving and Transitional Provisions) Order 2015 (SI 2015/373).

Note

Add at end:

3A–362.2 It was brought into force in Wales on October 21, 2014 by the Anti–social behaviour, Crime and Policing Act 2014 (Commencement No.2 and Transitional Provisions) (Wales) Order 2014 (SI 2014/2830) (W.286).

Note

Add at end:

3A–379.2 It was brought into force in Wales on October 21, 2014 by the Anti–social behaviour, Crime and Policing Act 2014 (Commencement No.2 and Transitional Provisions) (Wales) Order 2014 (SI 2014/2830) (W.286).

Note

Add at end:

3A–389.2 It was brought into force in Wales on October 21, 2014 by the Anti–social behaviour, Crime and Policing Act 2014 (Commencement No.2 and Transitional Provisions) (Wales) Order 2014 (SI 2014/2830) (W.286).

Regulations

Add at end:

3A–389.5 For the procedure for review in Wales see the Secure Tenancies (Absolute Ground for Possession for Anti–social Behaviour) (Review Procedure) (Wales) Regulations 2014 (SI 2014/3278) (W.335).

SECTION 79   SCHEDULE 1

TENANCIES WHICH ARE NOT SECURE TENANCIES

Accommodation for homeless persons

In paragraph 4, after "(homelessness)" add:

3A–487 or Part 2 of the Housing (Wales) Act 2014 (homelessness)

Note

At the end of the first paragraph, before the full stop, add:

3A–497 and Housing (Wales) Act 2014 Sch.3 para.1, with effect from 27 April 2015 (SI 2015/1271)

Housing Act 1988

Part I

Rented Accommodation

Chapter I

Assured Tenancies

"prescribed"

For "the Assured Tenancies and Agricultural Occupancies (Forms) Regulations 1997 (SI 1997/194). Note that a notice conforms with the regulations if it is "substantially to the same effect" as that prescribed (para.2)." substitute:
   the Assured Tenancies and Agricultural Occupancies (Forms) (England) Regula- **3A–763**
tions 2015 (SI 2015/620).

Fixing of terms of statutory periodic tenancy

In the first paragraph, for "Assured Tenancies and Agricultural Occupancies (Forms) Regulations 1997 (SI 1997/194)" substitute:
   Assured Tenancies and Agricultural Occupancies (Forms) (England) Regulations **3A–764**
2015 (SI 2015/620))

Note

For "That amendment is not yet in force." substitute:
   The amendment was brought into force on March 23, 2015 by the Anti–social Be- **3A–765.1**
haviour, Crime and Policing Act 2014 (Commencement No.8, Saving and Transitional
Provisions) Order 2015 (SI 2015/373).

Orders for possession

In the second paragraph, for "Protocol for Possession Claims Based on Rent Arrears" substitute:
   Pre–Action Protocol for Possession Claims by Social Landlords **3A–776**

"prescribed"

For "Assured Tenancies and Agricultural Occupancies (Forms) Regulations 1997 (SI 1997/194)" substitute:
   Assured Tenancies and Agricultural Occupancies (Forms) (England) Regulations **3A–790**
2015 (SI 2015/620)

Notice of proceedings for possession

In the first paragraph, delete from "The relevant form is contained" to "as well as the ground itself." and substitute:
   The relevant form is contained in the Assured Tenancies and Agricultural Oc- **3A–791**
cupancies (Forms) (England) Regulations 2015 (SI 2015/620). The relevant form
(Form 3) states that the landlord must, inter alia, "give the full text . . . of each ground
which is being relied upon". It is similar to the form of notice used in connection with
public sector secure tenancies (Housing Act 1985 s.83). An earlier form provided that
"Particulars of the grounds relied upon have to be included as well as the ground
itself. The current form requires a full explanation of why each ground is being relied
upon".

Note

In the last line, for "prescribe the new forms to be used in Wales" substitute:
   prescribe the forms to be used in Wales **3A–827**

"prescribed"

In the first paragraph, for "Assured Tenancies and Agricultural Occupancies (Forms) Regulations 1997 (SI 1997/194). Note that a notice conforms with the regulations if it is "substantially to the same effect" as that prescribed (para.2)." substitute:
   Assured Tenancies and Agricultural Occupancies (Forms) (England) Regulations **3A–833**
2015 (SI 2015/620)

CHAPTER II

ASSURED SHORTHOLD TENANCIES

Recovery of possession on expiry or termination of assured shorthold tenancy

Add new s.21(4ZA):

3A–889   (4ZA) In the case of a dwelling–house in England, subsection (4)(a) above has effect with the omission of the requirement for the date specified in the notice to be the last day of a period of the tenancy.

Add new s.21(4B), (4C), (4D), (4E):

(4B) A notice under subsection (1) or (4) may not be given in relation to an assured shorthold tenancy of a dwelling–house in England—

   (a) in the case of a tenancy which is not a replacement tenancy, within the period of four months beginning with the day on which the tenancy began, and

   (b) in the case of a replacement tenancy, within the period of four months beginning with the day on which the original tenancy began.

(4C) Subsection (4B) does not apply where the tenancy has arisen due to section 5(2).

(4D) Subject to subsection (4E), proceedings for an order for possession under this section in relation to a dwelling–house in England may not be begun after the end of the period of six months beginning with the date on which the notice was given under subsection (1) or s.21(4).

(4E) Where—

   (a) a notice under subsection (4) has been given in relation to a dwelling–house in England, and

   (b) paragraph (b) of that subsection requires the date specified in the notice to be more than two months after the date the notice was given,

   proceedings for an order for possession under this section may not be begun after the end of the period of four months beginning with the date specified in the notice.

In subsection (6), for "subsection (5(b)" substitute:

   subsections (4B)(b) and (5)(b)

Add new s.21(8) and (9):

(8) The Secretary of State may by regulations made by statutory instrument pre-scribe the form of a notice under subsection (1) or (4) given in relation to an assured shorthold tenancy of a dwelling–house in England.

(9) A statutory instrument containing regulations made under subsection (8) is subject to annulment in pursuance of a resolution of either House of Parliament.

Note

Add at end:

3A–890   Subsections (4ZA), (4B)–(4E) were inserted and subs.(6) was amended by the Deregulation Act 2015 ss.35, 36(2), with effect from 1 October 2015 (SI 2015/994). Subsections (8) and (9) were inserted by the Deregulation Act 2015 s.37, with effect from 1 July 2015 (SI 2015/994). The amendments made by ss.35 to 37 will only apply to assured shorthold tenancies of dwelling houses in England granted after the provi-sion was brought into force. See Deregulation Act s.41.

Recovery of possession on expiry or termination of assured shorthold tenancy

Delete the second paragraph and substitute:

3A–896   There are currently no requirements as to the form of the notice, although (i) it should be in writing (s.21(1)(b) and s.21(4)(a), as amended by the Housing Act 1996 s.98) and (ii) subsection (8) which is not yet in force, gives the Secretary of State power to make regulations prescribing the form of notice.

At the end of the eighth paragraph, add:
Note the provisions of Deregulation Act 2015 ss.33 and 34 (see para.3A–1846) which protect assured shorthold tenants from retaliatory eviction by landlords, in some circumstances where the condition of property is poor or unsafe. Those provisions will only apply to assured shorthold tenancies of dwelling houses in England granted after the provision was brought into force. See Deregulation Act 2015 s.41.

Add new paragraphs at end:
Note: some of the contents of the preceding paragraphs will no longer apply when amendments made by Deregulation Act 2015 are brought into force. Those amendments:

- **introduce the power to prescribe the form of s.21 notices;**
- **remove the requirement for s.21(4) notices to end on the last day of a period of the tenancy; and**
- **introduce time restrictions in relation to the giving of s.21 notices and the bringing of possession proceedings, following the service of a section 21 notice.**

Those amendments will only apply to assured shorthold tenancies of dwelling houses in England granted after the provision was brought into force. See Deregulation Act 2015 s.41.

Add new s.21A:

Compliance with prescribed legal requirements

21A.—(1) A notice under subsection (1) or (4) of section 21 may not be given in relation to an assured shorthold tenancy of a dwelling–house in England at a time when the landlord is in breach of a prescribed requirement. **3A–897.1**

(2) The requirements that may be prescribed are requirements imposed on landlords by any enactment and which relate to—
    (a) the condition of dwelling–houses or their common parts,
    (b) the health and safety of occupiers of dwelling–houses, or
    (c) the energy performance of dwelling–houses.

(3) In subsection (2) "enactment" includes an enactment contained in subordinate legislation within the meaning of the Interpretation Act 1978.

(4) For the purposes of subsection (2)(a) "common parts" has the same meaning as in Ground 13 in Part 2 of Schedule 2.

(5) A statutory instrument containing regulations made under this section is subject to annulment in pursuance of a resolution of either House of Parliament.

Add new paragraph 3A–897.2:

Note

This section was inserted by the Deregulation Act 2015 s.38, so far as is necessary for enabling the exercise on or after that day of any power to make provision by regulations made by statutory instrument with effect from 1 July 2015; otherwise with effect from 1 October 2015 (SI 2015/994). It only applies to assured shorthold tenancies of dwelling houses in England granted after the provision was brought into force. See the Deregulation Act 2015 s.41. **3A–897.2**

Add new paragraph 3A–897.3:

"statutory instrument containing Regulations"
At present there are no regulations. **3A–897.3**

Add new s.21B:

Requirement for landlord to provide prescribed information

21B.—(1) The Secretary of State may by regulations require infor- **3A–897.4**

mation about the rights and responsibilities of a landlord and a tenant under an assured shorthold tenancy of a dwelling–house in England (or any related matters) to be given by a landlord under such a tenancy, or a person acting on behalf of such a landlord, to the tenant under such a tenancy.

(2) Regulations under subsection (1) may—

    (a) require the information to be given in the form of a document produced by the Secretary of State or another person,

    (b) provide that the document to be given is the version that has effect at the time the requirement applies, and

    (c) specify cases where the requirement does not apply.

(3) A notice under subsection (1) or (4) of section 21 may not be given in relation to an assured shorthold tenancy of a dwelling–house in England at a time when the landlord is in breach of a requirement imposed by regulations under subsection (1).

(4) A statutory instrument containing regulations made under subsection (1) is subject to annulment in pursuance of a resolution of either House of Parliament.

Add new paragraph 3A–897.5:

Note

3A–897.5   This section was inserted by the Deregulation Act 2015 s.39, so far as is necessary for enabling the exercise on or after that day of any power to make provision by regulations made by statutory instrument with effect from 1 July 2015; otherwise with effect from 1 October 2015 (SI 2015/994). It only applies to assured shorthold tenancies of dwelling houses in England granted after the provision was brought into force. See the Deregulation Act 2015 s.41.

Add new paragraph 3A–897.6:

"statutory instrument containing Regulations"

3A–897.6   At present there are no regulations.

Add new s.21C:

Repayment of rent where tenancy ends before end of a period

3A–897.7   **21C.**—(1) A tenant under an assured shorthold tenancy of a dwelling–house in England is entitled to a repayment of rent from the landlord where—

    (a) as a result of the service of a notice under section 21 the tenancy is brought to an end before the end of a period of the tenancy,

    (b) the tenant has paid rent in advance for that period, and

    (c) the tenant was not in occupation of the dwelling–house for one or more whole days of that period.

(2) The amount of repayment to which a tenant is entitled under subsection (1) is to be calculated in accordance with the following formula—

$$R \times \frac{D}{P}$$

where—

- R is the rent paid for the final period;
- D is the number of whole days of the final period for which the tenant was not in occupation of the dwelling–house; and

- P is the number of whole days in that period.

(3) If the repayment of rent described in subsections (1) and (2) has not been made when the court makes an order for possession under section 21, the court must order the landlord to repay the amount of rent to which the tenant is entitled.

(4) Nothing in this section affects any other right of the tenant to a repayment of rent from the landlord.

Add new paragraph 3A–897.8:

Note

This section was inserted by the Deregulation Act 2015 s.40, with effect from 1 October 2015 (SI 2015/994). It only applies to assured shorthold tenancies of dwelling houses in England granted after the provision was brought into force. See the Deregulation Act 2015 s.41.   **3A–897.8**

CHAPTER IV

PROTECTION FROM EVICTION

"landlord"

Add at end:

The words of s.27 are wide enough to cover local authority landlords (*Lambeth LBC v Loveridge* [2014] UKSC 65; 3 December 2014).   **3A–909**

The measure of damages

After the first paragraph, add as a new paragraph:

Section 28(1) requires the court to make two valuations of the landlord's interest. Valuation (a) is based on the assumption that the tenant continues to have the same right to occupy the premises, and the landlord continues to be subject to the same restrictions on recovering possession, as before the eviction occurred. Valuation (b) is based on the assumption that the tenant's right to occupy and the restrictions on recovering possession have ceased (*Lambeth LBC v Loveridge* [2014] UKSC 65; 3 December 2014).   **3A–918**

CHAPTER VI

GENERAL PROVISIONS

Delete paragraph 3A–941 and substitute:

"prescribed"

See the Assured Tenancies and Agricultural Occupancies (Forms) (England) Regulations 2015 (SI 2015/620).   **3A–941**

SECTION 7   SCHEDULE 2

GROUNDS FOR POSSESSION OF DWELLING-HOUSES LET ON ASSURED TENANCIES

Note

Add at end:

It was brought into force in Wales on October 21, 2014 by the Anti–social behaviour, Crime and Policing Act 2014 (Commencement No.2 and Transitional Provisions) (Wales) Order 2014 (SI 2014/2830) (W.286).   **3A–991.1**

Housing Act 1996

Delete paragraphs 3A–1195 to 3A–1246.

Housing Act 1996—Pt VII

In the second paragraph, delete "There is a separate Welsh Code of Guidance issued by the Welsh Assembly Government."   **3A–1247**

Add new paragraph 3A–1247.1:

Note

The homelessness provisions of the Housing Act 1996 no longer apply in Wales.   **3A–1247.1**

They have been replaced by the Housing (Wales) Act 2014 (Part 2) which among other things placed a stronger duty on local authorities in Wales to prevent homelessness and allows them to use suitable accommodation in the private sector. Most of the provisions of Part 2 of that Act were brought into force on 27 April 2015. See the Housing (Wales) Act 2014 (Commencement No.3 and Transitory, Transitional and Saving Provisions) Order 2015 (SI 2015/1272) which implemented all of Part 2 of the Housing (Wales) Act 2014 with the exception of section 75(3) (intentionally homeless households with children) and the partial exception of section 78 (deciding to have regard to intentionality). The Order also makes transitory, transitional and saving provisions as a result of the commencement of Part 2.

See too

- The Housing (Wales) Act 2014 (Consequential Amendments) Regulations 2015 (SI 2015/752)
- The Homelessness (Intentionality) (Specified Categories) (Wales) Regulations 2015 (SI 2015/1265) (W.85)
- The Homelessness (Review Procedure) (Wales) Regulations 2015 (SI 2015/1266) (W.86)
- The Homelessness (Suitability of Accommodation) (Wales) Order 2015 (SI 2015/1268) (W.87)

Due to space constraints, it is not possible to include the Housing (Wales) Act 2014 in this work.

Domestic violence

At the end of the second paragraph, add:

3A–1255   See too *Hussain v Waltham Forest LBC* [2015] EWCA Civ 14, 20 January 2015.

Other violence

3A–1256   *Delete "In Wales, this amendment was brought into force on September 30, 2002 by the Homelessness Act 2002 (Commencement) (Wales) Order 2002 (SI 2002/1736) (w.166) (c.53)."*

Note

3A–1261   *Delete "In Wales, this amendment was brought into force on September 30, 2002 by the Homelessness Act 2002 (Commencement) (Wales) Order 2002 (SI 2002/1736) (w.166) (c.53)."*

GENERAL FUNCTIONS IN RELATION TO HOMELESSNESS OR THREATENED

HOMELESSNESS

Duty of local housing authority to provide advisory services

In s.179(1), after "Every local housing authority" add:

3A–1266   in England

Add new paragraph 3A–1266.1:

Note

3A–1266.1   Subsection (1) amended by the Housing (Wales) Act 2014 Sch.3 para.5, with effect from 27 April 2015 (SI 2015/1272).

Assistance for voluntary organisations

In s.180(1), after "local housing authority" add:

3A–1268   in England

Add new paragraph 3A–1268.1:

Note

3A–1268.1   Subsection (1) amended by the Housing (Wales) Act 2014 Sch.3 para.6, with effect from 27 April 2015 (SI 2015/1272).

Guidance by the Secretary of State

In s.182(1), after "social services authority" add:

in England   **3A–1271**

Add new paragraph 3A–1271.1:

Note

Subsection (1) amended by the Housing (Wales) Act 2014 Sch.3 para.7, with effect **3A–1271.1**
from 27 April 2015 (SI 2015/1272).

APPLICATION FOR ASSISTANCE IN CASE OF HOMELESSNESS OR THREATENED

HOMELESSNESS

Application for assistance

In s.183(1), after "local housing authority" add:

in England   **3A–1275**

Note

Add at end:
and Housing (Wales) Act 2014 Sch.3 para.8, with effect from 27 April 2015 (SI 2015/ **3A–1276**
1272).

Persons from abroad not eligible for housing assistance

In the second paragraph, delete "(For Wales, see the Homelessness (Wales) Regulations 2006 (SI **3A–1296**
2006/2624) (w.227).)"

Provision of information by Secretary of State

In s.187(1), after "local housing authority" add:

in England   **3A–1300**

Note

Add at end:
and Housing (Wales) Act 2014 Sch.3 para.9, with effect from 27 April 2015 (SI 2015/ **3A–1301**
1272).

Delete paragraph 3A–1321.

Duties to persons becoming homeless intentionally

At the end of the fifth paragraph, add:
However, in *Haile v Waltham Forest LBC* [2015] UKSC 34; 20 May 2015, after noting **3A–1337**
that s.193(1) is meant to prevent "queue jumping" by persons who, by intentionally
rendering themselves homeless, would obtain a priority in the provision of housing to
which they would not otherwise be entitled, the Supreme Court stated that it is in relation to the current state of being homeless that one asks, did the applicant become
homeless intentionally? Section 193(1) is therefore concerned with whether homelessness was caused by intentional conduct. This depends, first, on whether a homeless
person deliberately did or failed to do anything in consequence of which he ceased to
occupy accommodation meeting the requirements of s.191(1). If yes, the further question arises under s.193(1) whether the current homelessness was caused by that
intentional conduct. Section 193(1) is read as meaning the local authority "are not
satisfied that [the applicant is homeless because] he became homeless intentionally".

Eviction following arrears

At the end of the first paragraph, add:
and *Enfield LBC v Najim* [2015] EWCA Civ 319, 4 March 2015 (reviewing officer **3A–1339**

entitled to find that non–renewal of the tenancy was the reasonable result of the failure to pay rent when due).

Duty to persons with priority need who are not homeless intentionally

In s.193(10), for "appropriate authority" substitute:

3A–1361   Secretary of State

Delete s.193(12).

Note

Add at end:

3A–1362   Subsection (1) was amended and subs.(12) was repealed by the Housing (Wales) Act 2014 Sch.3 para.10, with effect from 27 April 2015 (SI 2015/1272).

"secure that accommodation is available for occupation"

In the first paragraph, after "who normally resides with him as a member of his family"." add:

3A–1375   The question of whether the accommodation offered is 'suitable' for the applicant and each member of her household clearly requires the local authority to have regard to the need to safeguard and promote the welfare of any children in her household (Children Act 2004 s.11). Its suitability to meet their needs is a key component in its suitability generally. In my view, it is not enough for the decision–maker simply to ask whether any of the children are approaching GCSE or other externally assessed examinations. Disruption to their education and other support networks may be actively harmful to their social and educational development, but the authority also have to have regard to the need to promote, as well as to safeguard, their welfare. The decision maker should identify the principal needs of the children, both individually and collectively, and have regard to the need to safeguard and promote them when making the decision (*Nzolameso v City of Westminster* [2015] UKSC 22, 2 April 2015).

At the end of the fourth paragraph, add:

As to the provision of out of area accommodation, see *Nzolameso v City of Westminster* [2015] UKSC 22, 2 April 2015. Local authorities have a statutory duty to accommodate within their area so far as this is reasonably practicable. 'Reasonable practicability' imports a stronger duty than simply being reasonable. But if it is not reasonably practicable to accommodate 'in borough', they must generally, and where possible, try to place the household as close as possible to where they were previously living. There will be some cases where this does not apply, for example where there are clear benefits in placing the applicant outside the district, because of domestic violence or to break links with negative influences within the district, and others where the applicant does not mind where she goes or actively wants to move out of the area. The combined effect of the Homelessness (Suitability of Accommodation) (England) Order 2012 (SI 2012/2601) and the Supplementary Guidance was meant to change the legal landscape as it was when previous cases dealing with an 'out of borough' placement policy, such as *R. (Yumsak) v Enfield London Borough Council* [2002] EWHC 280 (Admin); [2003] H.L.R. 1, and *R. (Calgin) v Enfield London Borough Council* [2005] EWHC 1716 (Admin); [2006] H.L.R. 58, were decided.

Delete the seventh paragraph starting "In R. (Ymsak) v Enfield LBC".

Section 194—Power exercisable after minimum period of duty under s.193

Note

3A–1379   *Delete "In Wales, this amendment was brought into force on September 30, 2002 by the Homelessness Act 2002 (Commencement) (Wales) Order 2002 (SI 2002/1736) (w.166) (c.53)."*

Duty where other suitable accommodation available

Delete "In Wales, this amendment was brought into force on September 30, 2002 by the Home- **3A–1392**
lessness Act 2002 (Commencement) (Wales) Order 2002 (SI 2002/1736) (w.166) (c.56))."

REFERRAL TO ANOTHER LOCAL HOUSING AUTHORITY

Referral of case to another local housing authority

Add new s.198(4A):

(4A) Subsection (4) is to be construed, in a case where the other **3A–1396**
authority is an authority in Wales, as if the reference to "this Part"
were a reference to Part 2 of the Housing (Wales) Act 2014.

In s.198(5), after "conditions for referral of a case" add:

which does not involve a referral to a local housing authority in
Wales

Add new s.198(5A):

(5A) The question whether the conditions for referral of a case
involving a referral to a local housing authority in Wales shall be
decided by agreement between the notifying authority and the notified authority or, in default of agreement, in accordance with such
arrangements as the Secretary of State and the Welsh Ministers may
jointly direct by order.

In s.198(6)(b), after "Secretary of State" add:

      or, in the case of an order under subsection (5A), to the
      Secretary of State and the Welsh Ministers

In s.198(7), for "No such order shall" substitute:

An order under this section shall not

In s.198(7), add at end:

and, in the case of a joint order, a resolution of the National Assembly for Wales.

Note

Add at end:

Subsections (4A) and (5A) were inserted and subs.(5), (6) and (7) were amended by **3A–1397**
the Housing (Wales) Act 2014 Sch.3 para.11, with effect from 27 April 2015 (SI 2015/
1272).

Note

Delete "and in Wales on March 30, 2009 by the Housing and Regeneration Act 2008 (Com- **3A–1406**
mencement No.1) (Wales) Order 2009 (SI 2009/773) (w.65) (c.48)"

Duties to applicant whose case is considered for referral or referred

Delete s.200(4) and substitute:

(4) If it is decided that those conditions are met and the notified **3A–1410**
authority is not an authority in Wales, the notified authority are
subject to the duty under section 193 (the main housing duty); for
provision about cases where it is decided that those conditions are
met and the notified authority is an authority in Wales, see section 83
of the Housing (Wales) Act 2014 (cases referred from a local housing
authority in England).

Note

Add at end:

3A–1411   Subsection (4) was amended by the Housing (Wales) Act 2014 Sch.3 para.12, with effect from 27 April 2015 (SI 2015/1272).

Add new s.201A:

Cases referred from a local housing authority in Wales

3A–1416.1   **201A.**—(1) This section applies where an application has been referred by a local housing authority in Wales to a local housing authority in England under section 80 of the Housing (Wales) Act 2014 (referral of case to another local housing authority).

(2) If it is decided that the conditions in that section for referral of the case are met, the notified authority are subject to the duty under section 193 of this Act in respect of the person whose case is referred (the main housing duty); for provision about cases where it is decided that the conditions for referral are not met, see section 82 of the Housing (Wales) Act 2014 (duties to applicant whose case is considered for referral or referred).

(3) References in this Part to an applicant include a reference to a person to whom a duty is owed by virtue of subsection (2).

Add new paragraph 3A–1416.2:

Note

3A–1416.2   Inserted by Housing (Wales) Act 2014 Sch.3 para.13, with effect from 27 April 2015 (SI 2015/1272).

Co–operation between relevant housing authorities and bodies

In s.213(1), after "local housing authority" add:

3A–1475   in England

Note

Add at end:

3A–1475.1   Subsection (1) was amended by the Housing (Wales) Act 2014 Sch.3 para.14, with effect from 27 April 2015 (SI 2015/1272).

Part VIII

Miscellaneous and general provisions

Note

For "That amendment is not yet in force." substitute:

3A–1489   The amendment was brought into force on March 23, 2015 by the Anti–social Behaviour, Crime and Policing Act 2014 (Commencement No.8, Saving and Transitional Provisions) Order 2015 (SI 2015/373).

Relevant authority

3A–1494   *Delete "or Housing for Wales".*

Guidance

3A–1495   *Delete (in both instances) "or, in Wales, by the National Assembly for Wales".*

SCHEDULE 15

Arrest for anti–social behaviour: powers of High Court and county court to remand

Delete paragraphs 3A–1497 and 3A–1497.1.

Crime and Disorder Act 1998

Delete paragraphs 3A–1502 to 3A–1526.

Housing Act 2004

Editorial introduction

Add at end:
The original scheme has been amended by both the Localism Act 2011 and the **3A–1614**
Deregulation Act 2015.

Delete paragraph 3A–1617 and substitute:

"regulations"
See Housing (Tenancy Deposit Schemes) Order 2007 (SI 2007/796) and Housing **3A–1617**
(Tenancy Deposits) (Prescribed Information) Order 2007 (SI 2007/797) as amended by
the Deregulation Act 2015 s.30.

Proceedings relating to tenancy deposits

In s.214(1), after "a shorthold tenancy"add:
on or after 6 April 2007 **3A–1622**

Note

After "from April 6, 2012 (SI 2012/628, art.8(d)" add:
, and by Deregulation Act 2015 s.31(2), with effect from 26 March 2015 **3A–1623**

Sanctions for non–compliance

Delete s.215(1) and substitute:

(1) Subject to subsection (2A), if (whether before, on or after 6 **3A–1628**
April 2007) a tenancy deposit has been paid in connection with a
shorthold tenancy, no section 21 notice may be given in relation to
the tenancy at a time when the deposit is not being held in accordance with an authorised scheme.

(1A) Subject to subsection (2A), if a tenancy deposit has been paid
in connection with a shorthold tenancy on or after 6 April 2007, no
section 21 notice may be given in relation to the tenancy at a time
when section 213(3) has not been complied with in relation to the
deposit.

In s.215(2A), after "Subsections (1)" add
, (1A)

Note

Add at end:
Subsection (1) substituted and subs.(2A) amended by the Deregulation Act 2015 **3A–1629**
s.31(3), with effect from 26 March 2015.

Add new s.215A:

Statutory periodic tenancies: deposit received before 6 April 2007

215A.—(1) This section applies where— **3A–1633.1**
  (a) before 6 April 2007, a tenancy deposit has been received
      by a landlord in connection with a fixed term shorthold
      tenancy,

187

(b) on or after that date, a periodic shorthold tenancy is deemed to arise under section 5 of the Housing Act 1988 on the coming to an end of the fixed term tenancy,

(c) on the coming to an end of the fixed term tenancy, all or part of the deposit paid in connection with the fixed term tenancy is held in connection with the periodic tenancy, and

(d) the requirements of section 213(3), (5) and (6) have not been complied with by the landlord in relation to the deposit held in connection with the periodic tenancy.

(2) If, on the commencement date—

(a) the periodic tenancy is in existence, and

(b) all or part of the deposit paid in connection with the fixed term tenancy continues to be held in connection with the periodic tenancy,

section 213 applies in respect of the deposit that continues to be held in connection with the periodic tenancy, and any additional deposit held in connection with that tenancy, with the modifications set out in subsection (3).

(3) The modifications are that, instead of the things referred to in section 213(3) and (5) being required to be done within the time periods set out in section 213(3) and (6)(b), those things are required to be done—

(a) before the end of the period of 90 days beginning with the commencement date, or

(b) (if earlier) before the first day after the commencement date on which a court does any of the following in respect of the periodic tenancy—

(i) determines an application under section 214 or decides an appeal against a determination under that section;

(ii) makes a determination as to whether to make an order for possession in proceedings under section 21 of the Housing Act 1988 or decides an appeal against such a determination.

(4) If, on the commencement date—

(a) the periodic tenancy is no longer in existence, or

(b) no deposit continues to be held in connection with the periodic tenancy, the requirements of section 213(3), (5) and (6) are treated as if they had been complied with by the landlord in relation to any deposit that was held in connection with the periodic tenancy.

(5) In this section "the commencement date" means the date on which the Deregulation Act 2015 is passed.

Add new paragraphs 3A–1633.2 to 3A–1633.6:

Note

3A–1633.2   This section was inserted by Deregulation Act 2015 s.32. It came into force on the date that the Act received the Royal Assent – i.e. 26 March 2015.

"tenancy deposit"

3A–1633.3   See s.212(8).

"shorthold tenancy"

3A–1633.4   See s.212(8) and (9) and Housing Act 1988 s.19.

the commencement date
   See s.215A(5) – i.e. 26 March 2015.   3A–1633.5

Editorial Note
   The purpose of ss.215A to 215C is to reverse the effect of Court of Appeal decision   3A–1633.6
in *Superstrike v Rodrigues* [2013] EWCA Civ 669 in which it was held that if a fixed term
tenancy expires and the tenant continues to occupy under a statutory periodic tenancy,
any deposit paid in respect of the fixed term must be treated as having been paid by
the tenant and received by the landlord afresh at the start of the statutory periodic
tenancy.

Add new s.215B:

Shorthold tenancies: deposit received on or after 6 April 2007

215B.—(1) This section applies where—   3A–1633.7
   (a) on or after 6 April 2007, a tenancy deposit has been
      received by a landlord in connection with a shorthold
      tenancy ("the original tenancy"),
   (b) the initial requirements of an authorised scheme have been
      complied with by the landlord in relation to the deposit
      (ignoring any requirement to take particular steps within
      any specified period),
   (c) the requirements of section 213(5) and (6)(a) have been
      complied with by the landlord in relation to the deposit
      when it is held in connection with the original tenancy
      (ignoring any deemed compliance under section 215A(4)),
   (d) a new shorthold tenancy comes into being on the coming
      to an end of the original tenancy or a tenancy that re-
      places the original tenancy (directly or indirectly),
   (e) the new tenancy replaces the original tenancy (directly or
      indirectly), and
   (f) when the new tenancy comes into being, the deposit
      continues to be held in connection with the new tenancy,
      in accordance with the same authorised scheme as when
      the requirements of section 213(5) and (6)(a) were last
      complied with by the landlord in relation to the deposit.
   (2) In their application to the new tenancy, the requirements of
section 213(3), (5) and (6) are treated as if they had been complied
with by the landlord in relation to the deposit.
   (3) The condition in subsection (1)(a) may be met in respect of a
tenancy even if the tenancy deposit was first received in connection
with an earlier tenancy (including where it was first received before 6
April 2007).
   (4) For the purposes of this section, a tenancy replaces an earlier
tenancy if—
   (a) the landlord and tenant immediately before the coming to
      an end of the earlier tenancy are the same as the landlord
      and tenant at the start of the new tenancy, and
   (b) the premises let under both tenancies are the same or
      substantially the same.

Add new paragraphs 3A–1633.8 to 3A–1633.11:

Note

   This section was inserted by Deregulation Act 2015 s.32. It came into force on the   3A–1633.8
date that the Act received the Royal Assent – i.e. 26 March 2015.

"tenancy deposit"

3A–1633.9   See s.212(8).

"shorthold tenancy"

3A–1633.10   See s.212(8) and 212(9) and Housing Act 1988 s.19.

Editorial Note

3A–1633.11   Section 215B was passed to ensure that every time a tenancy becomes a statutory periodic tenancy or is renewed, the landlord is not obliged to comply with the tenancy deposit protection requirements afresh at the start of the new tenancy if the deposit remains protected in accordance with the same authorised scheme from one tenancy to the next.

Add new s.215C:

Sections 215A and 215B: transitional provisions

3A–1633.12   **215C.**—(1) Sections 215A and 215B are treated as having had effect since 6 April 2007, subject to the following provisions of this section.

(2) Sections 215A and 215B do not have effect in relation to—

    (a) a claim under section 214 of this Act or section 21 of the Housing Act 1988 in respect of a tenancy which is settled before the commencement date (whether or not proceedings in relation to the claim have been instituted), or

    (b) proceedings under either of those sections in respect of a tenancy which have been finally determined before the commencement date.

(3) Subsection (5) applies in respect of a tenancy if—

    (a) proceedings under section 214 in respect of the tenancy have been instituted before the commencement date but have not been settled or finally determined before that date, and

    (b) because of section 215A(4) or 215B(2), the court decides—

        (i) not to make an order under section 214(4) in respect of the tenancy, or

        (ii) to allow an appeal by the landlord against such an order.

(4) Subsection (5) also applies in respect of a tenancy if—

    (a) proceedings for possession under section 21 of the Housing Act 1988 in respect of the tenancy have been instituted before the commencement date but have not been settled or finally determined before that date, and

    (b) because of section 215A(4) or 215B(2), the court decides—

        (i) to make an order for possession under that section in respect of the tenancy, or

        (ii) to allow an appeal by the landlord against a refusal to make such an order.

(5) Where this subsection applies, the court must not order the tenant or any relevant person (as defined by section 213(10)) to pay the landlord's costs, to the extent that the court reasonably considers those costs are attributable to the proceedings under section 214 of this Act or (as the case may be) section 21 of the Housing Act 1988.

(6) Proceedings have been "finally determined" for the purposes of this section if —

    (a) they have been determined by a court, and

(b) there is no further right to appeal against the determination.

(7) There is no further right to appeal against a court determination if there is no right to appeal against the determination, or there is such a right but—

(a) the time limit for making an appeal has expired without an appeal being brought, or

(b) an appeal brought within that time limit has been withdrawn.

(8) In this section "the commencement date" means the date on which the Deregulation Act 2015 is passed.

Add new paragraphs 3A–1633.13 to 3A–1633.14:

Note

This section was inserted by Deregulation Act 2015 s.32. It came into force on the **3A–1633.13** date that the Act received the Royal Assent – i.e. 26 March 2015.

the commencement date

See s.215C(8) – i.e. 26 March 2015.   **3A–1633.14**

Policing and Crime Act 2009

PART 4

INJUNCTIONS: GANG–RELATED VIOLENCE AND DRUG–DEALING ACTIVITY

POWER TO GRANT INJUNCTIONS

Delete s.34 and substitute:

Injunctions to prevent gang–related violence

34.—(1) A court may grant an injunction under this section against **3A–1719** a respondent aged 14 or over if the first and second conditions are met.

(2) The first condition is that the court is satisfied on the balance of probabilities that the respondent has engaged in or has encouraged or assisted—

(a) gang–related violence, or

(b) gang–related drug–dealing activity.

(3) The second condition is that the court thinks it is necessary to grant the injunction for either or both of the following purposes—

(a) to prevent the respondent from engaging in, or encouraging or assisting, gang–related violence or gang–related drug–dealing activity;

(b) to protect the respondent from gang–related violence or gang–related drug–dealing activity.

(4) An injunction under this section may (for either or both of those purposes)—

(a) prohibit the respondent from doing anything described in the injunction;

(b) require the respondent to do anything described in the injunction.

(5) For the purposes of this section, something is "gang–related" if it occurs in the course of, or is otherwise related to, the activities of a group that—

> (a) consists of at least three people, and
>
> (b) has one or more characteristics that enable its members to be identified by others as a group.

(6) In this section *"violence"* includes a threat of violence.

(7) In this Part *"drug–dealing activity"* means the unlawful production, supply, importation or exportation of a controlled drug.

"Production", *"supply"* and *"controlled drug"* here have the meanings given by section 37(1) of the Misuse of Drugs Act 1971.

Note

Delete Note and substitute:

3A–1719.1   This section was substituted, and the words in the Part heading were inserted by, the Serious Crime Act 2015 s.51, Sch.4 para.83, with effect from 1 June 2015 (SI 2015/820).

Contents of injunctions

In s.35(2)(e), after "using the internet to facilitate or encourage violence" add:

3A–1720   or drug–dealing activity

Add new paragraph 3A–1720.1:

Note

3A–1720.1   Subsection (2)(e) was amended by the Serious Crime Act 2015 Sch.4 para.84, with effect from 1 June 2015 (SI 2015/820).

Interpretation

In s.49(1), after the entry for "violence" add:

3A–1735   "drug–dealing activity" has the meaning given by section 34(7).

Add new paragraph 3A–1735.1:

Note

3A–1735.1   Subsection (1) was amended by the Serious Crime Act 2015 Sch.4 para.85, with effect from 1 June 2015 (SI 2015/820).

SCHEDULE 5A—BREACH OF INJUNCTION: POWERS OF COURT IN RESPECT OF UNDER–18S

PART 3

DETENTION ORDERS

Delete paragraphs 3A–1757 to 3A–1758.1.

Anti-social Behaviour, Crime and Policing Act 2014

Note

Delete Note and substitute:
This section was brought into force on March 23, 2015 by the Anti–social Behaviour, **3A–1778**
Crime and Policing Act 2014 (Commencement No.8, Saving and Transitional Provisions) Order 2015 (SI 2015/373).

Editorial introduction

In the second paragraph, after "Welsh Ministers or under arrangements made between the Welsh Ministers and that person or body (see section 5)." add:
In the first instance, an application for such an injunction or interim injunction in **3A–1781**
the county court will be allocated to a District Judge (Practice Direction 2B – Allocation of Cases to Levels of Judiciary para.8.1).

Sentences for breach of injunctions

At the beginning of the first paragraph, add:
An application for an order committing a person to prison or attaching a power of **3A–1782**
arrest to an injunction or remanding a person pursuant to Part 1 of the Anti–social
Behaviour, Crime and Policing Act 2014 may be listed before a district judge (Practice
Direction 2B – Allocation of Cases to Levels of Judiciary para.8.3).

In the sixth paragraph, after "Sevketoglu v Sevketoglu [2003] EWCA Civ 1570" add:
and *R. (James) v HM Prison Birmingham* [2015] EWCA Civ 58, 9 February 2015

Note

Delete Note and substitute:
This section was brought into force on March 23, 2015 by the Anti–social Behaviour, **3A–1784**
Crime and Policing Act 2014 (Commencement No.8, Saving and Transitional Provisions) Order 2015 (SI 2015/373).

Note

Delete Note and substitute:
This section was brought into force on March 23, 2015 by the Anti–social Behaviour, **3A–1789**
Crime and Policing Act 2014 (Commencement No.8, Saving and Transitional Provisions) Order 2015 (SI 2015/373).

Note

Delete Note and substitute:
This section was brought into force on March 23, 2015 by the Anti–social Behaviour, **3A–1791**
Crime and Policing Act 2014 (Commencement No.8, Saving and Transitional Provisions) Order 2015 (SI 2015/373).

Add new paragraph 3A–1791.1:
An application for an order attaching a power of arrest to an injunction pursuant to **3A–1791.1**
Part 1 of the Anti–social Behaviour, Crime and Policing Act 2014 may be listed before
a district judge (Practice Direction 2B – Allocation of Cases to Levels of Judiciary
para.8.3).

Note

Delete Note and substitute:
This section was brought into force on March 23, 2015 by the Anti–social Behaviour, **3A–1793**
Crime and Policing Act 2014 (Commencement No.8, Saving and Transitional Provisions) Order 2015 (SI 2015/373).

Add new paragraph 3A–1795.1:
In the first instance, an application for such an injunction or interim injunction in **3A–1795.1**
the county court will be allocated to a District Judge (Practice Direction 2B – Allocation of Cases to Levels of Judiciary para.8.1).

Note

Delete Note and substitute:

3A–1797   This section was brought into force on March 23, 2015 by the Anti–social Behaviour, Crime and Policing Act 2014 (Commencement No.8, Saving and Transitional Provisions) Order 2015 (SI 2015/373).

Note

Delete Note and substitute:

3A–1799   This section was brought into force on March 23, 2015 by the Anti–social Behaviour, Crime and Policing Act 2014 (Commencement No.8, Saving and Transitional Provisions) Order 2015 (SI 2015/373).

Add new paragraph 3A–1799.1:

3A–1799.1   In the first instance, an application for such an injunction or interim injunction in the county court will be allocated to a District Judge (Practice Direction 2B – Allocation of Cases to Levels of Judiciary para.8.1).

Note

Delete Note and substitute:

3A–1801   This section was brought into force on March 23, 2015 by the Anti–social Behaviour, Crime and Policing Act 2014 (Commencement No.8, Saving and Transitional Provisions) Order 2015 (SI 2015/373).

Note

Delete Note and substitute:

3A–1803   This section was brought into force on March 23, 2015 by the Anti–social Behaviour, Crime and Policing Act 2014 (Commencement No.8, Saving and Transitional Provisions) Order 2015 (SI 2015/373).

Note

Delete Note and substitute:

3A–1805   This section was brought into force on March 23, 2015 by the Anti–social Behaviour, Crime and Policing Act 2014 (Commencement No.8, Saving and Transitional Provisions) Order 2015 (SI 2015/373).

Note

Delete Note and substitute:

3A–1807   This section was brought into force on March 23, 2015 by the Anti–social Behaviour, Crime and Policing Act 2014 (Commencement No.8, Saving and Transitional Provisions) Order 2015 (SI 2015/373).

Remands and Bail

Add at end:

3A–1808   An application for an order remanding a person pursuant to Part 1 of the Anti–social Behaviour, Crime and Policing Act 2014 may be listed before a district judge (Practice Direction 2B – Allocation of Cases to Levels of Judiciary para.8.3).

Note

Delete Note and substitute:

3A–1810   This section was brought into force on March 23, 2015 by the Anti–social Behaviour, Crime and Policing Act 2014 (Commencement No.8, Saving and Transitional Provisions) Order 2015 (SI 2015/373).

Note

Delete Note and substitute:

3A–1812   This section was brought into force on March 23, 2015 by the Anti–social Behaviour,

Crime and Policing Act 2014 (Commencement No.8, Saving and Transitional Provisions) Order 2015 (SI 2015/373).

Note

Delete Note and substitute:
This section was brought into force on March 23, 2015 by the Anti–social Behaviour, **3A–1817** Crime and Policing Act 2014 (Commencement No.8, Saving and Transitional Provisions) Order 2015 (SI 2015/373).

Note

Delete Note and substitute:
This section was brought into force on March 23, 2015 by the Anti–social Behaviour, **3A–1821** Crime and Policing Act 2014 (Commencement No.8, Saving and Transitional Provisions) Order 2015 (SI 2015/373).

Note

Delete Note and substitute:
This section was brought into force on March 23, 2015 by the Anti–social Behaviour, **3A–1825** Crime and Policing Act 2014 (Commencement No.8, Saving and Transitional Provisions) Order 2015 (SI 2015/373).

Note

Delete Note and substitute:
This section was brought into force on March 23, 2015 by the Anti–social Behaviour, **3A–1827** Crime and Policing Act 2014 (Commencement No.8, Saving and Transitional Provisions) Order 2015 (SI 2015/373).

Delete paragraph 3A–1828 and substitute:

"rules of court"
Where the injunction is sought against a person under the age of 18, the applica- **3A–1828** tion must be made in a local youth court. The procedure on such youth court applications is contained in the Magistrates' Courts (Injunctions: Anti–Social Behaviour) Rules 2015 (SI 2015/423).

Note

Delete Note and substitute:
This section was brought into force on March 23, 2015 by the Anti–social Behaviour, **3A–1830** Crime and Policing Act 2014 (Commencement No.8, Saving and Transitional Provisions) Order 2015 (SI 2015/373).

Note

Delete Note and substitute:
This section was brought into force on March 23, 2015 by the Anti–social Behaviour, **3A–1833** Crime and Policing Act 2014 (Commencement No.8, Saving and Transitional Provisions) Order 2015 (SI 2015/373).

Note

Delete Note and substitute:
This section was brought into force on March 23, 2015 by the Anti–social Behaviour, **3A–1835** Crime and Policing Act 2014 (Commencement No.8, Saving and Transitional Provisions) Order 2015 (SI 2015/373).

SECTION 11   SCHEDULE 1

REMANDS UNDER SECTIONS 9 AND 10

Note

Delete Note and substitute:
This schedule was brought into force on March 23, 2015 by the Anti–social Behav- **3A–1845** iour, Crime and Policing Act 2014 (Commencement No.8, Saving and Transitional Provisions) Order 2015 (SI 2015/373).

Add new paragraphs 3A–1846 to 3A–1861:

Deregulation Act 2015

3A–1846

(2015 c.20)

Preventing retaliatory eviction

3A–1847   **33.**—(1) Where a relevant notice is served in relation to a dwelling–house in England, a section 21 notice may not be given in relation to an assured shorthold tenancy of the dwelling–house—

(a) within six months beginning with the day of service of the relevant notice, or

(b) where the operation of the relevant notice has been suspended, within six months beginning with the day on which the suspension ends.

(2) A section 21 notice given in relation to an assured shorthold tenancy of a dwelling–house in England is invalid where—

(a) before the section 21 notice was given, the tenant made a complaint in writing to the landlord regarding the condition of the dwelling–house at the time of the complaint,

(b) the landlord—

(i) did not provide a response to the complaint within 14 days beginning with the day on which the complaint was given,

(ii) provided a response to the complaint that was not an adequate response, or

(iii) gave a section 21 notice in relation to the dwelling–house following the complaint,

(c) the tenant then made a complaint to the relevant local housing authority about the same, or substantially the same, subject matter as the complaint to the landlord,

(d) the relevant local housing authority served a relevant notice in relation to the dwelling–house in response to the complaint, and

(e) if the section 21 notice was not given before the tenant's complaint to the local housing authority, it was given before the service of the relevant notice.

(3) The reference in subsection (2) to an adequate response by the landlord is to a response in writing which—

(a) provides a description of the action that the landlord proposes to take to address the complaint, and

(b) sets out a reasonable timescale within which that action will be taken.

(4) Subsection (2) applies despite the requirement in paragraph (a) for a complaint to be in writing not having been met where the tenant does not know the landlord's postal or e–mail address.

(5) Subsection (2) applies despite the requirements in paragraphs (a) and (b) not having been met where the tenant made reasonable efforts to contact the landlord to complain about the condition of the dwelling–house but was unable to do so.

(6) The court must strike out proceedings for an order for possession under section 21 of the Housing Act 1988 in relation to a dwelling–house in England if, before the order is made, the section 21 notice that would otherwise require the court to make an order for possession in relation to the dwelling–house has become invalid under subsection (2).

(7) An order for possession of a dwelling–house in England made under section 21 of the Housing Act 1988 must not be set aside on the ground that a relevant notice was served in relation to the dwelling–house after the order for possession was made.

(8) Subsection (1) does not apply where the section 21 notice is given after—

(a) the relevant notice has been wholly revoked under section 16 of the Housing Act 2004 as a result of the notice having been served in error,

(b) the relevant notice has been quashed under paragraph 15 of Schedule 1 to that Act,

(c) a decision of the relevant local housing authority to refuse to revoke the relevant notice has been reversed under paragraph 18 of Schedule 1 to that Act, or

(d) a decision of the relevant local housing authority to take the action to which the relevant notice relates has been reversed under section 45 of that Act.

(9) Subsection (2) does not apply where the operation of the relevant notice has been suspended.

(10) References in this section and section 34 to a relevant notice served, or complaint made, in relation to a dwelling–house include a relevant notice served, or complaint made, in relation to any common parts of the building of which the dwelling–house forms a part.

(11) But subsection (10) applies only if—

(a) the landlord has a controlling interest in the common parts in question, and

(b) the condition of those common parts is such as to affect the tenant's enjoyment of the dwelling–house or of any common parts which the tenant is entitled to use.

(12) In this section and section 34 a reference to a complaint to a landlord includes a complaint made to a person acting on behalf of the landlord in relation to the tenancy.

(13) In this section and section 34—

"assured shorthold tenancy" means a tenancy within section 19A or 20 of the Housing Act 1988;

"common parts", in relation to a building, includes—

(a) the structure and exterior of the building, and

(b) common facilities provided (whether or not in the building) for persons who include one or more of the occupiers of the building;

"controlling interest" means an interest which is such as to entitle the landlord to decide whether action is taken in relation to a complaint within this section or a relevant notice;

"dwelling–house" has the meaning given by section 45 of the Housing Act 1988;

"relevant local housing authority", in relation to a dwelling–house, means the local housing authority as defined in section 261(2) and (3) of the Housing Act 2004 within whose area the dwelling–house is located;

"relevant notice" means—

(a) a notice served under section 11 of the Housing Act 2004 (improvement notices relating to category 1 hazards),

(b) a notice served under section 12 of that Act (improvement notices relating to category 2 hazards), or

(c) a notice served under section 40(7) of that Act (emergency remedial action);

"section 21 notice" means a notice given under section 21(1)(b) or (4)(a) of the Housing Act 1988 (recovery of possession on termination of shorthold tenancy).

Note

3A–1848 This section is not yet in force. It will only apply to assured shorthold tenancies of dwelling houses in England granted after the provision was brought into force. See s.41.

"assured shorthold tenancy"

3A–1849 See Housing Act 1988 ss.19A and 20.

"a section 21 notice"

3A–1850 See Housing Act 1988.

"relevant local housing authority"

3A–1851 See s.33(13).

"dwelling–house"

3A–1852 See Housing Act 1988 s.45.

"a relevant notice"

3A–1853 See s.33(13).

Editorial note

3A–1854 Sections 33 and 34 provide protection for assured shorthold tenants against retaliatory eviction by landlords, where the condition of property is poor or unsafe. Where a relevant notice is served on the landlord, the landlord is prevented from evicting the tenant by giving a Housing Act 1988 s.21 notice for six months, from the date of service of the relevant notice. A relevant notice is defined as an improvement notice served under section 11 or section 12 of the Housing Act 2004, or a notice of emergency remedial action served under section 40(7) of the Housing Act 2004. Section 33(2) provides that a s.21 notice is invalid if, before the notice was served, the tenant had made a complaint about the condition of the property to the landlord, the landlord did not provide an adequate or timely response to the complaint or served a section 21 notice on the tenant, and the tenant then contacted the local housing authority about the matters raised with the landlord, who served a relevant notice in relation to the dwelling. When a landlord has been prevented from obtaining possession by virtue of the section, the landlord is required to serve a fresh section 21 notice to regain possession of the dwelling. Courts must strike out notices which are invalid.

Further exemptions to section 33

3A–1855 **34.**—(1) Subsections (1) and (2) of section 33 do not apply where the condition of the dwelling–house or common parts that gave rise to the service of the relevant notice is due to a breach by the tenant of—

    (a) the duty to use the dwelling–house in a tenant–like manner, or

    (b) an express term of the tenancy to the same effect.

(2) Subsections (1) and (2) of section 33 do not apply where at the time the section 21 notice is given the dwelling–house is genuinely on the market for sale.

(3) For the purposes of subsection (2), a dwelling–house is not genuinely on the market for sale if, in particular, the landlord intends to sell the landlord's interest in the dwelling–house to—

    (a) a person associated with the landlord,

    (b) a business partner of the landlord,

    (c) a person associated with a business partner of the landlord, or

    (d) a business partner of a person associated with the landlord.

(4) In subsection (3), references to a person who is associated with another person are to be read in accordance with section 178 of the Housing Act 1996.

(5) For the purposes of subsection (3), a business partner of a person ("P") is a person who is—

    (a) a director, secretary or other officer of a company of which P is also a director, secretary or other officer,

    (b) a director, secretary or other officer of a company in which P has a shareholding or other financial interest,

    (c) a person who has a shareholding or other financial interest in a company of which P is a director, secretary or other officer,

    (d) an employee of P,

    (e) a person by whom P is employed, or

    (f) a partner of a partnership of which P is also a partner.

(6) Subsections (1) and (2) of section 33 do not apply where the landlord is a private registered provider of social housing.

(7) Subsections (1) and (2) of section 33 do not apply where—

    (a) the dwelling–house is subject to a mortgage granted before the beginning of the tenancy,

    (b) the mortgagee is entitled to exercise a power of sale conferred on the mortgagee by the mortgage or by section 101 of the Law of Property Act 1925, and

    (c) at the time the section 21 notice is given the mortgagee requires possession of the dwelling–house for the purpose of disposing of it with vacant possession in exercise of that power.

(8) In subsection (7)—

    (a) "mortgage" includes a charge, and

    (b) "mortgagee" includes a receiver appointed by the mortgagee under the terms of the mortgage or in accordance with the Law of Property Act 1925.

Note

    This section is not yet in force. It will only apply to assured shorthold tenancies of **3A–1856** dwelling houses in England granted after the provision was brought into force. See s.41.

"common parts"

3A–1857   See s.33(13).

"business partner"

3A–1858   See s.34(5).

"mortgage and mortgagee"

3A–1859   See s.34(8).

Editorial note

3A–1860   Section 34 provides that the provisions in s.33 preventing retaliatory eviction do not apply where

- the condition of the dwelling was due to the tenant's breach of duty to use the dwelling in a tenant–like manner, or breach of an express term of the tenancy; or
- the landlord has a genuine intention to sell to a person that they are not associated with; or
- the landlord is a private registered provider of social housing; or
- a mortgagee is in possession of the landlord's interest in the dwelling and the mortgagee needs to be able to exercise their power of sale with vacant possession.

Application of sections 33 to 40

3A–1861   **41.**—(1) Subject to subsections (2) and (3), a provision of sections 33 to 40 applies only to an assured shorthold tenancy of a dwelling–house in England granted on or after the day on which the provision comes into force.

(2) Subject to subsection (3), a provision of sections 33 to 40 does not apply to an assured shorthold tenancy that came into being under section 5(2) of the Housing Act 1988 after the commencement of that provision and on the coming to an end of an assured shorthold tenancy that was granted before the commencement of that provision.

(3) At the end of the period of three years beginning with the coming into force of a provision of sections 33 to 38 or section 40, that provision also applies to any assured shorthold tenancy of a dwelling–house in England—

(a) which is in existence at that time, and

(b) to which that provision does not otherwise apply by virtue of subsection (1) or (2).

3B BUSINESS TENANCIES

Landlord and Tenant Act 1954

"excluded tenancies"

Add new paragraph at end:

3B–100   See also Defence Reform Act 2014 where the Secretary of State has let land to a contractor, or a sub–tenancy of any such land—protection excluded.

s.30(1)(f) intention of landlord to demolish or reconstruct

In the second paragraph, before the sentence beginning "The intention must be" add:

3B–182   The changes made to Part II of the 1954 Act by the Regulatory Reform (Business Tenancies) (England and Wales) Order 2003 did not change the relevant date to prove the landlord's intention under s.30(1)(f) of the 1954 Act. This remains the date of the hearing (*Hough v Greathall Ltd* [2015] EWCA Civ 23).

3C CONTEMPT OF COURT

A. An Outline of the Law of Contempt of Court

2. Principal forms of contempt liability

At the end of the third paragraph, add:

By the Criminal Justice and Courts Act 2015 s.74(2), with effect from April 13, 2015 **3C–13** (SI 2015/778), insofar as it extends to England and Wales, this section was repealed. By s.74(1) of the 2015 Act additions were made to the Juries Act 1974, in particular ss.20D to 20G, for the purpose of making it a criminal offence for a person intentionally to disclose a jury's deliberations, or to solicit or to obtain such information (see further paras 3C–65 & 3C–66 below). It is a contempt of court for a member of a jury to fail to surrender an electronic communications device in accordance with an order made by a judge under the Juries Act 1974 s.15A (also added by the 2015 Act). Proceedings for contempt under s.15A may only be instituted by or with the consent of the Attorney General (s.15A(6)).

Contempt of Court Act 1981

OTHER ASPECTS OF LAW AND PROCEDURE

Confidentiality of jury's deliberations : Scotland and Northern Ireland

Delete s.8(1) and substitute:

(1) In Scotland and Northern Ireland, subject to subsection (2) **3C–65** below, it is a contempt of court to obtain, disclose or solicit any particulars of statements made, opinions expressed, arguments advanced or votes cast by members of a jury in the course of their deliberations in any legal proceedings.

Confidentiality of jury's deliberations

Add new paragraph at beginning:

As it extends to England and Wales, this section was repealed by the Criminal **3C–66** Justice and Courts Act 2015 s.74(2) with effect from April 13, 2015 (SI 2015/778). By s.74(1) of that Act additions were made to the Juries Act 1974 (ss.20D to 20G) for the purpose of making it a criminal offence for a person intentionally to disclose a jury's deliberations, or to solicit or to obtain such information.

Term of imprisonment or fine for contempt

After the first paragraph, add as a new paragraph:

A committal for contempt must be for "a fixed term" (s.14(1)). In determining such **3C–87** term in a case of civil contempt it is open to a judge to reflect a period spent on remand by the contemnor. Thus, where a contemnor had spent seven days on remand, a committal to prison for (say) "three months less seven days" would satisfy the requirement that a committal must be for "a fixed term" (*R. (James) v Governor of Birmingham Prison* [2015] EWCA Civ 58, February 9, 2015, CA, unrep., where explained that any credit for time served on remand had to be reflected in the committal order).

Delete the last paragraph and substitute:

For commentary on sentences for breaches of injunctions made under the Anti–Social Behaviour, Crime and Policing Act 2014, see para.3A–1782 above. Note also commentary in para.3A–1207 on sentences for breach of the Housing Act 1996 s.153A (replaced by the 2014 Act).

3D PROCEEDINGS UNDER THE HUMAN RIGHTS ACT 1998

Human Rights Act 1988

Section 2(1)

In the first paragraph, after "(a seven–judge Court of Appeal)" add:

3D–9 and *R. (Haney) v Secretary of State for Justice* [2014] UKSC 66; [2015] 2 W.L.R. 76 at [18]–[23] and [30]–[37]

In the second paragraph, after "at para.19" add:

and *Breyer Group Plc v Department of Energy and Climate Change* [2015] EWCA Civ 408; [2015] W.L.R. (D) 192 at [42]–[49]

In the sixth paragraph beginning "The exercise is", after "Lord Nicholls at para.40" add:

3D–16 and *K (Children) (Unrepresented Father: Cross–Examination of Child), Re* [2015] EWCA Civ 543 at [27]–[31]

Before the last paragraph, add as a new paragraph:

3D–19 Where the case law of the European Court of Human Rights has said that the issue of compatibility of an issue with the Convention lies within the margin of appreciation of the state, then with the constitutional settlement of the UK, the court has constitutional authority to make a declaration of incompatibility in relation to that matter if it considers the domestic law breaches the Convention: *R. (Nicklinson) v Ministry of Justice* [2014] UKSC 38; [2014] 3 F.L.R. 1; [2014] 3 W.L.R. 200; [2014] 3 All E.R. 843 at [76], [191], [229], [326].

In the first paragraph, add at beginning:

3D–22 No declaration may be made in private law proceedings without the Crown first being notified and given an opportunity to make representations: *Coventry v Lawrence (No.2)* [2014] UKSC 46; [2014] P.T.S.R. 1014; [2014] 3 W.L.R. 55; [2014] 4 All E.R. 517 at [42]–[44].

Section 6(2)

In the first paragraph, after "[2005] UKHL 29" add

3D–26 ; [2005] 1 W.L.R. 673

At the end of the third paragraph, add:

3D–41 and *R. v Gas and Electricity Markets Authority* [2013] EWCA Civ 70; [2013] J.P.L. 1037 at [26]–[27]. But in *Breyer Group Plc v Department of Energy and Climate Change* [2015] EWCA Civ 408; [2015] W.L.R. (D) 192 at [42]–[49], the Court of Appeal held (following the consistent approach of the European Court of Human Rights to the concept of "property" under Article 1 Protocol 1) that damages could not be claimed under the Convention for loss of expectation of future income unless it was in the form of capitalisable goodwill.

There may be cases where no judicial remedy is needed, if the state has changed a law which violated a right before the matter is determined by the court. Acceptance by the court that the complaint was well–founded may be a sufficient remedy to constitute just satisfaction: *R. (T) v Chief Constable of Greater Manchester* [2014] UKSC 35; [2015] 1 A.C. 49; [2014] 3 W.L.R. 96; [2014] 4 All E.R. 159 at [66] [157–158].

At the end of the last paragraph, for "Ruddy v Chief Constable, Strathclyde Police & Another [2012] UKSC 57" substitute::

Ruddy v Chief Constable, Strathclyde Police [2012] UKSC 57; [2013] H.R.L.R. 10

Add at end:

3D–48 Section 12 HRA does not apply to applications under s.11 of the Contempt of Court Act 1981 because they are not applications for relief made against any person: *BBC, Re* [2014] UKSC 25, [2015] 1 A.C. 558, [2014] 2 W.L.R. 1281, [2014] 2 All E.R. 1037 at [62]–[68].

Note

Add at end:

Although it is the responsibility of the UK government in international law to **3D–68** ensure that the Channel Islands comply with such international obligations as apply to them, the Human Rights Act 1998 does not apply to Channel Islands legislation as it applies in that Channel Island, because an Order in Council made in exercise of the royal prerogative is not included in the definition of primary legislation in s.21 HRA: *R. (Barclay) v Secretary of State for Justice* [2014] UKSC 54; [2015] 1 A.C. 276; [2014] 3 W.L.R. 1142 at [27]–[39] and [48].

3E INSOLVENCY PROCEEDINGS

PRACTICE DIRECTION—INSOLVENCY PROCEEDINGS

Jurisdiction and distribution of business

Before the last paragraph entitled "Distribution of Business" add:

The Insolvency (Amendment) Rules 2015 (SI 2015/443) have amended, with effect **3E–22** from April 6, 2015, r.7.11 Insolvency Rules 1986 so as to allow the High Court in London to transfer certain cases to the County Court sitting at Central London. Following consultation with users and others, the Chancellor has agreed the following criteria which the registrars will apply when considering whether to retain a case in the High Court or transfer it to Central London:

Note on listing and criteria for the transfer of work from the registrars to The County Court sitting in Central London

(1) All winding up petitions must be issued and listed for initial hearing in the Royal Courts of Justice sitting in the Rolls Building.

(2) All bankruptcy petitions must be listed and allocated in accordance with rule 6.9A Insolvency Rules 1986.

(3) Save as provided above, all High Court proceedings which are to be listed before a registrar in accordance with the Practice Direction—Insolvency Proceedings will continue to be issued and listed in the Royal Courts of Justice sitting in the Rolls Building. In each case consideration will be given by a registrar at an appropriate stage to whether the proceedings should remain in the High Court or be transferred to the County Court sitting in Central London.

(4) When deciding whether proceedings which have been issued in the High Court should be transferred to the County Court sitting in Central London, the registrar should have regard to the following factors:

    (a) the complexity of the proceedings;

    (b) whether the proceedings raise new or controversial points of law;

    (c) the likely date and length of the hearing;

    (d) public interest in the proceedings;

    (e) (where it is ascertainable) the amount in issue in the proceedings.

(5) As a general rule, and subject to 4 (a)–(d) above, where the amount in issue in the proceedings is £100,000 or less, the proceedings should be transferred to the County Court sitting in Central London.

(6) Subject to paragraph 4 (a)–(e), the following will be transferred to be heard in the County Court sitting in Central London:

    (a) private examinations ordered to take place under ss.236 or 366 Insolvency Act 1986 (but not necessarily the application for the private examination);

    (b) applications to extend the term of office of an administrator (para.76 Sch.B1 Insolvency Act 1986);

    (c) applications for permission to distribute the prescribed part (para.65(3) Sch.B1 Insolvency Act 1986);

    (d) applications to disqualify a director and applications for a bankruptcy restrictions order where it appears likely that an order will be made for a period not exceeding five years.

(7) With effect from 6 April 2015 the following proceedings will be issued and heard in the County Court sitting in Central London:

(a) applications for the restoration of a company to the register (s.1029ff. Companies Act 2006);

(b) applications to extend the period allowed for the delivery of particulars relating to a charge (s.859F Companies Act 2006);

(c) applications to rectify the register by reason of omission or mis-statement in any statement or notice delivered to the registrar of companies (s.859M Companies Act 2006) or to replace an instrument or debenture delivered to the registrar of companies (s.859N Companies Act 2006).

Delete title "Distribution of Business" and substitute:

Distribution of business—judge/registrar/district judge

Company voluntary arrangements (Part I Insolvency Act 1986)

Company voluntary arrangements without moratorium

For "The meetings must then be held at the time, date and place proposed (s.3(2)." substitute:

3E–31   The meetings must then be held at the time, date and place proposed (s.3).

Administration orders (Part II Insolvency Act 1986)

Add new paragraph at end:

3E–39   Note that with effect from 6 April 2015 the High Court in London no longer deals with applications to extend administrations which will generally be transferred to the County Court in Central London (see the Note on listing and criteria for the transfer of work from the registrars to The County Court sitting in Central London (para.3E–22)).

Winding–up petitions (Parts IV and V Insolvency Act 1986)

Winding up unregistered companies

Add new paragraph at end:

3E–77   A club may not generally be wound up under the Insolvency Act as an unregistered company (*St James' Club, Re* 42 E.R. 920; (1852) 2 De G.M. & G. 383, in which the Lord Chancellor held that a members' social club was not an association for the purposes of the then Joint Stock Companies Winding–Up Act 1948; see also as to the modern law *International Tin Council, Re* [1989] Ch. 309; [1988] 3 W.L.R. 1159, *Western Counties Construction v Witney Town Football and Social Club* [1993] B.C.C. 874). However, in *National Union of Flint Glassworkers, Re* [2006] B.C.C. 828, Norris J. held that the court did have an equitable jurisdiction to wind up any organisation where there was no other method of winding up available.

3G   DATA PROTECTION ACT 1998

Introduction

In the list of cases, add at end:

3G–1   C212/13 *Rynes*

Data Protection Act 1998

PART I

PRELIMINARY

Editorial note

At the end of the penultimate paragraph, add:

3G–9   In C212/13 *Rynes* the CJEU confirmed that CCTV cameras which recorded the entrance to a domestic premises and the public footpath adjacent to it could not be exempt because the cameras captured footage outside the domestic premises.

Part II

Rights of data subjects and others

Editorial note

At the beginning of the fourth paragraph, add:
Subject access rights do not displace other provisions.   **3G–11**

After the fifth paragraph, add as new paragraph:
In *Kololo v Commissioner of Police for The Metropolis* [2015] EWHC 600 (QB) the court rejected a submission by the Metropolitan Police that Mr Kololo, an overseas national, should be denied the right of subject access on the grounds that the access regime under the Crime (International Cooperation) Act 2003 was an alternative legal mechanism.

At the end of the seventh paragraph, add:
In *Ranger v House of Lords Appointments Commission* [2015] EWHC 45 (QB) the High Court confirmed a refusal of subject access by the Lords Appointment Commission on the basis of Sch.7 para.3.

Editorial note

At the end of the fifth paragraph, add:
The provisions are enforced by the Information Commissioner.   **3G–17**

Editorial note

At the end of the second paragraph, add:
In the Court of Appeal, the Court held that damages could be recovered without **3G–21** the need to show financial loss and disapplied s.13(2) as incompatible with the Directive, see *Vidall–Hall v Google Inc* [2015] EWCA Civ 311.

At the end of the eight paragraph, add:
In *Crook v Chief Constable of Essex Police* [2015] EWHC 988 (QB) Mr Crook was awarded damages of £67,750 in total, being £57,750 for loss of earnings plus £3,000 general, £2,000 for distress plus £3,000 for a claim in breach of confidence, Art.8 and breach of the Act. The release of personal data of which he complained was neither necessary not proportionate.

Editorial note

At the end of the seventh paragraph, add:
In *Mosley v Google Inc* [2015] EWHC 59 (QB) the Court declined to strike out a case **3G–23** brought by Mr Mosley for the erasure of images relating to him despite the argument by Google Inc that to achieve erasure they would have to monitor content contrary to Directive 2000/3 (the E–commerce Directive).

Part V

Enforcement

Editorial note

Add at end:
The power to serve assessment notices was extended to NHS bodies by the Data **3G–24.1.1** Protection (Assessment Notices Designation of National Health Service Bodies) Order 2014 (SI 2014/3282). The Order came into effect on February 1, 2015.

Part VI

Miscellaneous and general

Note

Add at end:
The Privacy and Electronic Communications (EC Directive) Amendment Regula- **3G–57.1**

tions 2015 (SI 2015/312) effective April 6, 2015, allows the Commissioner to impose fines for nuisance calls or spam texts without having to show the calls or texts causing "substantial damage or distress."

SCHEDULE 1

Notes to Schedule 1

Add at end:

3G–62.0.23 In *R. (Catt) v Commissioner of Police for the Metropolis* [2015] UKSC 9 the Supreme Court confirmed in a case on Article 8 of the Human Rights Act that retention of some information on Mr Catt was not unlawful. The Court commented that complaints about data retention should more appropriately be made to the Commissioner than by way of judicial review.

3J DIRECTORS DISQUALIFICATION PROCEEDINGS

Editorial note

Add new paragraph 3J–3.1:

Prospective changes

3J–3.1 Part 9 of the Small Business, Enterprise and Employment Act 2015 makes provision for a number of substantial changes to CDDA 1986. The changes include an extension of the limitation period for bringing proceedings from 2 years to 3 years, and new provisions under which applications for disqualification orders can be made. These will come into force on a day to be appointed. When they come into force, consequential changes to the Practice Direction and commentary will be required. No day for the changes to come into force has yet been appointed.

PRACTICE DIRECTION—DIRECTORS DISQUALIFICATION PROCEEDINGS

11. Uncontested disposals

In paragraph 11.1, for "paragraph 9.4" substitute:

3J–33 paragraph 8.4

Add new paragraph 3J–45.1:

Office of Fair Trading

3J–45.1 The Office of Fair Trading was dissolved in 2014 and its functions transferred to the Competition and Markets Authority.

Add new paragraph 3J–56.2:

Office of Fair Trading

3J–56.2 The Office of Fair Trading was dissolved in 2014 and its functions transferred to the Competition and Markets Authority.

Evidence in section 8A applications

Add new paragraph at end:

3J–59 It should be noted that the references in para.29.2(4) to para.28.2(2); in para.29.3(3) to para.28.3(2) and para.29.4(3) to para.28.4(2) should be to paras 29.2(2), 29.3(2) and 29.4(2), respectively.

3K CIVIL RECOVERY PROCEEDINGS

PRACTICE DIRECTION—CIVIL RECOVERY PROCEEDINGS

Exclusions for legal costs

At the end of the second paragraph, add:

Exclusions can be made for the benefit of respondents sued by the claimant. They **3K–6.2** can also be made in favour of victims who intervene under s.281 to prevent recovery of the property, claim it is theirs and so should be vested in them: *National Crime Agency v Robb* [2014] EWHC 4384 (Ch).

3L EUROPEAN PROCEDURES (CPR PART 78)

PART 78—EUROPEAN PROCEDURES

Making a claim

Add new paragraph at end:

In *eco cosmetics GmbH & Co KG v Dupuy (C–119/13)* [2015] 1 W.L.R. 678, ECJ, refer- **3L–5** ences by a German court to the ECJ for preliminary rulings raised questions concerning the EOP procedure, in particular, the question whether the EOP Regulation must be interpreted as meaning that the procedures referred to in arts 16 to 20 are applicable where an order for payment has not been served in accordance with the minimum standards laid down in arts 13 to 15 (see paras 3L–69—3L–71 below). The ruling given on the reference was that (1) the Regulation must be interpreted as meaning that arts 16 to 20 are not so applicable where there has been such irregularity, (2) where it is only after an EOP has been declared enforceable that such an irregularity is exposed the defendant must have the opportunity to raise that irregularity, which, if it is duly established, will invalidate the declaration of enforceability, (3) as, in such an event, the Regulation is silent as to the possible remedies available to the defendant, the procedural issues (as art.26 provides) are governed by national law.

3M PREVENTION OF TERRORISM PROCEEDINGS

PART 76—PROCEEDINGS UNDER THE PREVENTION OF TERRORISM ACT 2005

Consideration of Secretary of State's objection

In rule 76.29(1)(a), after "special advocate" add:

or to the form in which it is proposed to be made 3M–42

PART 79—PROCEEDINGS UNDER THE COUNTER–TERRORISM ACT 2008 AND PART 1 OF THE TERRORIST ASSET–FREEZING ETC. ACT 2010

Consideration of the Treasury's objection

In rule 79.21(1), after "proposed communication by the special advocate" add:

or to the form in which it is proposed to be made 3M–86

PART 80—PROCEEDINGS UNDER THE TERRORISM PREVENTION AND INVESTIGATION MEASURES ACT 2011

Consideration of the Secretary of State's objection or application

In rule 80.25(1)(a), after "special advocate" add:

3M–136   **or to the form in which it is proposed to be made**

After the existing Part 80, add new Part 88:

PART 88—PROCEEDINGS UNDER THE COUNTER–TERRORISM AND SECURITY ACT 2015

Contents

3M–145   *I. Application of this Part*

II. Permission Applications, Reviews and References to the High Court Relating to Temporary Exclusion Orders

III. Appeals to the Court of Appeal

IV. General Provisions

Editorial introduction

The Counter–Terrorism and Security Act 2015 (c.6) received the Royal Assent on **3M–146** February 12, 2015, and came into force on the following day. Chapter 2 of Part 1 of the Act (ss.2 to 15) gives the Secretary of State power, if certain conditions are met, to impose, on an individual who has a right of abode in the United Kingdom and who is reasonably suspected of involvement in terrorist activity abroad, a temporary exclusion order (TEO), requiring that individual not to return to the United Kingdom except in accordance with a permit to return (or as a result of deportation to the United Kingdom). Section 3 (Temporary exclusion orders: prior permission of the court) makes provision for the role of the court in providing prior permission to the Secretary of State to impose a TEO. The prior permission of the court is required, except in circumstances of particular urgency, in which case the Secretary of State may impose a TEO but must refer the matter to the court immediately after doing so. An individual on whom a TEO has been imposed may also apply to the court to review the Secretary of State's decision that the conditions for the TEO were met, the decision to impose the TEO, or the decision to impose conditions on an individual after return. Where the principal place of residence of the individual is neither Scotland nor Northern Ireland, the statutory jurisdiction is exercisable by the High Court.

Rules in Part 88 detail the function of the court, allows the court to consider the application even if the person is not aware of the proposal to impose a TEO on him or her, and requires the court to apply judicial review principles in determining it. That section also introduces Sch.2 (Urgent temporary exclusion orders: reference to the court etc). Section 12 (Temporary exclusion orders: proceedings and appeals against convictions) introduces Sch.3 (Temporary exclusion orders: proceedings) and Sch.4 (Temporary exclusion orders: appeals against convictions). Schedule 3 details the provisions that can be made by rules of court in relation to temporary exclusion order proceedings, and the provisions that must be made in relation to disclosure. Schedule 4 details the appeal proceedings available to an individual where a TEO or associated in–country measure under it is quashed or altered and the individual has already been convicted of an offence under s.10(1) or (3) of the Act in connection with the TEO or measure.

For the purpose of implementing Chapter 2 of Pt 1 of the Act, the Civil Procedure (Amendment) Rules 2015 (SI 2015/406) amend the CPR by inserting Part 88 (Proceedings under the Counter–Terrorism Act 2015). This Part contains rules about proceedings in relation to TEO proceedings generally, and particularly where sensitive material is in issue and it is necessary to ensure that such material is not disclosed where such disclosure would be contrary to the public interest. This includes modification of the application of other Parts of the CPR for the purposes of those proceedings). Rule 1.2 (Application by the court of the overriding objective) is modified (see r.88.2). The statutory instrument was made on February 26, 2015, and came into effect on the following day. The instrument was made, not by the Rule Committee, but by the Lord Chancellor in exercise of power conferred by paras 2 to 4 and 6 of Sch.3 to the 2015 Act.

In its structure, and in much of its detail, Part 88 is similar to Part 79 (Proceedings under the Counter–Terrorism Act 2008) and Part 80 (Proceedings under the Terrorism Prevention and Investigation Measures Act 2011). The art is not supplemented by a Practice Direction.

The Temporary Exclusion Orders (Notices) Regulations 2015 (SI 2015/438) make provision under s.13(1) and (2) of the 2015 Act for the giving of notice to a person on whom the Secretary of State has decided to impose a TEO under s.2 or obligations under s.9. These Regulations deal with the timing and method of giving notice and provide for notice to be deemed to have been given in prescribed circumstances.

I. Application of this Part

Scope and interpretation

3M–147   **88.1—(1) This Part contains rules about—**

(a) **TEO proceedings in the High Court; and**

(b) **appeals to the Court of Appeal against an order of the High Court in such proceedings.**

(2) In this Part—

(a) **"the Act" means the Counter–Terrorism and Security Act 2015;**

(b) **"closed material" means any relevant material that the Secretary of State objects to disclosing to a relevant party on the grounds that disclosure is contrary to the public interest;**

(c) **"legal representative" is to be construed in accordance with paragraph 4(4)(b) of Schedule 3 to the Act;**

(d) **"TEO" means a temporary exclusion order (which has the same meaning as in section 2 of the Act);**

(e) **"open material" means any relevant material that the Secretary of State does not object to disclosing to a relevant party on the grounds that disclosure is contrary to the public interest;**

(f) **"relevant material" means the material described in paragraph 3(1)(a) to (c) of Schedule 3 to the Act;**

(g) **"relevant party" means any party to the proceedings other than the Secretary of State;**

(h) **"special advocate" means a person appointed under paragraph 10(1) of Schedule 3 to the Act;**

(i) **"TEO proceedings" has the same meaning as in paragraph 1 of Schedule 3 to the Act;**

(j) **"TEO subject" means an individual on whom the Secretary of State has imposed, or is proposing to impose, a TEO.**

(3) For the purposes of this Part, disclosure is contrary to the public interest if it is made contrary to the interests of national security, the international relations of the United Kingdom or the detection and prevention of crime, or in any other circumstances where disclosure is likely to harm the public interest.

Modification to the overriding objective

3M–148   **88.2—(1) Where any of the rules in this Part applies, the overriding objective in Part 1, and so far as possible any other rule, must** be read and given effect in a way which is compatible with the duty set out in paragraph (2).

(2) The court must ensure that information is not disclosed contrary to the public interest.

(3) Subject to paragraph (2), the court must satisfy itself that the material available to it enables it properly to determine proceedings.

II. Permission Applications, Reviews and References to the High Court Relating to Temporary Exclusion Orders

Scope of this section

88.3 This section contains rules about— 3M–149
  (a) applications under section 3(1)(b) of the Act (application for permission to impose a TEO);
  (b) references under paragraph 3(1) of Schedule 2 to the Act (reference of the imposition of measures imposed without permission); and
  (c) applications to the High Court under section 11 of the Act (applications to the court to review decisions of the Secretary of State relating to a TEO).

Application for permission to impose a TEO

88.4 An application under section 3(1)(b) of the Act for permis- 3M–150 sion to impose a TEO must be made by the Secretary of State filing with the court—
  (a) a statement of reasons to support the application;
  (b) any relevant material of which the Secretary of State is aware at that stage; and
  (c) any written submissions.

Reference of TEO imposed without permission

88.5 A reference under paragraph 3(1) of Schedule 2 to the Act of 3M–151 the imposition of a TEO imposed without permission must be made by the Secretary of State filing with the court—
  (a) a statement of reasons for imposing the TEO;
  (b) any relevant material of which the Secretary of State is aware at that stage; and
  (c) any written submissions.

Application for review under section 11 of the Act

88.6 Rules 88.7 to 88.14 apply to a review under section 11 of the 3M–152 Act.

Applications (general) and modification of Part 8

88.7—(1) An application to the court to review a decision under 3M–153 section 11 of the Act ("a review application") must be made pursuant to Part 8, as modified by this Part, and subject to paragraph (2).

(2) The following rules do not apply to a review application—

(a) rule 8.1(3) (court may order claim to continue as if claimant had not used Part 8 procedure);

(b) rule 8.2A (issue of claim form without naming defendants);

(c) rule 8.4 (consequence of not filing an acknowledgment of service);

(d) rule 8.5 (filing and serving written evidence);

(e) rule 8.6 (evidence—general); and

(f) rule 8.8 (defendant objects to use of Part 8).

Review application

3M–154   88.8—(1) A review application must be started by a claim form.

(2) The claim form must set out—

(a) the details of the decision which it is sought to review;

(b) details of how the TEO subject is affected by the TEO; and

(c) the grounds on which the TEO subject seeks to review the decision.

(3) The TEO subject must file with the claim form—

(a) a copy of—

(i) the written notice under section 4 of the Act of the imposition of the TEO; or

(ii) where relevant, any notice under section 9 of the Act imposing any or all of the permitted conditions; and

(b) any evidence, including witness statements, on which the TEO subject relies at that stage.

Fixing of directions hearing date

3M–155   88.9—(1) When the court issues the claim form it must fix a date for a directions hearing.

(2) Unless the court directs otherwise, the directions hearing will be not less than 14 days but not more than 28 days after the date of issue of the claim form.

Service of the claim form and accompanying documents

3M–156   88.10 The court must—

(a) serve on the Secretary of State and any special advocate (if one has been appointed)—

(i) the claim form; and

(ii) the documents specified in rule 88.8(3); and

(b) send to all parties and to any special advocate a notice of the directions hearing date (where such date is not endorsed on the claim form).

Acknowledgment of service

3M–157   88.11 Where a special advocate has been appointed, the Secretary of State must serve on that special advocate a copy of the acknowledgment of service filed under rule 8.3.

Directions hearing

88.12 At the directions hearing the court may give case manage- 3M–158
ment directions, in particular—

    (a) for the holding of a further hearing to determine the application;

    (b) fixing a date, time and place for the further hearing at which the parties, their legal representatives (if any) and any special advocate can be present; and

    (c) as to the order in which, and the time within which, the following are to be filed and served—

        (i) any response to the application to be filed and served by the Secretary of State under rule 88.13(1), (2) and (4);

        (ii) any application to be made under rule 88.13(5);

        (iii) any information to be filed and served by the Secretary of State pursuant to an order under rule 88.13(7);

        (iv) any evidence to be filed and served by the TEO subject under rule 88.14(1);

        (v) any evidence to be filed and served by the Secretary of State under rule 88.14(2);

        (vi) any application by the Secretary of State under rule 88.13(3), 88.13(8) or 88.14(3); and

        (vii) any further evidence, including witness statements, written submissions or skeleton arguments, to be filed and served by the parties and any special advocate.

Response by the Secretary of State

88.13—(1) Where the Secretary of State intends to oppose the 3M–159
exercise of any of the court's powers under section 11(3) or (5) of
the Act, the Secretary of State must file with the court—

    (a) the grounds for opposing the exercise of those powers; and

    (b) any relevant evidence of which the Secretary of State is aware at that stage.

(2) Unless the Secretary of State objects to the grounds and evidence referred to in paragraph (1) being disclosed to the TEO subject and the TEO subject's legal representative, the Secretary of State must serve a copy of the grounds and evidence on the TEO subject at the same time as filing them.

(3) Where the Secretary of State objects to the grounds and evidence referred to in paragraph (1) being disclosed to the TEO subject and the TEO subject's legal representative, the Secretary of State must make an application in accordance with rule 88.27.

(4) Where a special advocate has been appointed, the Secretary of State must serve on the special advocate a copy of the grounds and evidence filed under paragraph (1).

(5) The TEO subject and any special advocate may apply to the court for an order directing the Secretary of State to file and serve further information about the Secretary of State's grounds filed under paragraph (1)(a).

(6) An application under paragraph (5) must set out—

(a) what information is sought; and

(b) why the information sought is necessary for the determination of the review application.

(7) The court may make an order on an application under paragraph (5) where it considers that the information sought—

(a) is necessary for the determination of the review application; and

(b) may be provided without disproportionate cost, time or effort.

(8) Where the Secretary of State objects to serving on the TEO subject and the TEO subject's legal representative the information sought under paragraph (5), the Secretary of State must make an application in accordance with rule 88.27.

Filing and service of evidence

3M–160   88.14—(1) Where the TEO subject wishes to rely on evidence in support of the review application and—

(a) such evidence was not filed with the court with the claim form; or

(b) such evidence was filed with the court with the claim form but the TEO subject wishes to rely on further evidence,

the TEO subject must file and serve that evidence, including any witness statement, on the Secretary of State and any special advocate.

(2) Where the TEO subject serves evidence in support of the application, the Secretary of State must file and serve, subject to paragraph (3), any further evidence, including any witness statement, on the TEO subject and any special advocate.

(3) Where the Secretary of State wishes to withhold disclosure of any closed material from the TEO subject and the TEO subject's legal representative, the Secretary of State must make an application in accordance with rule 88.27.

(4) The Secretary of State must serve any closed material on the special advocate.

(5) The parties and, where relevant, any special advocate must file and serve any further evidence, including witness statements, written submissions or skeleton arguments, as directed by the court.

III. Appeals to the Court of Appeal

Modification of Part 52 (appeals)

3M–161   88.15—(1) Part 52 (appeals) applies to an appeal to the Court of Appeal against an order of the High Court in TEO proceedings subject to—

(a) rule 88.2;

(b) the rules in Section IV of this Part; and

(c) paragraphs (2) and (3) of this rule.

(2) The following rules do not apply to appeals to the Court of Appeal—
  (a) rule 52.4(1) (appellant's notice); and
  (b) rule 52.5 (respondent's notice).
(3) Rule 52.2 (all parties to comply with Practice Directions 52A to 52E) applies, but the parties are not required to comply with paragraphs 3(3), 7.2 and 27 of Practice Direction 52C.

IV. General Provisions

Scope of this section
88.16 This section applies to—   3M–162
  (a) TEO proceedings in the High Court; and
  (b) appeals to the Court of Appeal against an order of the High Court in such proceedings.

Address for filing proceedings
88.17—(1) Any TEO proceedings must be filed at the Administra- 3M–163 tive Court Office, Room C315, Royal Courts of Justice, Strand, London WC2A 2LL.
(2) Any appeals to the Court of Appeal against an order of the High Court in TEO proceedings must be filed at the Civil Appeals Office, Room E307, Royal Courts of Justice, Strand, London WC2A 2LL.

Applications for anonymity
88.18—(1) The TEO subject or the Secretary of State may apply 3M–164 for an order requiring anonymity for the TEO subject.
(2) An application under paragraph (1) may be made at any time, irrespective of whether any TEO proceedings have been commenced.
(3) An application may be made without notice to the other party.
(4) The reference in this rule to an order requiring anonymity for the TEO subject is to be construed in accordance with paragraph 6(3) of Schedule 3 to the Act.

Notification of hearings
88.19 Unless the court directs otherwise, it must serve notice of 3M–165 the date, time and place fixed for any hearing on—
  (a) every party, whether or not entitled to attend that hearing; and
  (b) if one has been appointed for the purposes of the hearing, the special advocate or those instructing the special advocate.

Proceedings which must be determined at a hearing
88.20—(1) The following proceedings must be determined at a 3M–166 hearing—

(a) a review application under section 11 of the Act (review of decisions relating to temporary exclusion orders);

(b) an appeal to the Court of Appeal from a decision or order of the High Court made in the proceedings mentioned in sub–paragraph (a) above; and

c) a hearing under rule 88.28(2) (consideration of the Secretary of State's objection or application).

(2) Paragraph (1)(b) does not apply where—

(a) the appeal is withdrawn by the appellant;

(b) the Court of Appeal allows the appeal with consent; or

(c) the Court of Appeal strikes out the appeal.

Hearings in private

3M–167   88.21—(1) If the court considers it necessary for any party and that party's legal representative to be excluded from any hearing or part of a hearing in order to secure that information is not disclosed contrary to the public interest, it must—

(a) direct accordingly; and

(b) conduct the hearing, or that part of it from which that party and that party's legal representative are excluded, in private but attended by a special advocate to represent the interests of the excluded party.

(2) The court may conduct a hearing or part of a hearing in private for any other good reason.

Appointment of a special advocate

3M–168   88.22—(1) Subject to paragraph (2), the Secretary of State must immediately give notice of the proceedings to the Attorney General (who, under paragraph 10(1) of Schedule 3 to the Act, has the power to appoint a special advocate), on—

(a) making an application under section 3(1)(b) of the Act (application for permission to impose a TEO);

(b) making a reference under paragraph 3(1) of Schedule 2 to the Act (reference of urgent TEO imposed without permission); or

(c) being served with a copy of any applications, claim or notice of appeal in proceedings to which this Part applies.

(2) Paragraph (1) applies unless—

(a) the Secretary of State does not intend to—

(i) oppose the application, claim or appeal; or

(ii) withhold closed material from a relevant party; or

(b) a special advocate has already been appointed to represent the interests of the relevant party in the proceedings and that special advocate is not prevented from communicating with that party by virtue of rule 88.24 (special advocate: communicating about proceedings).

(3) Where any proceedings to which this Section applies are pending but no special advocate has been appointed, a relevant party or the Secretary of State may request that the Attorney General appoint a special advocate.

Functions of a special advocate

88.23 The functions of a special advocate are to represent the 3M–169 interests of a relevant party by—

   (a) making submissions to the court at any hearing or part of a hearing from which the relevant party and the relevant party's legal representative are excluded;

   (b) adducing evidence and cross–examining witnesses at any such hearing or part of a hearing;

   (c) making applications to the court or seeking directions from the court where necessary; and

   (d) making written submissions to the court.

Special advocate: communicating about proceedings

88.24—(1) The special advocate may communicate with the rele- 3M–170 vant party or the relevant party's legal representative at any time before the Secretary of State serves closed material on the special advocate.

(2) After the Secretary of State serves closed material on the special advocate, the special advocate must not communicate with any person about any matter connected with the proceedings, except in accordance with paragraph (3) or (6)(b) or with a direction of the court pursuant to a request under paragraph (4).

(3) The special advocate may, without directions from the court, communicate about the proceedings with—

   (a) the court;

   (b) the Secretary of State or any person acting for the Secretary of State;

   (c) the Attorney General or any person acting for the Attorney General; or

   (d) any other person, except the relevant party or the relevant party's legal representative, with whom it is necessary for administrative purposes for the special advocate to communicate about matters not connected with the substance of the proceedings.

(4) The special advocate may request directions from the court authorising the special advocate to communicate with the relevant party or the relevant party's legal representative or with any other person.

(5) Where the special advocate makes a request for directions under paragraph (4)—

   (a) the court must notify the Secretary of State of the request and of the content of the proposed communication and the form in which it is proposed to be made; and

   b) the Secretary of State must, within a period specified by the court, file with the court and serve on the special advocate notice of any objection which the Secretary of State has to the proposed communication or to the form in which it is proposed to be made.

(6) Paragraph (2) does not prohibit the relevant party from communicating with the special advocate after the Secretary of State has served material on the special advocate, but—

    (a) the relevant party may only communicate with the special advocate in writing through the relevant party's legal representative; and

    (b) the special advocate must not reply to the communication other than in accordance with directions of the court, except that the special advocate may without such directions send a written acknowledgment of receipt to the relevant party's legal representative.

Modification of the general rules of evidence and disclosure

3M–171   88.25—(1) Part 31 (disclosure and inspection of documents), Part 32 (evidence) and Part 33 (miscellaneous rules about evidence) do not apply to any proceedings to which this Part applies.

(2) Subject to the other rules in this Part, the evidence of a witness may be given either—

    (a) orally before the court; or

    (b) in writing, in which case it must be given in such manner and at such time as the court directs.

(3) The court may also receive evidence in documentary or any other form.

(4) The court may receive evidence that would not, but for this rule, be admissible in a court of law.

(5) Every party is entitled to adduce evidence and to cross–examine witnesses during any hearing or part of a hearing from which that party and that party's legal representatives are not excluded.

(6) A special advocate is entitled to adduce evidence and to cross–examine a witness only during a hearing or part of a hearing from which the relevant party and the relevant party's legal representatives are excluded.

(7) The court may require a witness to give evidence on oath.

Filing and service of relevant material

3M–172   88.26 The Secretary of State must—

    (a) make a reasonable search for relevant material; and

    (b) file and serve that material in accordance with the rules in this Part.

Closed material

3M–173   88.27—(1) The Secretary of State—

    (a) must apply to the court for permission to withhold closed material from a relevant party or the relevant party's legal representative in accordance with this rule; and

    (b) may not rely on closed material at a hearing on notice unless a special advocate has been appointed to represent the interests of the relevant party.

(2) The Secretary of State must file with the court and, at such time as the court directs, serve on the special advocate—

    (a) the closed material;

    (b) a statement of the Secretary of State's reasons for withholding that material from the relevant party and the relevant party's legal representatives; and

(c) if the Secretary of State considers it possible to provide a summary of that material without disclosing information contrary to the public interest, a summary of that material in a form which can be served on the relevant party.

(3) The Secretary of State may at any time amend or supplement material filed under this rule, but only with—

(a) the agreement of the special advocate; or

(b) the permission of the court.

Consideration of the Secretary of State's objection or application

88.28—(1) This rule applies where the Secretary of State has—   3M–174

(a) objected under rule 88.24(5)(b) (special advocate: communicating about proceedings) to a proposed communication by the special advocate or to the form in which it is proposed to be made; or

(b) applied under rule 88.27 (closed material) for permission to withhold closed material.

(2) The court must fix a hearing for the Secretary of State and the special advocate to make oral representations, unless—

(a) the special advocate gives notice that he or she does not challenge the application or objection;

(b) the court has previously considered—

(i) an objection under rule 88.24(5)(b) to the same or substantially the same proposed communication; or

(ii) an application under rule 88.27(1) for permission to withhold the same or substantially the same material; and

is satisfied that it would be just to give permission or uphold the objection without a hearing; or

(c) the Secretary of State and the special advocate consent to the court deciding the objection or application without a hearing.

(3) If the special advocate does not challenge the objection or the application, he or she must give notice of that fact to the court and the Secretary of State no later than the end of—

(a) 14 days after the date on which the Secretary of State serves on the special advocate the notice under rule 88.24(5)(b) or the material under rule 88.27(2); or

(b) such other period as the court may direct.

(4) Where the court fixes a hearing under this rule, the Secretary of State and the special advocate must before the hearing file with the court a schedule identifying the issues which cannot be agreed between them, which must also—

(a) give brief reasons for their contentions in relation to each issue; and

(b) set out any proposals for the court to resolve those issues.

(5) A hearing under this rule shall take place in the absence of the relevant party and the relevant party's legal representative.

(6) Where the court gives permission to the Secretary of State to withhold sensitive material, the court must—

    (a) consider whether to direct the Secretary of State to serve a summary of that material on the relevant party and the relevant party's legal representative; but

    (b) ensure that any such summary does not contain material the disclosure of which would be contrary to the public interest.

(7) Where the court has not given permission to the Secretary of State to withhold sensitive material from, or has directed the Secretary of State to serve a summary of that material on, the relevant party and the relevant party's legal representative—

    (a) the Secretary of State shall not be required to serve that material or summary; but

    (b) if the Secretary of State does not do so, at a hearing on notice the court may—

        (i) if it considers that the material or anything that is required to be summarised might be of assistance to the relevant party in relation to a matter under consideration by the court, direct that the matter is withdrawn from its consideration or that the Secretary of State makes such concessions or takes such other steps as the court may direct; and

        (ii) in any other case, direct that the Secretary of State must not rely in the proceedings on that material or (as the case may be) on what is required to be summarised.

(8) The court must give permission to the Secretary of State to withhold sensitive material where it considers that disclosure of that material would be contrary to the public interest.

Order of filing and serving material and written submissions

3M–175   88.29 Subject to any directions given by the court, the parties must file and serve any material and written submissions, and the special advocate must file and serve any written submissions, in the following order—

    (a) the Secretary of State must file with the court any relevant material of which the Secretary of State is aware;

    (b) the Secretary of State must serve on—

        (i) the relevant party or the relevant party's legal representative; and

        (ii) the special advocate (as soon as one is appointed) or those instructing the special advocate,

any open material;

    (c) the relevant party must file with the court and serve on the Secretary of State and special advocate (if one is appointed) or those instructing the special advocate any written evidence which the relevant party wishes the court to take into account at the hearing;

    (d) the Secretary of State must file with the court any further relevant material;

    (e) the Secretary of State must serve on—

> (i) the relevant party or the relevant party's legal representative; and
> (ii) the special advocate (as soon as one is appointed) or those instructing the special advocate,

any open material filed with the court under sub–paragraph (d);

> (f) the Secretary of State must serve on the special advocate (if one has been appointed) any closed material;
> (g) the parties and the special advocate (if one has been appointed) must file and serve any written submissions as directed by the court.

(Rules 88.27 and 88.28 will apply where any closed material is filed by the Secretary of State.)

Failure to comply with directions

88.30—(1) Where a party or the special advocate fails to comply **3M–176** with a direction of the court, the court may serve on that person a notice which states—

> (a) the respect in which that person has failed to comply with the direction;
> (b) a time limit for complying with the direction; and
> (c) that the court may proceed to determine the proceedings before it on the material before it if that person fails to comply with the direction within that time limit.

(2) Where a party or the special advocate fails to comply with the direction after such a notice, the court may proceed in accordance with paragraph (1)(c).

Judgments

88.31—(1) Where the court gives judgment in any proceedings to **3M–177** which this Part applies, it may withhold any, or any part, of its reasons if and to the extent that it is not possible to give those reasons without disclosing information contrary to the public interest.

(2) Where the judgment of the court does not include the full reasons for its decision, the court must serve on the Secretary of State and the special advocate a separate written judgment giving those reasons.

Application by the Secretary of State for reconsideration of decision

88.32—(1) If the court proposes, in any proceedings to which this **3M–178** Part applies, to serve on a relevant party—

> (a) notice of any order or direction made or given in the absence of the Secretary of State; or
> (b) any written judgment;

then before the court serves any such notice or judgment on the relevant party, it must first serve notice on the Secretary of State of its intention to do so.

(2) The Secretary of State may, within 5 days of being served

with notice under paragraph (1), apply to the court to reconsider the terms of the order or direction or to review the terms of the proposed judgment if the Secretary of State considers that—

    a) the Secretary of State's compliance with the order or direction; or

    (b) the notification to the relevant party of any matter contained in the judgment, order or direction,

would cause information to be disclosed contrary to the public interest.

(3) Where the Secretary of State makes an application under paragraph (2), the Secretary of State must at the same time serve on the special advocate (if one has been appointed)—

    (a) a copy of the application; and

    (b) a copy of the notice served on the Secretary of State pursuant to paragraph (1).

(4) Rule 88.28 (consideration of Secretary of State's objection or application), except for paragraphs (6) and (7) of that rule, applies where a special advocate has been appointed and with any necessary modifications to the consideration of an application under paragraph (2) of this rule.

(5) The court must not serve notice or a written judgment on the relevant party as mentioned in paragraph (1) before the time for the Secretary of State or relevant person to make an application under paragraph (2) has expired.

Supply of court documents

3M–179   88.33 Unless the court otherwise directs, rule 5.4 (Register of Claims), rule 5.4B (supply of documents from court records—a party) and rule 5.4C (supply of court documents—a non–party) do not apply to any proceedings to which this Part applies.

SECTION 4

SUPREME COURT OF THE UNITED KINGDOM AND JUDICIAL COMMITTEE OF THE PRIVY COUNCIL

4A SUPREME COURT OF THE UNITED KINGDOM APPEALS

Supreme Court Rules 2009

Effect of rules 46 to 53

At the end of the first paragraph, add:

4A–46.1   Recovery of an after the event insurance premium cannot be recovered from the losing party to an appeal: *McGraddie v McGraddie* [2015] UKSC 1.

PRACTICE DIRECTION 1—GENERAL NOTE AND JURISDICTION

Delete paragraphs 1.2.17 to 1.2.19 and substitute:

Leapfrog Appeals

1.2.17 Appeals in civil matters may exceptionally be permitted to 4A–59
be made direct to the Supreme Court under sections 12 to 16 of the
Administration of Justice Act 1969, sections 14A to 14C of the
Tribunals, Courts and Enforcement Act 2007, sections 37A to 37C of
the Employment Tribunals Act 1996 and under sections 7B to 7D of
the Special Immigration Commission Act 1997. These appeals are
generally called leapfrog appeals.

1.2.18 Such appeals are permitted only if the relevant statutory
conditions are satisfied and the Supreme Court grants permission.

1.2.19 The relevant statutory conditions are set out in section 12(3)
and (3A) of the Administration of Justice Act 1969, section 14A(4)
and (5) of the Tribunals, Courts and Enforcement Act 2007, section
37A(4) and (5) of the Employment Tribunals Act 1996 and section
7B(4) and (5) of the Special Immigration Commission Act 1997.

PRACTICE DIRECTION 2—THE REGISTRY OF THE SUPREME COURT

Time limits

At the end of paragraph 2.1.13, add:

The Registrar may reject an application for permission to appeal 4A–67
solely on the ground that it is out of time.

*In paragraph 2.1.15, for "The Registrar may reject an application for permission to appeal solely
on the ground that it is out of time." substitute:*

A Respondent who has applied for public funding or other party
who has difficulty in complying with a relevant time limit should
contact the Registry.

Special cases: contempt of court and leapfrog appeals

*In paragraph 2.1.16(b), delete "a "leapfrog appeal" from the High Court must be filed within
one month from the date on which the High Court judge grants a certificate under section 12 of
the Administration of Justice Act 1969." and substitute:*

a "leapfrog appeal" must be filed within one month from the 4A–68
date on which the certificate is granted under sections 12 to 16
of the Administration of Justice Act 1969, sections 14A to 14C
of the Tribunals, Courts and Enforcement Act 2007, sections
37A to 37C of the Employment Tribunals Act 1996 or sections
7B to 7D of the Special Immigration Commission Act 1997.

PRACTICE DIRECTION 3—APPLICATIONS FOR PERMISSION TO APPEAL

Leapfrog appeals

Delete paragraph 3.6.1 and substitute:

3.6.1 In certain cases an appeal lies direct to the Supreme Court; 4A–82
see paragraph 1.2.17 of Practice Direction 1. A certificate must first
be obtained and the permission of the Supreme Court then given

before the appeal may proceed.[1] Such appeals are known as "leapfrog" appeals.

PRACTICE DIRECTION 6—THE APPEAL HEARING

Fixing the hearing date

In paragraph 6.2.2, for "Counsel should agree an order of speeches or timetable for the hearing and submit it to the Registry on the working day before the hearing." substitute:

4A–97 Counsel should agree an order of speeches and timetable for the hearing and submit it to the Registry at least 3 working days before the hearing.

Authorities

At the end of paragraph 6.5.1, add:

4A–102 The following paragraphs give guidance on the arrangement and order of the volumes but where the parties consider that a different order or arrangement would be of greater assistance to the Court, that order or arrangement should be adopted.

Form and content of authorities volumes

In paragraph 6.5.2, after "...authorities should appear in alphabetical order." add:

(The indexes must be included in the pagination.)

PRACTICE DIRECTION 8—MISCELLANEOUS MATTERS

Effect of application by respondent for public funding/legal aid

In paragraph 8.12.5, for "the Registrar should be informed within the original time limit for filing the statement and appendix." substitute:

4A–126 they should inform the Registrar as soon as possible and in any event within the original time limit for filing the statement and appendix, particularly if they anticipate any possible difficulty in complying with a relevant time limit.

Delete paragraph 8.17.1 and substitute:

Broadcasting

4A–131 **8.17.1** The President and the Justices of the Supreme Court will normally accede to a request from a broadcaster to make available audio or video footage of proceedings before the Court (either live or after the event) where such use does not affect the administration of justice and the recording and broadcasting is conducted in accordance with the protocol[2] which has been agreed with representatives

---

[1] Sections 12 to 16 of the Administration of Justice Act 1969 (as amended by the Criminal Justice and Courts Act 2015) provide circumstances in which decisions of the High Court or the Divisional Court may be "leapfrogged" to the Supreme Court. Sections 14A to 14C of the Tribunals, Courts and Enforcement Act 2007 and sections 37A to 37C of the Employment Tribunals Act 1996 (inserted by the Criminal Justice and Courts Act 2015) provide circumstances in which decisions of certain tribunals which have High Court equivalent jurisdiction may be "leapfrogged" to the Supreme Court and sections 7B to 7D of the Special Immigration Appeals Commission Act 1997 (inserted by the Criminal Justice and Courts Act 2015) provide circumstances in which SIAC decisions may be "leapfrogged" to the Supreme Court.

[2] The protocol ensures that certain types of proceedings and some aspects of

of several UK broadcasters. Permission to broadcast proceedings must be sought from the President or the presiding Justice on each occasion and requires his or her express approval. Where the President or the presiding Justice grants permission, he may impose such conditions as he considers to be appropriate including the obtaining of consent from all the parties involved in the proceedings.

PRACTICE DIRECTION 13—COSTS

SECTION 3: GUIDELINE HOURLY RATES FOR SOLICITORS

Delete box headed "The National 2/3 rates apply to" and substitute:

The National 2 rates apply to   4A–177

Bath, Cheltenham and Gloucester, Taunton, Yeovil
Birmingham Outer
Bradford (Dewsbury, Halifax, Huddersfield, Keighly & Skipton)
Bury
Chelmsford North, Cambridge County, Peterborough, Bury St E, Norfolk, Lowestoft
Cheshire & North Wales
Coventry, Rugby, Nuneaton, Stratford and Warwick
Cumbria
Devon, Cornwall
Exeter, Plymouth
Grimsby, Skegness
Hull (City)
Kidderminster
Leeds Outer, Wakefield & Pontefract
Leigh
Lincoln
Luton, Bedford, St Albans, Hitchin, Hertford
Manchester Outer, Oldham, Bolton, Tameside
Newcastle (other than City Centre)
Northampton & Leicester
Nottingham & Derbyshire
Sheffield, Doncaster and South Yorkshire
Shrewsbury, Telford, Ludlow, Oswestry
South & West Wales
Southport
Stafford, Stoke, Tamworth
St Helens
Stockport, Altrincham, Salford
Swansea, Newport, Cardiff (Outer)
Teeside
Wigan
Wolverhampton, Walsall, Dudley & Stourbridge
Worcester, Hereford, Evesham and Redditch
York, Harrogate

proceedings such as private discussions between parties and their advisers are not recorded, televised or filmed. It also regulates the use of extracts of proceedings and prevents their use in certain types of programmes (such as party political broadcasts) and in any form of advertising or publicity.

SECTION 5

EUROPEAN JURISDICTION

Regulation (EU) No 1215/2012 of the European Parliament and of the Council of 12 December 2012 on jurisdiction and the recognition and enforcement of judgments in civil and commercial matters

Add new paragraphs 5–316.1 to 5–316.8:

Article 71a

5–316.1 1. For the purposes of this Regulation, a court common to several Member States as specified in paragraph 2 (a 'common court') shall be deemed to be a court of a Member State when, pursuant to the instrument establishing it, such a common court exercises jurisdiction in matters falling within the scope of this Regulation.

2. For the purposes of this Regulation, each of the following courts shall be a common court:

(a) the Unified Patent Court established by the Agreement on a Unified Patent Court signed on 19 February 2013 (the 'UPC Agreement'); and

(b) the Benelux Court of Justice established by the Treaty of 31 March 1965 concerning the establishment and statute of a Benelux Court of Justice (the 'Benelux Court of Justice Treaty').

Note

5–316.2 Article 71a was inserted by Council Regulation (EU) No 542/2014 of 15 May 2014.

Article 71b

5–316.3 The jurisdiction of a common court shall be determined as follows:

1. a common court shall have jurisdiction where, under this Regulation, the courts of a Member State party to the instrument establishing the common court would have jurisdiction in a matter governed by that instrument;

2. where the defendant is not domiciled in a Member State, and this Regulation does not otherwise confer jurisdiction over him, Chapter II shall apply as appropriate regardless of the defendant's domicile.

Application may be made to a common court for provisional, including protective, measures even if the courts of a third State have jurisdiction as to the substance of the matter;

3. where a common court has jurisdiction over a defendant under point 2 in a dispute relating to an infringement of a European patent giving rise to damage within the Union, that court may also exercise jurisdiction in relation to damage arising outside the Union from such an infringement.

Such jurisdiction may only be established if property belonging to the defendant is located in any Member State party to the instrument establishing the common court and the dispute has a sufficient connection with any such Member State.

Note

5–316.4 Article 71b was inserted by Council Regulation (EU) No 542/2014 of 15 May 2014.

Article 71c

1. Articles 29 to 32 shall apply where proceedings are brought in a **5–316.5** common court and in a court of a Member State not party to the instrument establishing the common court.

2. Articles 29 to 32 shall apply where, during the transitional period referred to in Article 83 of the UPC Agreement, proceedings are brought in the Unified Patent Court and in a court of a Member State party to the UPC Agreement.

Note

Article 71c was inserted by Council Regulation (EU) No 542/2014 of 15 May 2014.   **5–316.6**

Article 71d

This Regulation shall apply to the recognition and enforcement of: **5–316.7**

(a) judgments given by a common court which are to be recognised and enforced in a Member State not party to the instrument establishing the common court; and

(b) judgments given by the courts of a Member State not party to the instrument establishing the common court which are to be recognised and enforced in a Member State party to that instrument.

However, where recognition and enforcement of a judgment given by a common court is sought in a Member State party to the instrument establishing the common court, any rules of that instrument on recognition and enforcement shall apply instead of the rules of this Regulation.

Note

Article 71d was inserted by Council Regulation (EU) No 542/2014 of 15 May 2014.   **5–316.8**

Delete Annex I and substitute:

Annex I

5–327

25.2.2015   EN   Official Journal of the European Union   L 54/3

ANNEX

'ANNEX I

CERTIFICATE CONCERNING A JUDGMENT IN CIVIL AND COMMERCIAL MATTERS

Article 53 of Regulation (EU) No 1215/2012 of the European Parliament and of the Council on jurisdiction and the recognition and enforcement of judgments in civil and commercial matters

1.	COURT OF ORIGIN
1.1.	Name:
1.2.	Address:
1.2.1.	Street and number/PO box:
1.2.2.	Place and postal code:
1.2.3.	Member State:

AT ☐ BE ☐ BG ☐ CY ☐ CZ ☐ DK ☐ DE ☐ EE ☐ EL ☐ ES ☐ FI ☐ FR ☐ HR ☐ HU ☐ IE ☐ IT ☐ LT☐
LU ☐ LV ☐ MT ☐ NL ☐ PL ☐ PT ☐ RO ☐ SE ☐ SI ☐ SK ☐ UK ☐

1.3.	Telephone:
1.4.	Fax:
1.5.	E-mail (if available):
2.	CLAIMANT(S) (^{1})
2.1.	Surname and given name(s)/name of company or organisation:
2.2.	Identification number (if applicable and if available):
2.3.	Date (dd/mm/yyyy) and place of birth or, if legal person, of incorporation/formation/registration (if relevant and if available):
2.4.	Address:
2.4.1.	Street and number/PO box:
2.4.2.	Place and postal code:
2.4.3.	Country:

AT ☐ BE ☐ BG ☐ CY ☐ CZ ☐ DK ☐ DE ☐ EE ☐ EL ☐ ES ☐ FI ☐ FR ☐ HR ☐ HU ☐ IE ☐ IT ☐ LT☐
LU ☐ LV ☐ MT ☐ NL ☐ PL ☐ PT ☐ RO ☐ SE ☐ SI ☐ SK ☐ UK ☐ Other (please specify (ISO-code)) ☐

2.5.	E-mail (if available):
3.	DEFENDANT(S) (^{2})
3.1.	Surname and given name(s)/name of company or organisation:
3.2.	Identification number (if applicable and if available):
3.3.	Date (dd/mm/yyyy) and place of birth or, if legal person, of incorporation/formation/registration (if relevant and if available):
3.4.	Address:
3.4.1.	Street and number/PO box:
3.4.2.	Place and postal code:
3.4.3.	Country:

AT ☐ BE ☐ BG ☐ CY ☐ CZ ☐ DK ☐ DE ☐ EE ☐ EL ☐ ES ☐ FI ☐ FR ☐ HR ☐ HU ☐ IE ☐ IT ☐ LT☐
LU ☐ LV ☐ MT ☐ NL ☐ PL ☐ PT ☐ RO ☐ SE ☐ SI ☐ SK ☐ UK ☐ Other (please specify (ISO-code)) ☐

3.5.	E-mail (if available):

4.	THE JUDGMENT
4.1.	Date (dd/mm/yyyy) of the judgment:
4.2.	Reference number of the judgment:
4.3.	The judgment was given in default of appearance:
4.3.1.	☐ No
4.3.2.	☐ Yes (please indicate the date (dd/mm/yyyy) on which the document instituting the proceedings or an equivalent document was served on the defendant):
4.4.	The judgment is enforceable in the Member State of origin without any further conditions having to be met:
4.4.1.	☐ Yes (please indicate the date (dd/mm/yyyy) on which the judgment was declared enforceable, if applicable):
4.4.2.	☐ Yes, but only against the following person(s) (please specify):
4.4.3.	☐ Yes, but limited to part(s) of the judgment (please specify):
4.4.4.	☐ The judgment does not contain an enforceable obligation
4.5.	As of the date of issue of the certificate, the judgment has been served on the defendant(s):
4.5.1.	☐ Yes (please indicate the date of service (dd/mm/yyyy) if known):
4.5.1.1.	The judgment was served in the following language(s):

BG ☐ ES ☐ CS ☐ DK ☐ DE ☐ ET ☐ EL ☐ EN ☐ FR ☐ HR ☐ GA ☐ IT ☐ LV ☐ LT ☐ HU ☐ MT ☐ NL ☐ PL ☐ PT ☐ RO ☐ SK ☐ SL ☐ FI ☐ SV ☐ Other (please specify (ISO-code)) ☐

4.5.2.	☐ Not to the knowledge of the court
4.6.	Terms of the judgment and interest:
4.6.1.	Judgment on a monetary claim (^{3})
4.6.1.1.	Short description of the subject-matter of the case:
4.6.1.2.	The court has ordered:

.... (surname and given name(s)/name of company or organisation) (^{4})

to make a payment to:

.... (surname and given name(s)/name of company or organisation)

4.6.1.2.1.	If more than one person has been held liable for one and the same claim, the whole amount may be collected from any one of them:
4.6.1.2.1.1.	☐ Yes
4.6.1.2.1.2.	☐ No
4.6.1.3.	Currency:

☐ euro (EUR) ☐ Bulgarian lev (BGN) ☐ Czech koruna (CZK) ☐ Danish krone (DKK) ☐ kuna (HRK) ☐ Hungarian forint (HUF) ☐ Polish zloty (PLN) ☐ pound sterling (GBP) ☐ Romanian leu (RON) ☐ Swedish krona (SEK) ☐ other (please specify (ISO code)):

| 4.6.1.4. | Principal amount: |
| 4.6.1.4.1. | ☐ Amount to be paid in one sum |

25.2.2015 | EN | Official Journal of the European Union | L 54/5

4.6.1.4.2. ☐ Amount to be paid in instalments (⁵)

Due date (dd/mm/yyyy)	Amount

4.6.1.4.3. ☐ Amount to be paid regularly

4.6.1.4.3.1. ☐ per day

4.6.1.4.3.2. ☐ per week

4.6.1.4.3.3. ☐ other (state frequency):

4.6.1.4.3.4. From date (dd/mm/yyyy) or event:

4.6.1.4.3.5. If applicable, until (date (dd/mm/yyyy) or event):

4.6.1.5. Interest, if applicable:

4.6.1.5.1. Interest:

4.6.1.5.1.1. ☐ Not specified in the judgment

4.6.1.5.1.2. ☐ Yes, specified in the judgment as follows:

4.6.1.5.1.2.1. Amount:

or:

4.6.1.5.1.2.2. Rate ... %

4.6.1.5.1.2.3. Interest due from .... (date (dd/mm/yyyy) or event) to .... (date (dd/mm/yyyy) or event) (⁶)

4.6.1.5.2. ☐ Statutory interest (if applicable) to be calculated in accordance with (please specify relevant statute):

4.6.1.5.2.1. Interest due from .... (date (dd/mm/yyyy) or event) to .... (date (dd/mm/yyyy) or event) (⁶)

4.6.1.5.3. ☐ Capitalisation of interest (if applicable, please specify):

4.6.2. Judgment ordering a provisional, including a protective, measure:

4.6.2.1. Short description of the subject matter of the case and the measure ordered:

4.6.2.2. The measure was ordered by a court having jurisdiction as to the substance of the matter:

4.6.2.2.1. ☐ Yes

4.6.3. Other type of judgment:

4.6.3.1. Short description of the subject-matter of the case and the ruling by the court:

4.7. Costs (⁷):

4.7.1. Currency:

☐ euro (EUR) ☐ Bulgarian lev (BGN) ☐ Czech koruna (CZK) ☐ Danish krone (DKK) ☐ kuna (HRK) ☐ Hungarian forint (HUF) ☐ Polish zloty (PLN) ☐ pound sterling (GBP) ☐ Romanian leu (RON) ☐ Swedish krona (SEK) ☐ other (please specify (ISO code)):

4.7.2. The following person(s) against whom enforcement is sought has/have been ordered to bear the costs:

4.7.2.1. Surname and given name(s)/name of company or organisation: (⁸)

4.7.2.2. If more than one person has been ordered to bear the costs, the whole amount may be collected from any one of them:

4.7.2.2.1.	☐ Yes
4.7.2.2.2.	☐ No
4.7.3.	The costs of which recovery is sought are as follows: (⁵)
4.7.3.1.	☐ The costs have been fixed in the judgment by way of a total amount (please specify amount):
4.7.3.2.	☐ The costs have been fixed in the judgment by way of a percentage of total costs (please specify percentage of total):
4.7.3.3.	☐ Liability for the costs has been determined in the judgment and the exact amounts are as follows:
4.7.3.3.1.	☐ Court fees:
4.7.3.3.2.	☐ Lawyers' fees:
4.7.3.3.3.	☐ Cost of service of documents:
4.7.3.3.4.	☐ Other:
4.7.3.4.	☐ Other (please specify):
4.7.4.	Interest on costs:
4.7.4.1.	☐ Not applicable
4.7.4.2.	☐ Interest specified in the judgment
4.7.4.2.1.	☐ Amount:
	or
4.7.4.2.2.	☐ Rate ... %
4.7.4.2.2.1.	Interest due from .... (date (dd/mm/yyyy) or event) to .... (date (dd/mm/yyyy) or event) (⁶)
4.7.4.3.	☐ Statutory interest (if applicable) to be calculated in accordance with (please specify relevant statute):
4.7.4.3.1.	Interest due from .... (date (dd/mm/yyyy) or event) to .... (date (dd/mm/yyyy) or event): (⁶)
4.7.4.4.	☐ Capitalisation of interest (if applicable, please specify):

Done at: ...

Signature and/or stamp of the court of origin:

(¹) Insert information for all claimants if the judgment concerns more than one.
(²) Insert information for all defendants if the judgment concerns more than one.
(³) If the judgment only concerns costs relating to a claim which has been decided in an earlier judgment, leave point 4.6.1. blank and go to point 4.7.
(⁴) If more than one person has been ordered to make a payment, insert information for all persons.
(⁵) Insert information for each instalment.
(⁶) Insert information for all periods if more than one.
(⁷) This point also covers situations where the costs are awarded in a separate judgment.
(⁸) Insert information for all persons if more than one.
(⁹) In the event that the costs may be recovered from several persons, insert the breakdown for each person separately.

———

Add new paragraph 5–327.1:

Note

    Annex I was substituted by Council Regulation (EU) No 2015/281 of 26 November **5–327.1** 2014.

Delete Annex II and substitute:

Annex II

5–328

25.2.2015 ⬜ EN ⬜ Official Journal of the European Union L 54/7

ANNEX II

CERTIFICATE CONCERNING AN AUTHENTIC INSTRUMENT/COURT SETTLEMENT ([1]) IN CIVIL AND COMMERCIAL MATTERS

Article 60 of Regulation (EU) No 1215/2012 of the European Parliament and of the Council on jurisdiction and the recognition and enforcement of judgments in civil and commercial matters

1.	COURT OR COMPETENT AUTHORITY ISSUING THE CERTIFICATE
1.1.	Name:
1.2.	Address:
1.2.1.	Street and number/PO box:
1.2.2.	Place and postal code:
1.2.3.	Member State:

AT ⬜ BE ⬜ BG ⬜ CY ⬜ CZ ⬜ DK ⬜ DE ⬜ EE ⬜ EL ⬜ ES ⬜ FI ⬜ FR ⬜ HR ⬜ HU ⬜ IE ⬜ IT ⬜ LT ⬜ LU ⬜ LV ⬜ MT ⬜ NL ⬜ PL ⬜ PT ⬜ RO ⬜ SE ⬜ SI ⬜ SK ⬜ UK ⬜

1.3.	Telephone:
1.4.	Fax:
1.5.	E-mail (if available):
2.	AUTHENTIC INSTRUMENT
2.1.	Authority which has drawn up the authentic instrument (if different from the authority issuing the certificate)
2.1.1.	Name and designation of authority:
2.1.2.	Address:
2.2.	Date (dd/mm/yyyy) on which the authentic instrument was drawn up by the authority referred to in point 2.1:
2.3.	Reference number of the authentic instrument (if applicable):
2.4.	Date (dd/mm/yyyy) on which the authentic instrument was registered in the Member State of origin (to be filled in only if the date of registration determines the legal effect of the instrument and this date is different from the date indicated in point 2.2):
2.4.1.	Reference number in the register (if applicable):
3.	COURT SETTLEMENT
3.1.	Court which approved the court settlement or before which the court settlement was concluded (if different from the court issuing the certificate)
3.1.1.	Name of court:
3.1.2.	Address:
3.2.	Date (dd/mm/yyyy) of the court settlement:
3.3.	Reference number of the court settlement:
4.	PARTIES TO THE AUTHENTIC INSTRUMENT/COURT SETTLEMENT:
4.1.	Name(s) of creditor(s) (surname and given name(s)/name of company or organisation) ([2]):
4.1.1.	Identification number (if applicable and if available):
4.1.2.	Date (dd/mm/yyyy) and place of birth or, if legal person, of incorporation/formation/registration (if relevant and if available):
4.2.	Name(s) of debtor(s) (surname and given name(s)/name of company or organisation) ([3]):
4.2.1.	Identification number (if applicable and if available):
4.2.2.	Date (dd/mm/yyyy) and place of birth or, if legal person, of incorporation/formation/registration (if relevant and if available):
4.3.	Name of other parties, if any (surname and given name(s)/name of company or organisation) ([4]):

L 54/8 [EN] Official Journal of the European Union 25.2.2015

4.3.1.	Identification number (if applicable and if available):
4.3.2.	Date (dd/mm/yyyy) and place of birth or, if legal person, of incorporation/formation/registration (if relevant and if available):
5.	ENFORCEABILITY OF THE AUTHENTIC INSTRUMENT/COURT SETTLEMENT IN THE MEMBER STATE OF ORIGIN
5.1.	The authentic instrument/court settlement is enforceable in the Member State of origin:
5.1.1.	☐ Yes
5.2.	Terms of the authentic instrument/court settlement and interest
5.2.1.	Authentic instrument/court settlement relating to a monetary claim
5.2.1.1.	Short description of the subject matter:
5.2.1.2.	Under the authentic instrument/court settlement:

.... (surname and given name(s)/name of company or organisation) (^{6})

has to make a payment to:

.... (surname and given name(s)/name of company or organisation)

5.2.1.2.1.	If more than one person has been held liable for one and the same claim, the whole amount may be collected from any one of them:
5.2.1.2.1.1.	☐ Yes
5.2.1.2.1.2.	☐ No
5.2.1.3.	Currency:

☐ euro (EUR) ☐ Bulgarian lev (BGN) ☐ Czech koruna (CZK) ☐ Danish krone (DKK) ☐ kuna (HRK) ☐ Hungarian forint (HUF) ☐ Polish zloty (PLN) ☐ pound sterling (GBP) ☐ Romanian leu (RON) ☐ Swedish krona (SEK) ☐ other (please specify (ISO code)):

5.2.1.4.	Principal amount:
5.2.1.4.1.	☐ Amount to be paid in one sum
5.2.1.4.2.	☐ Amount to be paid in instalments (^{6})

Due date (dd/mm/yyyy)	Amount

5.2.1.4.3.	☐ Amount to be paid regularly
5.2.1.4.3.1.	☐ per day
5.2.1.4.3.2.	☐ per week
5.2.1.4.3.3.	☐ other (state frequency):
5.2.1.4.3.4.	From date (dd/mm/yyyy) or event:
5.2.1.4.3.5.	If applicable, until .... (date (dd/mm/yyyy) or event)
5.2.1.5.	Interest, if applicable
5.2.1.5.1.	Interest:
5.2.1.5.1.1.	☐ Not specified in the authentic instrument/court settlement
5.2.1.5.1.2.	☐ Yes, specified in the authentic instrument/court settlement as follows:

Section 5: European Jurisdiction

5.2.1.5.1.2.1.   Amount:

or

5.2.1.5.1.2.2.   Rate ... %

5.2.1.5.1.2.3.   Interest due from .... (date (dd/mm/yyyy) or event) to ....,............. (date (dd/mm/yyyy) or event) (^{7})

5.2.1.5.2.   ☐ Statutory interest (if applicable) to be calculated in accordance with (please specify relevant statute):

5.2.1.5.2.1.   Interest due from .... (date (dd/mm/yyyy) or event) to .... (date (dd/mm/yyyy) or event) (^{7})

5.2.1.5.3.   ☐ Capitalisation of interest (if applicable, please specify):

5.2.2.   Authentic instrument/court settlement relating to a non-monetary enforceable obligation:

5.2.2.1.   Short description of the enforceable obligation

5.2.2.2.   The obligation referred to in point 5.2.2.1. is enforceable against the following person(s) (^{8}) (surname and given name(s)/name of company or organisation):

Done at: ...

Signature and/or stamp of the court or competent authority issuing the certificate:

(^{1})   Delete as appropriate throughout the certificate.
(^{2})   Insert information for all creditors if more than one.
(^{3})   Insert information for all debtors if more than one.
(^{4})   Insert information for other parties (if any).
(^{5})   If more than one person has been ordered to make a payment, insert information for all persons.
(^{6})   Insert information for each instalment.
(^{7})   Insert information for all periods if more than one.
(^{8})   Insert information for all persons if more than one.'

Add new paragraph 5–328.1:

Note

5–328.1   Annex II was substituted by Council Regulation (EU) No 2015/281 of 26 November 2014.

SECTION 6

ADMINISTRATION OF FUNDS, PROPERTY AND AFFAIRS

6A COURT FUNDS

Court Funds Rules 2011

Note

Delete "certified".   **6A–61**

INVESTMENTS ON BEHALF OF CHILDREN AND PROTECTED BENEFICIARIES

Wills, grants of probate or letters of administration

In the second sentence, for "http://www.nationalarchives.gov.uk/documentsonline/wills.asp" substitute:
   http://discovery.nationalarchives.gov.uk   **6A–213**

Birth, marriage and death certificates

In the first paragraph, after "email" add:
   (certificate.service@gro.gsi.gov.uk)   **6A–214**

Estates which have fallen to the Crown

In the second paragraph, for "The Treasury Solicitor" substitute:
   The Government Legal Department   **6A–216**

Funds held in court in Northern Ireland

Delete first sentence and substitute:
   For funds lodged in court in Northern Ireland since 1921, write to: the Court **6A–218**
Funds Office, Ground Floor, Laganside House, 23–27 Oxford Street, Belfast BT1 3LA
(Tel: 028 9072 8894/8849/8950/8891, email: courtfundsoffice@courtsni.gov.uk).

SECTION 7

LEGAL REPRESENTATIVES—COSTS AND LITIGATION FUNDING

7A1 LITIGATION FUNDING BEFORE APRIL 1, 2013

FUNDING ARRANGEMENTS

CONDITIONAL FEES

Add at end:

7A1–56   Upheld by the Court of Appeal: [2015] EWCA Civ 18.

7A2 LITIGATION FUNDING AFTER APRIL 1, 2013

INTRODUCTION

At the end of the sixth paragraph, add:

7A2–1   The Supreme Court has confirmed that, in the absence of agreement or specific statutory provision to the contrary, a party cannot recover an ATE premium as part of the costs of legal expenses: *McGraddie v McGraddie* [2015] UKSC 1.

SECTION 8

LIMITATION

Limitation Act 1980

Add new paragraph 8–91.1:

Section 33 and abuse of process

8–91.1   In *Lloyd v Humphries & Glasgow Ltd* [2015] EWHC 525 (QB) the court exercised its discretion under the Limitation Act 1980 s.33 to allow a claim for damages for mesothelioma to proceed after the expiry of the limitation period where the claimant had acted promptly and reasonably once he knew he had a cause of action and had taken all the legal and medical advice which it was reasonable for him to take. The fact that he had settled actions against two other former employers within the limitation period did not mean that it was an abuse of process to allow the later claim to proceed, as the employer against whom that later claim was being brought had resisted the proceedings pending the outcome of a House of Lords decision.

SECTION 9

JURISDICTIONAL AND PROCEDURAL LEGISLATION

9A   MAIN STATUTES

Senior Courts Act 1981

PART II

JURISDICTION

"criminal cause or matter"

At the end of the third paragraph, add:

That dictum was relied on by the Court of Appeal in *R. (Panesar) v Central Criminal* **9A–64.1**
Court [2014] EWCA Civ 1613, C.A., [2015] 1 W.L.R. 2577, CA, where the Court held
that it had no jurisdiction to entertain an appeal from the High Court dismissing an
application for judicial review of a Crown Court decision granting the Revenue's application for an order under the Criminal Justice and Police Act 2001 s.59(5)(b)
permitting the retention of material seized in execution of a search warrant
notwithstanding the fact that the warrant had been quashed.

Delete s.31 and substitute:

Application for judicial review

31.—(1) An application to the High Court for one or more of the **9A–101**
following forms of relief, namely—
   (a) a mandatory, prohibiting or quashing order,
   (b) a declaration or injunction under subsection (2); or
   (c) an injunction under section 30 restraining a person not
      entitled to do so from acting in an office to which that sec-
      tion applies,
      shall be made in accordance with rules of court by a pro-
      cedure to be known as an application for judicial review.
   (2) A declaration may be made or an injunction granted under
this subsection in any case where an application for judicial review,
seeking that relief, has been made and the High Court considers
that, having regard to—
   (a) the nature of the matters in respect of which relief may be
      granted by mandatory, prohibiting and quashing orders;
   (b) the nature of the persons and bodies against whom relief
      may be granted by such orders; and
   (c) all the circumstances of the case, it would be just and con-
      venient for the declaration to be made or the injunction to
      be granted, as the case may be.
   (2A) The High Court—
   (a) must refuse to grant relief on an application for judicial
      review, and
   (b) may not make an award under subsection (4) on such an
      application,
      if it appears to the court to be highly likely that the
      outcome for the applicant would not have been substan-
      tially different if the conduct complained of had not
      occurred.

(2B) The court may disregard the requirements in subsection (2A)(a) and (b) if it considers that it is appropriate to do so for reasons of exceptional public interest.

(2C) If the court grants relief or makes an award in reliance on subsection (2B), the court must certify that the condition in subsection (2B) is satisfied.

(3) No application for judicial review shall be made unless the leave of the High Court has been obtained in accordance with rules of court; and the court shall not grant leave to make such an application unless—

> (a) it considers that the applicant has a sufficient interest in the matter to which the application relates, and
>
> (b) the applicant has provided the court with any information about the financing of the application that is specified in rules of court for the purposes of this paragraph.

(3A) The information that may be specified for the purposes of subsection (3)(b) includes—

> (a) information about the source, nature and extent of financial resources available, or likely to be available, to the applicant to meet liabilities arising in connection with the application, and
>
> (b) if the applicant is a body corporate that is unable to demonstrate that it is likely to have financial resources available to meet such liabilities, information about its members and about their ability to provide financial support for the purposes of the application.

(3B) Rules of court under subsection (3)(b) that specify information identifying those who are, or are likely to be, sources of financial support must provide that only a person whose financial support (whether direct or indirect) exceeds, or is likely to exceed, a level set out in the rules has to be identified.

This subsection does not apply to rules that specify information described in subsection (3A)(b).

(3C) When considering whether to grant leave to make an application for judicial review, the High Court—

> (a) may of its own motion consider whether the outcome for the applicant would have been substantially different if the conduct complained of had not occurred, and
>
> (b) must consider that question if the defendant asks it to do so.

(3D) If, on considering that question, it appears to the High Court to be highly likely that the outcome for the applicant would not have been substantially different, the court must refuse to grant leave.

(3E) The court may disregard the requirement in subsection (3D) if it considers that it is appropriate to do so for reasons of exceptional public interest.

(3F) If the court grants leave in reliance on subsection (3E), the court must certify that the condition in subsection (3E) is satisfied.

(4) On an application for judicial review the High Court may award to the applicant damages, restitution or the recovery of a sum due if—

> (a) the application includes a claim for such an award arising from any matter to which the application relates; and

(b) the court is satisfied that such an award would have been made if the claim had been made in an action begun by the applicant at the time of making the application.

(5) If, on an application for judicial review, the High Court quashes the decision to which the application relates, it may in addition—

(a) remit the matter to the court, tribunal or authority which made the decision, with a direction to reconsider the matter and reach a decision in accordance with the findings of the High Court, or

(b) substitute its own decision for the decision in question.

(5A) But the power conferred by subsection (5)(b) is exercisable only if

(a) the decision in question was made by a court or tribunal,

(b) the decision is quashed on the ground that there has been an error of law, and

(c) without the error, there would have been only one decision which the court or tribunal could have reached.

(5B) Unless the High Court otherwise directs, a decision substituted by it under subsection (5)(b) has effect as if it were a decision of the relevant court or tribunal.

(6) Where the High Court considers that there has been undue delay in making an application for judicial review, the court may refuse to grant—

(a) leave for the making of the application; or

(b) any relief sought on the application,

if it considers that the granting of the relief sought would be likely to cause substantial hardship to, or substantially prejudice the rights of, any person or would be detrimental to good administration.

(7) Subsection (6) is without prejudice to any enactment or rule of court which has the effect of limiting the time within which an application for judicial review may be made.

(8) In this section "the conduct complained of", in relation to an application for judicial review, means the conduct (or alleged conduct) of the defendant that the applicant claims justifies the High Court in granting relief.

Note

Add at end:

Sub–sections (2A)–(2C), (3C)–(3F), (8) inserted by the Criminal Justice and Courts **9A–102** Act 2015 s.84(1), with effect from April 13, 2015 (SI 2015/778). Subsection (3) amended and subss.(3A), (3B) inserted by the Criminal Justice and Courts Act 2015 s.85(1), (2). Those amendments are not yet in force. Express provisions dealing with "information about the financing of the application" are contained in s.86 of the 2015 Act; see para.9A–1310 below.

Costs

Costs in civil division of Court of Appeal, High Court and county courts

Add new s.51(7A):

(7A) Where the court exercises a power under subsection (6) in relation to costs incurred by a party, it must inform such of the following as it considers appropriate— **9A–199**

(a) an approved regulator;

(b) the Director of Legal Aid Casework.

Add new s.51(12A):

(12A) In subsection (7A)—

"approved regulator" has the meaning given by section 20 of the Legal Services Act 2007;

"the Director of Legal Aid Casework" means the civil servant designated under section 4 of the Legal Aid, Sentencing and Punishment of Offenders Act 2012.

Note

Add at end:

9A–200   Subsections (7A), (12A) inserted by the Criminal Justice and Courts Act 2015 s.67, with effect from April 13, 2015 (SI 2015/778).

SCHEDULE 1

Distribution of Business in High Court

Queen's Bench Division

After paragraph 2(bd) insert:

9A–399   (be) all TEO proceedings (within the meaning given by paragraph 1 of Schedule 3 to the Counter–Terrorism and Security Act 2015 (proceedings relating to temporary exclusion orders));

Note

Add at end:

9A–399.1   Paragraph 2(be) inserted by the Counter–Terrorism and Security Act 2015 s.15(1), with effect from February 12, 2015.

Note

Add at end:

9A–401   Paragraph 3(l) inserted by the Civil Jurisdiction and Judgments (Protection Measures) Regulations 2014 (SI 2014/3296) reg.3(3), with effect from January 11, 2015.

Tribunals, Courts and Enforcement Act 2007

Right to appeal to Court of Appeal etc.

In s.13(6A)(a), after "principle" add:

9A–1007   or practice

Note

Add at end:

9A–1007.1   Paragraph (a) of s.13(6A) was amended by the Criminal Justice and Courts Act 2015 s.83(2). The amendment was brought into force on April 13, 2015 by the Criminal Justice and Courts Act 2015 (Commencement No.1, Saving and Transitional Provisions) Order 2015 (SI 2015/778).

Upper Tribunal's "judicial review" jurisdiction

Add new s.15(5A) and (5B):

9A–1009   (5A) In cases arising under the law of England and Wales, subsections (2A) and (2B) of section 31 of the Senior Courts Act 1981 apply to the Upper Tribunal when deciding whether to grant relief under subsection (1) as they apply to the High Court when deciding whether to grant relief on an application for judicial review.

(5B) If the tribunal grants relief in reliance on section 31(2B) of the Senior Courts Act 1981 as applied by subsection (5A), the tribunal must certify that the condition in section 31(2B) as so applied is satisfied.

Add new paragraph 9A–1009.1:

Note

Sub–sections (5A) and (5B) inserted by the Criminal Justice and Courts Act 2015 **9A–1009.1** s.84(4). That amendment is not yet in force.

Application for relief under section 15(1)

Delete s.16(3) and substitute:

(3) The tribunal may not grant permission (or leave) to make the **9A–1010** application unless—

- (a) it considers that the applicant has a sufficient interest in the matter to which the application relates, and
- (b) in cases arising under the law of England and Wales, the applicant has provided the tribunal with any information about the financing of the application that is specified in Tribunal Procedure Rules for the purposes of this paragraph.

(3A) The information that may be specified for the purposes of subsection (3)(b) includes—

- (a) information about the source, nature and extent of financial resources available, or likely to be available, to the applicant to meet liabilities arising in connection with the application, and
- (b) if the applicant is a body corporate that is unable to demonstrate that it is likely to have financial resources available to meet such liabilities, information about its members and about their ability to provide financial support for the purposes of the application.

(3B) Tribunal Procedure Rules under subsection (3)(b) that specify information identifying those who are, or are likely to be, sources of financial support must provide that only a person whose financial support (whether direct or indirect) exceeds, or is likely to exceed, a level set out in the rules has to be identified.

This subsection does not apply to rules that specify information described in subsection (3A)(b).

(3C) In cases arising under the law of England and Wales, when considering whether to grant permission to make the application, the tribunal—

- (a) may of its own initiative consider whether the outcome for the applicant would have been substantially different if the conduct complained of had not occurred, and
- (b) must consider that question if the respondent asks it to do so.

(3D) In subsection (3C) "the conduct complained of" means the conduct (or alleged conduct) of the respondent that the applicant claims justifies the tribunal in granting relief.

(3E) If, on considering the question mentioned in subsection (3C)(a) and (b), it appears to the tribunal to be highly likely that the outcome for the applicant would not have been substantially different, the tribunal must refuse to grant permission.

(3F) The tribunal may disregard the requirement in subsection (3E) if it considers that it is appropriate to do so for reasons of exceptional public interest.

(3G) If the tribunal grants permission in reliance on subsection (3F), the tribunal must certify that the condition in subsection (3F) is satisfied.

Add new s.16(6A) and (6B):

(6A) In cases arising under the law of England and Wales, subsections (2A) and (2B) of section 31 of the Senior Courts Act 1981 apply to the Upper Tribunal as regards the making of an award under subsection (6) as they apply to the High Court as regards the making of an award under section 31(4) of the Senior Courts Act 1981.

(6B) If the tribunal makes an award in reliance on section 31(2B) of the Senior Courts Act 1981 as applied by subsection (6A), the tribunal must certify that the condition in section 31(2B) as so applied is satisfied.

Add new paragraph 9A–1010.1:

Note

9A–1010.1   Subsection (3) amended by, and subss.(3A)–(3G), (6A), (6B) inserted by the Criminal Justice and Courts Act 2015 s.84(5) and s.85(3), (4), (6). That amendment is not yet in force.

Add new paragraphs 9A–1308 to 9A–1314.1:

Criminal Justice and Courts Act 2015

9A–1308

(2015 c.2)

ARRANGEMENT OF SECTIONS

PART IV

JUDICIAL REVIEW

Judicial Review in the High Court and the Upper Tribunal

SECT.

Introductory note

9A–1309   Provisions in Pt 4 of the Criminal Justice Act 2015 substantially reformed the law relating to judicial review. The Part contains nine sections (ss.84 to 92) presented under two headings; viz "Judicial review in the High Court and the Upper Tribunal" (ss.84 to 90) and "Planning Proceedings" (ss.91 and 92). Section 84 (Likelihood of substantially different outcome for appellant) amended the Senior Courts Act 1981 s.31 (Applications for judicial review) (see para.9A–101 above) and the Tribunal, Courts and Enforcement Act 2007 s.15 (The Upper Tribunal's "judicial review" jurisdiction) and s.16 (Application for relief under s.15(1)) (see paras 9A–1009 and 9A–1010 above). Section 91 (Procedure for certain planning challenges) introduced Sch.16 and s.92 (Periods of time for certain legal challenges) amended the Town and Country

242

Planning Act 1990 s.61N and s.106C and the Planning Act 2008 s.13 and s.118. Schedule 16 further amended the 1990 Act and also amended the Planning (Listed Buildings and Conservations Areas) Act 1990. Sections 86 to 90 (the texts of which are set out below) stand alone, but must be read with the Senior Courts Act 1981 s.31 and the Tribunals, Courts and Enforcement Act 2007 s.16 as amended by s.85, with relevant rules in the CPR (see e.g. r.46.15 (costs against interveners)) and in the Tribunal Procedure Rules, and with any Regulations made by the Lord Chancellor under s.88(9), s.89(3) and s.90(1).

Part IV

Judicial Review

Judicial Review in the High Court and the Upper Tribunal

Use of information about financial information

86.—(1) This section applies when the High Court, the Upper Tribunal or the Court of Appeal is determining by whom and to what extent costs of or incidental to judicial review proceedings are to be paid.   **9A–1310**

(2) The information to which the court or tribunal must have regard includes—

    (a) information about the financing of the proceedings provided in accordance with section 31(3)(b) of the Senior Courts Act 1981 or section 16(3)(b) of the Tribunals, Courts and Enforcement Act 2007, and

    (b) any supplement to that information provided in accordance with rules of court or Tribunal Procedure Rules.

(3) The court or tribunal must consider whether to order costs to be paid by a person, other than a party to the proceedings, who is identified in that information as someone who is providing financial support for the purposes of the proceedings or likely or able to do so.

(4) In this section "judicial review proceedings" means—

    (a) proceedings on an application for leave to apply for judicial review,

    (b) proceedings on an application for judicial review,

    (c) proceedings on an application for permission to apply for relief under section 15 of the Tribunals, Courts and Enforcement Act 2007 in a case arising under the law of England and Wales,

    (d) proceedings on an application for such relief in such a case,

    (e) any proceedings on an application for leave to appeal from a decision in proceedings described in paragraph (a), (b), (c) or (d), and

    (f) proceedings on an appeal from such a decision.

Note

This section is not yet in force. It will be brought into force by a commencement order.   **9A–1310.1**

Interveners and costs

87.—(1) This section applies where—   **9A–1311**

243

    (a) a person is granted permission to file evidence or make representations in judicial review proceedings, and

    (b) at that time, the person is not a relevant party to the proceedings.

(2) That person is referred to in this section as an "intervener".

(3) A relevant party to the proceedings may not be ordered by the High Court or the Court of Appeal to pay the intervener's costs in connection with the proceedings.

(4) Subsection (3) does not prevent the court making an order if it considers that there are exceptional circumstances that make it appropriate to do so.

(5) On an application to the High Court or the Court of Appeal by a relevant party to the proceedings, if the court is satisfied that a condition described in subsection (6) is met in a stage of the proceedings that the court deals with, the court must order the intervener to pay any costs specified in the application that the court considers have been incurred by the relevant party as a result of the intervener's involvement in that stage of the proceedings.

(6) Those conditions are that—

    (a) the intervener has acted, in substance, as the sole or principal applicant, defendant, appellant or respondent;

    (b) the intervener's evidence and representations, taken as a whole, have not been of significant assistance to the court;

    (c) a significant part of the intervener's evidence and representations relates to matters that it is not necessary for the court to consider in order to resolve the issues that are the subject of the stage in the proceedings;

    (d) the intervener has behaved unreasonably.

(7) Subsection (5) does not require the court to make an order if it considers that there are exceptional circumstances that make it inappropriate to do so.

(8) In determining whether there are exceptional circumstances that are relevant for the purposes of subsection (4) or (7), the court must have regard to criteria specified in rules of court.

(9) In this section, "judicial review proceedings" means—

    (a) proceedings on an application for leave to apply for judicial review,

    (b) proceedings on an application for judicial review,

    (c) any proceedings on an application for leave to appeal from a decision in proceedings described in paragraph (a) or (b), and

    (d) proceedings on an appeal from such a decision, and the proceedings described in paragraphs (a) to (d) are "stages" of judicial review proceedings.

(10) For the purposes of this section, "a relevant party" to judicial review proceedings means any of the following—

    (a) a person who is or has been an applicant or defendant in the proceedings described in subsection (9)(a), (b) or (c);

    (b) a person who is or has been an appellant or respondent in the proceedings described in subsection (9)(d);

    (c) any other person who is or has been directly affected by the proceedings and on whom the application for judicial review, or for leave to apply for judicial review, has been served.

(11) If a person who is an intervener in judicial review proceedings becomes a relevant party to the proceedings, the person is to be treated for the purposes of subsections (3) and (5) as having been a relevant party, rather than an intervener, at all times when involved in the proceedings.

Note

This section was brought into force on April 13, 2015 by the Criminal Justice and **9A–1311.1**
Courts Act 2015 (Commencement No.1, Saving and Transitional Provisions) Order 2015 (SI 2015/778).

Capping of costs

88.—(1) A costs capping order may not be made by the High Court **9A–1312**
or the Court of Appeal in connection with judicial review proceedings except in accordance with this section and sections 89 and 90.

(2) A "costs capping order" is an order limiting or removing the liability of a party to judicial review proceedings to pay another party's costs in connection with any stage of the proceedings.

(3) The court may make a costs capping order only if leave to apply for judicial review has been granted.

(4) The court may make a costs capping order only on an application for such an order made by the applicant for judicial review in accordance with rules of court.

(5) Rules of court may, in particular, specify information that must be contained in the application, including—

(a) information about the source, nature and extent of financial resources available, or likely to be available, to the applicant to meet liabilities arising in connection with the application, and

(b) if the applicant is a body corporate that is unable to demonstrate that it is likely to have financial resources available to meet such liabilities, information about its members and about their ability to provide financial support for the purposes of the application.

(6) The court may make a costs capping order only if it is satisfied that—

(a) the proceedings are public interest proceedings,

(b) in the absence of the order, the applicant for judicial review would withdraw the application for judicial review or cease to participate in the proceedings, and

(c) it would be reasonable for the applicant for judicial review to do so.

(7) The proceedings are "public interest proceedings" only if—

(a) an issue that is the subject of the proceedings is of general public importance,

(b) the public interest requires the issue to be resolved, and

(c) the proceedings are likely to provide an appropriate means of resolving it.

(8) The matters to which the court must have regard when determining whether proceedings are public interest proceedings include—

  (a) the number of people likely to be directly affected if relief
       is granted to the applicant for judicial review,
  (b) how significant the effect on those people is likely to be,
       and
  (c) whether the proceedings involve consideration of a point
       of law of general public importance.

(9) The Lord Chancellor may by regulations amend this section by
adding, omitting or amending matters to which the court must have
regard when determining whether proceedings are public interest
proceedings.

(10) Regulations under this section are to be made by statutory
instrument.

(11) A statutory instrument containing regulations under this section may not be made unless a draft of the instrument has been laid
before, and approved by a resolution of, each House of Parliament.

(12) In this section and sections 89 and 90—

"costs capping order" has the meaning given in subsection (2);

"the court" means the High Court or the Court of Appeal;

"judicial review proceedings" means—

  (a) proceedings on an application for leave to apply for
       judicial review,
  (b) proceedings on an application for judicial review,
  (c) any proceedings on an application for leave to appeal from
       a decision in proceedings described in paragraph (a) or
       (b), and
  (d) proceedings on an appeal from such a decision, and the
       proceedings described in paragraphs (a) to (d) are "stages"
       of judicial review proceedings.

(13) For the purposes of this section and section 89, in relation to
judicial review proceedings—

  (a) the applicant for judicial review is the person who is or
       was the applicant in the proceedings on the application
       for judicial review, and
  (b) references to relief being granted to the applicant for
       judicial review include the upholding on appeal of a deci-
       sion to grant such relief at an earlier stage of the
       proceedings.

Note

9A–1312.1   This section is not yet in force. It will be brought into force by a commencement
order.

Capping of costs orders and their terms

9A–1313   **89.**—(1) The matters to which the court must have regard when
considering whether to make a costs capping order in connection
with judicial review proceedings, and what the terms of such an order should be, include—

  (a) the financial resources of the parties to the proceedings,
       including the financial resources of any person who
       provides, or may provide, financial support to the parties;
  (b) the extent to which the applicant for the order is likely to
       benefit if relief is granted to the applicant for judicial
       review;

   (c) the extent to which any person who has provided, or may provide, the applicant with financial support is likely to benefit if relief is granted to the applicant for judicial review;

   (d) whether legal representatives for the applicant for the order are acting free of charge;

   (e) whether the applicant for the order is an appropriate person to represent the interests of other persons or the public interest generally.

(2) A costs capping order that limits or removes the liability of the applicant for judicial review to pay the costs of another party to the proceedings if relief is not granted to the applicant for judicial review must also limit or remove the liability of the other party to pay the applicant's costs if it is.

(3) The Lord Chancellor may by regulations amend this section by adding to, omitting or amending the matters listed in subsection (1).

(4) Regulations under this section are to be made by statutory instrument.

(5) A statutory instrument containing regulations under this section may not be made unless a draft of the instrument has been laid before, and approved by a resolution of, each House of Parliament.

(6) In this section—

"free of charge" means otherwise than for or in expectation of fee, gain or reward;

"legal representative", in relation to a party to proceedings, means a person exercising a right of audience or conducting litigation on the party's behalf.

Note

   This section is not yet in force. It will be brought into force by a commencement order.   **9A–1313.1**

Capping of costs: environmental cases

   90.—(1) The Lord Chancellor may by regulations provide that sec- **9A–1314** tions 88 and 89 do not apply in relation to judicial review proceedings which, in the Lord Chancellor's opinion, have as their subject an issue relating entirely or partly to the environment.

(2) Regulations under this section—

   (a) may make provision generally or only in relation to proceedings described in the regulations, and

   (b) may include transitional, transitory or saving provision.

(3) Regulations under this section are to be made by statutory instrument.

(4) A statutory instrument containing regulations under this section is subject to annulment in pursuance of a resolution of either House of Parliament.

Note

   This section is not yet in force. It will be brought into force by a commencement order.   **9A–1314.1**

9B OTHER STATUTES AND REGULATIONS

Administration of Justice Act 1969

Part II

Appeal from High Court to Supreme Court

Grant of certificate by trial Judge

Delete s.12(1) and subsitute:

9B–30 (1) Where on the application of any of the parties to any proceedings to which this section applies the judge is satisfied—

    (a) that the relevant conditions are fulfilled in relation to his decision in those proceedings or that the conditions in subsection (3A) ("the alternative conditions") are satisfied in relation to those proceedings, and

    (b) that a sufficient case for an appeal to the Supreme Court under this Part of this Act has been made out to justify an application for leave to bring such an appeal,

the judge, subject to the following provisions of this Part of this Act, may grant a certificate to that effect.

Add new s.12(3A):

(3A) The alternative conditions, in relation to a decision of the judge in any proceedings, are that a point of law of general public importance is involved in the decision and that—

    (a) the proceedings entail a decision relating to a matter of national importance or consideration of such a matter,

    (b) the result of the proceedings is so significant (whether considered on its own or together with other proceedings or likely proceedings) that, in the opinion of the judge, a hearing by the Supreme Court is justified, or

    (c) the judge is satisfied that the benefits of earlier consideration by the Supreme Court outweigh the benefits of consideration by the Court of Appeal.

Note

Add at end:

9B–31 Subsection (1) amended, and subs.(3A) inserted by the Criminal Justice and Courts Act 2015 s.63(2), (3), with effect from April 13, 2015 (SI 2015/778; for transitional provisions see art.4, Sch.2).

Late Payment of Commercial Debts (Interest) Act 1998

Period for which statutory interest runs

In s.4(8), in the definition of "public authority", for "regulation 3 of the Public Contracts Regulations 2006" substitute:

9B–1337 regulation 2(1) of the Public Contracts Regulations 2015

Note

Add at end:

9B–1337.1 Subsection (8) amended by the Public Contracts Regulations 2015 (SI 2015/102) Sch.6(1) para.1, with effect from February 26, 2015; for savings and transitional provisions see Pt 5 of SI 2015/102.

SECTION 10

10   COURT FEES

Civil Proceedings Fees Order 2008

REMISSIONS AND PART REMISSIONS

Delete art.5 and substitute:

5.—(1) Subject to paragraph (2), Schedule 2 applies for the purpose **10–5** of ascertaining whether a party is entitled to a remission or part remission of a fee prescribed by this Order.

(2) Schedule 2 does not apply to—
- (a) fee 1.2 if the fee relates to proceedings to recover a sum of money in cases brought by Money Claim OnLine users; or
- (b) fee 8.8 (fee payable on a consolidated attached of earnings order or an administration order).

Add new paragraph 10–5.1:

Note

Substituted by the Courts and Tribunals Fee Remissions Order 2013 (SI 2013/2302) **10–5.1** art.6(2) with effect from October 7, 2013 (for transitional provisions see art.13(1) thereof). Sub–section (2)(a) substituted by Civil Proceedings and Family Proceedings Fees (Amendment) Order 2015 (SI 2015/576) art.2(2) with effect from March 1, 2015.

In Sch.1, delete the column headers and the text (in both columns) from "1 Starting proceedings (High Court and county court)" to the end of the entry headed "Fees 1.1, 1.2 and 1.3" and substitute:

SCHEDULE 1

FEES TO BE TAKEN

10–7

Column 1 Number and description of fee	Column 2 Amount of fee (or manner of calculation)
1 Starting proceedings (High Court and County Court)	
1.1 On starting proceedings (including proceedings issued after permission to issue is granted but excluding CCBC cases brought by Centre users or cases brought by Money Claim OnLine users) to recover a sum of money where the sum claimed:	
(a) does not exceed £300;	£35
(b) exceeds £300 but does not exceed £500;	£50
(c) exceeds £500 but does not exceed £1,000;	£70
(d) exceeds £1,000 but does not exceed £1,500;	£80
(e) exceeds £1,500 but does not exceed £3,000;	£115
(f) exceeds £3,000 but does not exceed £5,000;	£205
(g) exceeds £5,000 but does not exceed £10,000;	£455
(h) exceeds £10,000 but does not exceed £200,000;	5% of the value of the claim
(i) exceeds £200,000 or is not limited.	£10,000
1.2 On starting proceedings in CCBC cases brought by Centre users or cases brought by Money Claim OnLine users, to recover a sum of money where the sum claimed:	

Column 1 *Number and description of fee*	Column 2 *Amount of fee (or manner of calculation)*
(a) does not exceed £300;	£25
(b) exceeds £300 but does not exceed £500;	£35
(c) exceeds £500 but does not exceed £1,000;	£60
(d) exceeds £1,000 but does not exceed £1,500;	£70
(e) exceeds £1,500 but does not exceed £3,000;	£105
(f) exceeds £3,000 but does not exceed £5,000;	£185
(g) exceeds £5,000 but does not exceed £10,000;	£410
(h) exceeds £10,000 but does not exceed £100,000.	4.5% of the value of the claim
Fee 1.1	
Where the claimant does not identify the value of the claim when starting proceedings to recover a sum of money, the fee payable is the one applicable to a claim where the sum is not limited.	
Fees 1.1 and 1.2.	
Where the claimant is making a claim for interest on a specified sum of money, the amount on which the fee is calculated is the total amount of the claim and the interest.	

Note

Delete Note and substitute:

10–7.1   Schedule 1 substituted by the Civil Proceedings Fees (Amendment) Order 2014 (SI 2014/874), with effect from April 22, 2014.

Entry 3.5 amended by the Civil Proceedings Fees (Amendment No.2) Order 2014 (SI 2014/1834) with effect from August 4, 2014.

Entry 8.1 amended by the Civil Proceedings Fees (Amendment No.3) Order 2014 (SI 2014/2059) with effect from August 4, 2014.

The column headings and the entries from "1 Starting proceedings (High Court and county court)" to the end of the entry headed "Fees 1.1, 1.2 and 1.3" substituted by the Civil Proceedings and Family Proceedings Fees (Amendment) Order 2015 (SI 2015/576) with effect from March 1, 2015.

SECTION 12

CPR: APPLICATION, AMENDMENTS AND INTERPRETATION

C. STATUTORY INSTRUMENTS AMENDING CPR

4. TRANSITIONAL ARRANGEMENTS IN AMENDING STATUTORY INSTRUMENTS

(b) 2014 to date

Delete the first paragraph and Rule 18 and substitute:

12–34   The Civil Procedure (Amendment No.3) Rules 2015 (SI 2015/877) contained a number of amendments clarifying and correcting the following rules: 76.29, 79.21, 80.25(1), 82.14, 88.2(2), 88.24, 88.28 and 88.9(1).

The Civil Procedure (Amendment No.2) Rules 2015 (SI 2015/670) contained two types of amendments. First, it introduced a simplified approach to cost assessment for children and protected parties under r.46.4. Secondly, it implemented reforms to r.54

(judicial review) consequent on statutory changes effected by Criminal Justice and Courts Act 2015, ss.84 and 87.

The Civil Procedure (Amendment) Rules 2015 (SI 2015/406) contained a new Pt 88, which provides rules governing proceedings under the Counter–Terrorism and Security Act 2015. Consequential modifications were also made to r.1.2(d).

The Civil Procedure (Amendment No. 8) Rules 2014 (SI 2014/3299) contained amendments to various rules. Most significantly it substituted a new Pt 36, as from April 6, 2015. It also included a new Pt 87, by way of replacement for RSC Ord. 54, governing applications for writs of habeas corpus. Additionally, it contained a number of revisions to Pt 21 (expenses incurred by a litigation friend), Pt 30 (transfer of specialist proceedings), Pt 45 (costs of medical reports in respect of claims under the RTA Protocol), and a new Section VI to Pt 74 concerning changes to the procedure for recognition and enforcement of protection measures. Transitional provisions provide for the continuing application of the new provisions relating to Pt 36 and applications for writs of habeas corpus to certain matters arising prior to April 6, 2015.

SECTION 14

ALTERNATIVE DISPUTE RESOLUTION

A. INTRODUCTION

2. APPELLATE JUDGES' STATEMENTS AND SPEECHES ON ADR—THE JACKSON REPORT—PROPOSALS FOR REFORM

In the second paragraph, for "http://webarchive.nationalarchives.gov.uk/20140509091326/ http://www.judiciary.gov.uk/Resources/JCO/Documents/Speeches/mr–littletonchambers– 080609.pdf [accessed October 31, 2014]" substitute:

> http://webarchive.nationalarchives.gov.uk/20131202164909/http://judiciary.gov.uk/media/ **14–3** speeches/2009/speech–lord–clarke–mor–09062009 [accessed May 25, 2015]

In the sixth paragraph, for "http://webarchive.nationalarchives.gov.uk/20140509091326/http:// www.judiciary.gov.uk/Resources/JCO/Documents/Speeches/mrkeating–lecture–19052010.pdf [accessed October 31, 2014]" substitute:

> http://webarchive.nationalarchives.gov.uk/20131202164909/http://judiciary.gov.uk/ Resources/JCO/Documents/Speeches/mr–keating–lecture–19052010.pdf [accessed May 25, 2014]

In the eighth paragraph, for "(See http://www.justice.gov.uk/downloads/guidance/mediation/drc– guidance–may2011.pdf [accessed October 31, 2014] and http://www.justice.gov.uk/downloads/ guidance/mediation/drc–may2011.pdf [accessed October 31, 2014].)" substitute:

> (See http://webarchive.nationalarchives.gov.uk/20130128112038/http://www.justice.gov.uk/ courts/mediation/dispute–resolution–commitment [accessed May 25, 2015]).

B. ADR IN THE CONTEXT OF THE CPR

1. CASE MANAGEMENT

(f) Judicial speeches—ADR case management post Halsey—power to direct ADR

In the fifth paragraph, for "(See http://webarchive.nationalarchives.gov.uk/20140509091326/ www.judiciary.gov.uk/Resources/JCO/Documents/Speeches/mr–speech–compensation–culture.pdf [accessed October 31, 2014].)" substitute:

> (See http://webarchive.nationalarchives.gov.uk/20131202164909/http://judiciary.gov.uk/ **14–9** media/speeches/2013/mr–speech–compensation–culture–fact–or–fantasy [accessed May 25, 2015].)

(h) Case management and cost sanctions

In the fourth paragraph, for "http://webarchive.nationalarchives.gov.uk/20140509091326/

14–11 *www.judiciary.gov.uk/Resources/JCO/Documents/Speeches/lj–jackson–speecheleventh–lecture–implementation–programme.pdf" [accessed October 31, 2014]" substitute:*
https://www.judiciary.gov.uk/wp–content/uploads/JCO/Documents/Speeches/lj–jackson–speech–eleventh–lecture–implementation–programme.pdf [accessed May 25, 2015]

After the seventh paragraph, add as a new paragraph:

In *Laporte v The Commissioner of Police of the Metropolis* [2015] EWHC 371 (QB) the court, having found that the defendant had failed, without adequate justification, to fully and adequately engage in the ADR process, which had a reasonable chance of success, imposed a costs sanction. Although the defendant was successful on every substantive issue and, although ADR made settlement a sufficiently likely possibility, it would not have been certain, the court ordered that he should only receive two thirds of his costs, to be assessed.

(i) Case management: facilitation of ADR procedures and criteria for referral to ADR

14–12 *Delete the last paragraph starting "Criteria for referral to mediation".*

(j) Case management: the stages at which ADR may be encouraged

In the fifth paragraph, for "On other occasions the circumstances of the litigation may make mediation appropriate." substitute:

14–13 On other occasions it is the circumstances of the litigation that may make mediation appropriate.

2. PREDOMINANCE OF MEDIATION AS AN ADR PROCEDURE

14–16 *Delete the last paragraph starting "The Civil Justice Council has issued".*

3. COSTS WHERE ADR DECLINED

Add new paragraph at end:

14–17 Similarly, in *Laporte v The Commissioner of Police of the Metropolis* [2015] EWHC 371 (QB) the defendant, who was successful on every substantive issue, was awarded only two thirds of his costs. This was the consequence of the court's finding that the defendant had failed, without adequate justification, to fully and adequately engage in the ADR process, notwithstanding that the outcome of such process was not certain.

Add new paragraph 14–17A:

14–17A ADR is as relevant to disputes about costs as it is to all other types of litigation. In particular an unreasonable refusal to mediate a costs dispute may, and in at least two cases has, resulted in a costs sanction. In *Lakehouse Contracts Ltd v UPR Services Ltd* [2014] EWHC 1223 (Ch) a failure to mediate was taken into account in dealing with the costs of a winding–up petition. In *Morris v Hay County Court* (Kingston upon Hull, 02 February 2015, unreported) the defendant paying party received two CPR r.47.20 offers prior to a detailed assessment but did not respond to them. The District Judge found that the defendant failed to failure to make any offer and/or to actively consider dispute resolution and concluded that this was a conduct issue. He said, following *Halsey v Milton Keynes General NHS Trust* [2004] EWCA Civ 576; [2004] 1 W.L.R. 3002 and *PGF II SA v OMFS Co 1 Ltd* [2013] EWCA Civ 1288; [2014] 1 W.L.R. 1386, that the parties were expected to engage in alternative dispute resolution. He considered it likely that further mediation could have achieved a far speedier conclusion and at less cost and concluded that the defendant's conduct was also conduct contrary to the overriding objective.

C. ADR IN PRE–ACTION PROTOCOLS AND COURT GUIDES

1. ADR IN PROTOCOLS

Delete paragraph 14–21 and substitute:

14–21 Pre–action conduct is dealt with by Practice Direction—Pre–Action Conduct, as amended in April 2015 (para.C1–001) and the various pre–action protocols listed below.

Paragraphs 8–11 deal with settlement and ADR. Paragraph 8 reminds parties that litigation should be regarded as a last resort and exhorts them to consider negotiation or some other form of ADR. The next paragraph cautions that there is a continuing duty to keep settlement under review. Paragraph 10 defines ADR and gives pointers to further information about it: "The Jackson ADR Handbook" and websites hosted by the MoJ and the Citizens Advisory Board. Paragraph 11 concludes the section with reminders that parties may be required to provide evidence that ADR has been considered and that a party's silence in response to an invitation to participate, or a refusal to participate, in ADR might be considered unreasonable by the court and could lead to the court ordering that party to pay additional court costs.

The various pre–action protocols all include provisions relating to ADR similar to those in the Practice Direction—Pre–Action Conduct as summarised above. The several protocols are distinguished by the fact that each covers distinctive forms of civil proceedings. Obviously, parties in person and the legal representatives of parties engaged in such proceedings are well advised to read carefully what is said about ADR in the appropriate protocol. (In some forms of proceedings arising out of commercial transactions methods of pre–action resolution are well established and habitually used by parties falling into dispute and the relevant pre–action protocols take account of that.)

The references to ADR in the several protocols are as follows (for complete texts, see Vol.1, Section C (Pre–Action Protocols)):

- *Pre–Action Protocol for Personal Injury Claims*, para.9;
- *Pre–Action Protocol for the Resolution of Clinical Disputes*, para.5;
- *Pre–Action Protocol for Construction and Engineering Disputes*, paras 5.1 to 5.7;
- *Pre–Action Protocol for Defamation*, paras 3.7 to 3.9;
- *Professional Negligence Pre–action Protocol*, para.12;
- *Pre–Action Protocol for Judicial Review*, para.9;
- *Pre–action Protocols for Disease and Illness Claims*, paras 2A.1 to 2A.4;
- *Pre–Action Protocol for Housing Disrepair Claims*, para.4;
- *Pre–Action Protocol for Possession Claims by Social Landlords*, para.2.10;
- *Pre–Action Protocol for Possession Claims (Mortgage)*, no ADR provision.

2. ADR IN COURT GUIDES

For *"http://www.judiciary.gov.uk/publications/longtrials–working–party–report/ [accessed October 31, 2015]"* substitute:

> *https://www.judiciary.gov.uk/publications/long–trials–working–party–report/* [accessed May **14–22** 25, 2015]

D. ADR IN PARTICULAR COURTS

2. MEDIATION IN COUNTY COURTS

In the first paragraph, delete *"a page of guidance on a website (http://www.justice.gov.uk/* **14–24** *guidance/mediation/index.htm [accessed October 31, 2014]) and"*.

In the second paragraph, delete from *"As mentioned in 14–3 above, the Ministry of Justice 2011"* to the end of the paragraph.

3. COURT OF APPEAL MEDIATION SCHEME (CAMS)

In the last paragraph, delete *"and http://www.thelawyer.com/coa–pilots–mediation–scheme–in–* **14–25** *bid–to–cutlitigation–costs/1012099.article [accessed October 31, 2014]"*.

F. JUDICIAL REFERRAL TO MEDIATION

Delete paragraphs 14–28 to 14–35.

SECTION 15

INTERIM REMEDIES

A. INTERIM INJUNCTIONS

1. JURISDICTION

(b) Foreign proceedings

In the first paragraph, after "substance of the matter." add:

15-5   With effect from January 10, 2015, Council Regulation (EU) No.44/2001 was replaced by Regulation (EU) No.1215/2012 of the European Parliament and of the Council of December 12, 2012, commonly known as the "recast" Judgments Regulation (see para.5–249 et seq above). In the recast, what was art.31 in the former Regulation, is art.35 (see para.5–280 above).

3. GUIDELINES—ADEQUACY OF DAMAGES AS A REMEDY AND THE BALANCE OF CONVENIENCE

(a) Stage 1—adequacy as a remedy of damages awarded at trial or payable under undertaking

In the last paragraph, for "B v D [2014] EWCA Civ 229, March 6, 2014, CA, unrep." substitute:

15-11   *AB v CD* [2014] EWCA Civ 229, [2015] 1 W.L.R. 771, CA

9. UNDERTAKING AS TO DAMAGES

(d) Extent of undertaking as to damages

Add at end:

15-29   The default position is that an applicant for an interim injunction is required to give an unlimited cross–undertaking in damages (though this price is not exacted where the applicant is a law enforcement agency simply enforcing the law in the public interest). The mere fact that litigation is being brought by a liquidator does not compel the conclusion that the cross–undertaking should be capped, but such is within the scope of the Judge's discretion, which should not be fettered by rigid judge–made rules (*JSC Mezhdunarodniy Promyshlenniy Bank v Pugachev* [2015] EWCA Civ 139, February 27, 2015, CA, unrep., at [68–73]). It is fairness rather than likelihood of loss that leads to the requirement of a cross–undertaking (also at [77]).

(e) Applicant unable to offer credible undertaking

Add new paragraph at end:

15-30   If an applicant for an injunction says that they do not wish to, or are not in a position to give an unlimited cross–undertaking in damages, the burden is on them to show that external funds are not available, and why they should be able to provide a cross–undertaking in a lesser amount (*JSC Mezhdunarodniy Promyshlenniy Bank v Pugachev* [2015] EWCA Civ 139, February 27, 2015, CA, unrep., at [85]).

(g) Fortifying undertaking

Delete paragraph 15–32 and substitute:

15-32   In a proper case, the court may impose a condition to the effect that the claimant's undertaking should be fortified by his giving security in a certain sum by the bond of an insurance company or by payment into court or by some other means, for example, by payment to the applicant's solicitor or to the solicitors for each party jointly to be held pending further order (*Baxter v Claydon* [1952] W.N. 376).

A defendant should apply for the security at the time when the injunction is granted and the undertaking is given. The court has no power subsequently to impose such an additional term on the grant of an injunction (*Commodity Ocean Transport Corp v Basford Unicorn Industries Ltd (The Mito)* [1987] 2 Lloyd's Rep. 197).

Where an injunction has been granted, the respondent may apply to the court for the security to be fortified by further or additional security. Before an application to fortify an undertaking can succeed a likelihood of a significant loss arising as a result of the injunction and a sound basis for belief that the undertaking will be insufficient must be shown (*Bhimji v Chatwani; Chatwani v Bhimji (No.2)* [1992] 1 W.L.R. 1158; [1992] B.C.L.C. 387). See also *Sinclair Investment Holdings SA v Cushnie* [2004] EWHC 218, (Ch), February 12, 2004, unrep. (Mann J.). For an explanation of the matters that the court should take into account where the defendant applies for an uplift by way of fortification of the security, see *Harley Street Capital Ltd v Tchigirinski* [2005] EWHC 2471 (Ch), May 24, 2005, unrep. (Mr Briggs Q.C.) ; *In the matter of Bloomsbury International Ltd* [2010] EWHC 1150 (Ch) (Floyd J.). In *Energy Venture Partners Ltd v Malabu Oil and Gas Ltd* [2015] 1 W.L.R. 2309, CA, the Court of Appeal reviewed and generally approved the relevant existing first instance authorities. The Court stated that (1) in determining whether fortification should be ordered in respect of an undertaking in damages a court is required to make an "intelligent estimate" of the likely amount of the loss for which a court would find the respondent should be compensated in the event of the undertaking being enforced, (2) loss will not qualify for compensation under an undertaking unless it has been caused by the grant of the injunction, (3) in making an intelligent estimate of the likely amount of loss the court must examine that causation issue, (4) it is for the respondent to show a sufficient level of risk of loss to require fortification, (5) it is not necessary for the respondent to establish the linked issues of likely loss and causation on a balance of probabilities, and it is in general unnecessary and inappropriate for a court to go into a detailed and prolonged assessment of those issues.

Where a defendant who might wish to seek fortification of a cross–undertaking is unable to show a consistent pattern of deal–making or engagement in business ventures which may be stultified by the injunction, he may, if a real opportunity is identified, take steps to secure permission from the claimant or the court to take advantage of it, and may make application for fortification at that time (*JSC Mezhdunarodniy Promyshlenniy Bank v Pugachev* [2015] EWCA Civ 139, February 27, 2015, CA, at [99]). It may be appropriate expressly to preserve the right to make such application in the order made on the return date.

Specimen clauses for giving security for the cross–undertaking in damages are at paragraphs (2) of Schedule B (freezing order) and (5) of Schedule C (search order) in the Annex to Practice Direction 25A. See further Vol. 1 para.25APD.10.

B. FREEZING INJUNCTIONS

3. JURISDICTION

(c) County courts

Delete the second paragraph beginning "The power of county courts". **15–59**

5. "DOMESTIC" FREEZING INJUNCTIONS

(a) Relevant factors

(iv) *Risk of judgment being unsatisfied*

In the second paragraph, for "Congentra AG v Sixteen Thirteen Marine SA [2008] EWHC 1613 (Com), July 15, 2008, unrep." substitute:

Congentra AG v Sixteen Thirteen Marine SA [2008] EWHC 1613 (Comm); [2008] 2 **15–69** Lloyd's Rep. 602

INDEX

LEGAL TAXONOMY
FROM SWEET & MAXWELL

This index has been prepared using Sweet and Maxwell's Legal Taxonomy. Main index entries conform to keywords provided by the Legal Taxonomy except where references to specific documents or non-standard terms (denoted by quotation marks) have been included. These keywords provide a means of identifying similar concepts in other Sweet & Maxwell publications and online services to which keywords from the Legal Taxonomy have been applied. Readers may find some minor differences between terms used in the text and those which appear in the index. Suggestions to *sweetandmaxwell.taxonomy@thomson.com.*

(All references are to paragraph number and all references to material in Volume 2 are enclosed in square parentheses)

Aarhus Convention on Access to Information 1998
costs limits on claims
nature of the claimant, 45.43.1

Abuse of process
breach of judgment, order or
undertaking to do or abstain from
doing an act, 81.4.9
collateral attacks upon earlier
decisions, 3.4.3.3
contempt of court, 81.4.9
other forms, 3.4.3.6
pointless litigation, 3.4.3.4
wasteful litigation, 3.4.3.4

Acceptance
Part 36 offers
generally, 36.11

Accountant General of the Supreme Court
investment, [6A–213] — [6A–218]

Accounts and inquiries
during proceedings
application, 25.3.5

Addition of parties
generally, 19.2.4
joinder
generally, 19.3.2

Administration
court, by, [3E–39]

Admiralty and Commercial Court Guide
introduction, [2A–39.0]

Admissions
pre–action admissions
general provision, 14.1A.2

Allocation of business
appeals
County Court, 2BPD.15
Chancery Division
Practice Direction, 2BPD.7
County Court
allocation to Circuit judges, 2BPD.12
allocation to District judges,
2BPD.11
appeals, 2BPD.15
distribution between Circuit judge
and District judge, 2BPD.13
freezing injunctions, 2BPD.8
human rights, 2BPD.14
District judges, to, 2BPD.11
early trials, 2BPD.3
freezing injunctions
County Court, 2BPD.8
High Court, 2BPD.5
High Court
Chancery Division, 2BPD.7
early trials, 2BPD.3
freezing injunctions, 2BPD.5
human rights, 2BPD.6
interim remedies, 2BPD.2
Masters, to, 2BPD.4
transfer, 2BPD.4
human rights
County Court, 2BPD.14
High Court, 2BPD.6
injunctions
County Court, 2BPD.8
High Court, 2BPD.2
interim remedies
High Court, 2BPD.2
Practice Direction
County Court, 2BPD.8 — 2BPD.15

Allocation of business—*cont.*
High Court, 2BPD.2 — 2BPD.7
pre–trial relief, 2BPD.2

Alternative dispute resolution
appellate judges' statements and
speeches, [14–3]
case management
generally, [14–9] — [14–13]
costs where declined, [14–17] —
[14–17A]
County Court, [14–24]
court guides, and
generally, [14–22]
Court of Appeal, [14–25]
mediation
County Court, [14–24]
Court of Appeal scheme, [14–25]
generally, [14–16]
small claims, [14–24]
personal injury protocol, C2–014
pre–action protocols, and
clinical disputes, C3–013
generally, [14–21]
introduction, C1–006
judicial review, C8–002
personal injury, C2–014
professional negligence, C7–012
professional negligence protocol,
C7–012
Small Claims Mediation Service,
[14–24]

Amendments
appellants' notices
point not raised below, 52.8.2
judgments
procedure, 3.10.3
respondents' notices
point not raised below, 52.8.2

Amendments (statements of case)
expiry of limitation periods, after
addition of new cause of action,
17.4.4 — 17.4.4.3
addition of new party, 19.5.11
generally, 17.4.1
substitution of new cause of action,
17.4.4 — 17.4.4.3
substitution of new party, 19.5 —
19.5.10 19.5.11

Antisocial behaviour
assured tenancies
demotion orders, [3A–765.1]
landlords' policies and procedures,
[3A–1488] — [3A–1495]
secure tenancies
demotion orders, [3A–350]
notice requirements, [3A–362.2]

**Antisocial Behaviour Crime and Polic-
ing Act 2014**
editorial introduction
generally, [3A–1781]
sentencing for breach of injunctions,
[3A–1781]

Antisocial behaviour injunctions
ABCPA 2014, under
'anti–social behaviour', [3A–1783] —
[3A–1787]
applications, [3A–1792] — [3A–1797]
breach, [3A–1802] — [3A–1810]
consultation requirements,
[3A–1816] — [3A–1818]
contents, [3A–1788] — [3A–1791.1]
court rules, [3A–1826] — [3A–1828]
definitions, [3A–1832] — [3A–1833]
discharge, [3A–1800] — [3A–1801]
editorial introduction, [3A–1781]
exclusion from home, [3A–1811] —
[3A–1815]
guidance, [3A–1829] — [3A–1831]
interim injunctions, [3A–1798] —
[3A–1799.1]
power of arrest, [3A–1790] —
[3A–1791.1]
remands, [3A–1836] — [3A–1845]
reporting restrictions, [3A–1824] —
[3A–1825]
special measures for witnesses,
[3A–1820] — [3A–1823]
variation, [3A–1800] — [3A–1801]

Appeal notices
amendments, 52.8.2

Appeals
arbitral proceedings
procedure, [2E–274]
time, [2E–271]
foreign judgments (enforcement)
generally, 74.8.1
insolvency proceedings
generally, 52.3.1
introduction
modification of Part, 52.0.3.1
leapfrog appeals
Practice Direction, [4A–59], [4A–82]
reopening
generally, 52.17.2
Upper Tribunal, from
generally, [9A–1007] — [9A–1007.1]

Appeals (county courts)
introduction
modification of Part, 52.0.3.1

Appeals (Court of Appeal)
introduction

Judicial review—*cont.*
public funding, C8–009
requests for information and
documents, C8–003
templates, C8–006
refusal of permission
service of order, 54.11
response letter
generally, C8–005
required information, C8–007
time limits
generally, 54.5
Upper Tribunal decisions
costs against interveners, [3A–1311]
costs capping orders, [3A–1312] —
[3A–1314]
introductory note, [3A–1309]
jurisdiction, [9A–1009] —
[9A–1010.1]
use of information about financial
information, [3A–1310]

Jurisdiction
Court of Appeal
restrictions on, [9A–64.1]
insolvency proceedings
generally, [3E–22]

Leapfrog appeals
Supreme Court, to
Practice Direction, [4A–59], [4A–82]

Legal advisers
County Court
definitions, 51KPD.1
jurisdiction that may be exercised,
51KPD.2, 51KPD.4
reconsideration of decision made,
51KPD.3

Legal aid
contempt of court
generally, 81.1.5

Legal representation
contempt of court
generally, 81.1.5
estate where no personal
representative, 19.8.1 — 19.8.3

Letters of claim
Clinical Disputes Protocol
generally, C3–010
template, C3–018
Housing Disrepair Cases Protocol
form, C10–013 — C10–014
generally, C10–005
Judicial Review Protocol
generally, C8–004
information required, C8–006
Personal Injury Claims Protocol

Letters of claim—*cont.*
contents, C2–008
generally, C2–008
specimen form, C2–018
status, C2–009
Professional Negligence Protocol,
C7–006

Letters of request (request from Regulation State)
definitions, 34.22
editorial introduction, 34.21.26

Limitation periods
addition of new cause of action
generally, 17.4.4 — 17.4.4.3
amendments after expiry of
addition of new cause of action,
17.4.4 — 17.4.4.3
generally, 17.4.1
substitution of new cause of action,
17.4.4 — 17.4.4.3
substitution of new parties, 19.5 —
19.5.11
Housing Disrepair Cases protocol,
C10–010
new cause of action
generally, 17.4.4 — 17.4.4.3
personal injury (discretionary
exclusion)
abolition of rule in Walkley, [8–91.1]
pre–action protocols, C1–009
substitution of new cause of action
generally, 17.4.4 — 17.4.4.3

Limited civil restraint orders
generally, 3.11.1

Listing
multi–track
generally, 29.2.6

Low value personal injury claims (employers' liability)
Stage 2 procedure, C15–013

Low value personal injury claims (road traffic accidents)
child settlements
generally, 21.10.2
claim notification form, C13–007
fixed costs (before April 1, 2013)
percentage increases, and, 45x.15.1
litigants in person, C13–006
Part 36 offers
costs consequences following
judgment, 36.29
pre–action protocol
general provisions, C13–006
scope, C13–005
stages of process, C13–007

Writs of control
wrongful seizure by enforcement
officer, 83.0.13

Writs of execution
wrongful seizure by enforcement
officer, 83.0.13

Written judgments
handing down
generally, 40.2.5